Essentials

of **Psychological Assessment** Series

Everything you need to know to administer, score, and interpret the major psychological tests.

I'd like to order the following *Essentials of Psychological Assessment:*

❑ WAIS®-IV Assessment (w/CD-ROM) / 978-0-471-73846-6 • $46.95
❑ WJ III™ Cognitive Abilities Assessment / 978-0-471-34466-7 • $36.95
❑ Cross-Battery Assessment, Second Edition
(w/CD-ROM) / 978-0-471-75771-9 • $46.95
❑ Nonverbal Assessment / 978-0-471-38318-5 • $36.95
❑ PAI® Assessment / 978-0-471-08463-1 • $36.95
❑ CAS Assessment / 978-0-471-29015-5 • $36.95
❑ MMPI-2™ Assessment / 978-0-471-34533-6 • $36.95
❑ Myers-Briggs Type Indicator® Assessment, Second Edition
978-0-470-34390-6 • $36.95
❑ Rorschach® Assessment / 978-0-471-33146-9 • $36.95
❑ Millon™ Inventories Assessment, Third Edition / 978-0-470-16862-2 • $36.95
❑ TAT and Other Storytelling Techniques / 978-0-471-39469-3 • $36.95
❑ MMPI-A™ Assessment / 978-0-471-39815-8 • $36.95
❑ NEPSY® Assessment / 978-0-471-32690-8 • $36.95
❑ Neuropsychological Assessment, Second Edition / 978-0-470-43747-6 • $36.95
❑ WJ III™ Tests of Achievement Assessment / 978-0-471-33059-2 • $36.95
❑ Evidence-Based Academic Interventions / 978-0-470-20632-4 • $36.95
❑ WRAML2 and TOMAL-2 Assessment / 978-0-470-17911-6 • $36.95
❑ WMS®-III Assessment / 978-0-471-38080-1 • $36.95
❑ Behavioral Assessment / 978-0-471-35367-6 • $36.95
❑ Forensic Psychological Assessment / 978-0-471-33186-5 • $36.95
❑ Bayley Scales of Infant Development II Assessment / 978-0-471-32651-9 • $36.95
❑ Career Interest Assessment / 978-0-471-35365-2 • $36.95
❑ WPPSI™-III Assessment / 978-0-471-28895-4 • $36.95
❑ 16PF® Assessment / 978-0-471-23424-1 • $36.95
❑ Assessment Report Writing / 978-0-471-39487-7 • $36.95
❑ Stanford-Binet Intelligence Scales (SB5) Assessment / 978-0-471-22404-4 • $36.95
❑ WISC®-IV Assessment, Second Edition (w/CD-ROM)
978-0-470-18915-3 • $46.95
❑ KABC-II Assessment / 978-0-471-66733-9 • $36.95
❑ WIAT®-II and KTEA-II Assessment / 978-0-471-70706-6 • $36.95
❑ Processing Assessment / 978-0-471-71925-0 • $36.95
❑ School Neuropsychological Assessment / 978-0-471-78372-5 • $36.95
❑ Cognitive Assessment with KAIT
& Other Kaufman Measures / 978-0-471-38317-8 • $36.95
❑ Assessment with Brief Intelligence Tests / 978-0-471-26412-5 • $36.95
❑ Creativity Assessment / 978-0-470-13742-0 • $36.95
❑ WNV™ Assessment / 978-0-470-28467-4 • $36.95
❑ DAS-II® Assessment (w/CD-ROM) / 978-0-470-22520-2 • $46.95
❑ Executive Function Assessment / 978-0-470-42202-1 • $36.95
❑ Conners Rating Scales™ Assessment / 978-0-470-34633-4 • $36.95

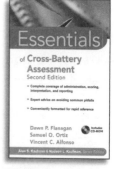

Please complete the order form on the back.
To order by phone, call toll free 1-877-762-2974
To order online: www.wiley.com/essentials
To order by mail: refer to order form on next page

WILEY

Essentials

of **Psychological Assessment** Series

ORDER FORM

Please send this order form with your payment (credit card or check) to:
John Wiley & Sons, Attn: J. Knott, 111 River Street, Hoboken, NJ 07030-5774

QUANTITY	TITLE	ISBN	PRICE

Shipping Charges:	Surface	2-Day	1-Day
First item	$5.00	$10.50	$17.50
Each additional item	$3.00	$3.00	$4.00

For orders greater than 15 items,
please contact Customer Care at 1-877-762-2974.

ORDER AMOUNT _____
SHIPPING CHARGES _____
SALES TAX _____
TOTAL ENCLOSED _____

NAME_____

AFFILIATION_____

ADDRESS_____

CITY/STATE/ZIP _____

TELEPHONE _____

EMAIL_____
❏ Please add me to your e-mailing list

PAYMENT METHOD:
❏ Check/Money Order   ❏ Visa   ❏ Mastercard   ❏ AmEx

Card Number _____Exp. Date_____

Cardholder Name *(Please print)* _____

Signature _____

*Make checks payable to **John Wiley & Sons.** Credit card orders invalid if not signed.*
All orders subject to credit approval. • Prices subject to change.

To order by phone, call toll free 1-877-762-2974
To order online: www.wiley.com/essentials

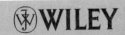

Essentials of
Evidence-Based
Academic Interventions

Essentials of Psychological Assessment Series

Series Editors, Alan S. Kaufman and Nadeen L. Kaufman

Essentials

of Evidence-Based

Academic Interventions

Barbara J. Wendling

Nancy Mather

John Wiley & Sons, Inc.

WILEY

Published by John Wiley & Sons, Inc., Hoboken, New Jersey.
Published simultaneously in Canada.

Library of Congress Cataloging-in-Publication Data:

Wendling, Barbara J.
    Essentials of evidence-based academic interventions / by Barbara J. Wendling and Nancy Mather.
      p. cm. — (Essentials of psychological assessment series)
    Includes bibliographical references and index.
    ISBN 978-0-470-20632-4 (pbk.)
    1. Learning disabled children—Education. 2. Learning disabilities—Testing. 3. Reading comprehension—Study and teaching. 4. Mathematics—Study and teaching—Evaluation.
    I. Mather, Nancy. II. Title.
    LC4704.5.W46 2009
    371.9—dc22

                2008016819

Printed in the United States of America

10 9 8 7 6 5

To Steve, my loving gentle bear,
my angel here on earth.——Barbara

To Michael,——to past years and future years
of love, laughter, and wildflowers . . .——Nancy

CONTENTS

SERIES PREFACE

I n the *Essentials of Psychological Assessment* series, we have attempted to provide the reader with books that will deliver key practical information in the most efficient and accessible style. The series features instruments in a variety of domains, such as cognition, personality, education, and neuropsychology. For the experienced clinician, books in the series will offer a concise yet thorough way to master utilization of the continuously evolving supply of new and revised instruments, as well as a convenient method for keeping up-to-date on the tried-and-true measures. The novice will find here a prioritized assembly of all the information and techniques that must be at one's fingertips to begin the complicated process of individual psychological diagnosis.

Wherever feasible, visual shortcuts to highlight key points are utilized alongside systematic, step-by-step guidelines. Chapters are focused and succinct. Topics are targeted for an easy understanding of the essentials of administration, scoring, interpretation, and clinical application. Theory and research are continually woven into the fabric of each book, but always to enhance clinical inference, never to sidetrack or overwhelm. We have long been advocates of what has been called *intelligent testing*—the notion that a profile of test scores is meaningless unless it is brought to life by the clinical observations and astute detective work of knowledgeable examiners. Test profiles must be used to make a difference in the child's or adult's life, or why bother to test? We want this series to help our readers become the best intelligent testers they can be.

The *Essentials of Evidence-Based Academic Interventions* is designed for assessment professionals and educators alike who are looking for a resource on effective instruction. With the focus on response-to-intervention and evidence-based instruction in both general and special education we felt it important to add a book to our *Essentials* series that deals with effective instruction and intervention. The authors of *Essentials of Evidence-Based Academic Interventions,* Barbara Wendling and Nancy Mather, are both worldwide experts in academic interventions. They have created a convenient resource that identifies effective instructional techniques and materials for the achievement domains of reading, writing, and mathematics, as well as the general principles of effective instruction and the relevance of cognitive abilities to academic interventions.

Each chapter provides an overview of the academic area and the relevant research, the characteristics of individuals struggling with each academic area, and the ways to implement specific instructional interventions. In addition, the text contains helpful web sites and examples of effective commercially available programs. This book makes the essentials of evidence-based instruction accessible to all assessment professionals and teachers.

Alan S. Kaufman, PhD, and Nadeen L. Kaufman, EdD, Series Editors
Yale University School of Medicine

One

GENERAL PRINCIPLES OF EVIDENCE-BASED INSTRUCTION

THE ROLE OF ASSESSMENT

The single most important factor in planning for a child with a learning disability is an intensive diagnostic study. Without a comprehensive evaluation of his deficits and assets, the educational program may be too general, or even inappropriate.

—*Johnson & Myklebust, 1967*

Results from comprehensive evaluations often reveal the various cognitive and linguistic factors that are affecting learning. With this information, evaluators are better equipped to use assessment results to help plan instruction. Understanding individual differences in attention, learning abilities, and memory is not only critical for informing instruction, but also for identifying individuals with specific learning disabilities. There is much debate about the need for comprehensive evaluation as part of the identification process for specific learning disabilities. Some argue that comprehensive evaluation is absolutely necessary, while others argue it is absolutely unnecessary. Some even make the case that the category of specific learning disabilities should be eliminated completely. Although confusion exists, Scruggs and Mastropieri (2002) advised that eliminating the construct of specific learning disabilities is like "throwing the baby out with the bathwater" (p. 165). A comprehensive evaluation is important to understanding an individual's strengths and weaknesses—a critical element not only for identifying specific learning disabilities but also for planning effective instruction.

Once the factors that are affecting learning and performance have been determined, both standardized and informal assessment results can help inform and improve instruction in several ways. First, assessment results can promote student learning. Teachers can ensure that students receive instruction at an appropriate level of difficulty with effective methods and materials. Learning is made accessible to students and teachers by knowing what skills and knowledge students have and have not mastered. Findings from the National Reading Panel (2000) indicate that teachers need to be able to assess individual students and then tailor instruction to their individual needs. This information helps the teacher focus on the specific instructional needs of each student. Assessment helps ensure that students receive targeted, carefully designed instruction rather than a one-size-fits-all approach.

Second, more frequent assessments, such as curriculum-based measures, can help students monitor their own learning—an important metacognitive goal. Students will know more clearly what is expected of them because they receive feedback on the criteria that need to be mastered. Third, assessment can document what students are able to do with information that is taught to them. Assessment is a powerful tool for improving teaching by revealing when instruction is working and when it is not. If students are not succeeding, instruction can be redirected, modified, or intensified as needed. Thus, assessment is viewed as a method or diagnostic process that helps determine the factors affecting learning, reveals the present levels of performance, helps establish the goals of intervention, and helps evaluators determine the most effective instructional methods.

The implementation of effective instruction is critical for both general and special education. Under No Child Left Behind (NCLB, 2001), educators must consider results of scientifically based research, if available, before making instructional decisions. In the Individuals with Disabilities Education Improvement Act (IDEA, 2004), response to intervention (using scientifically based instruction) is specified as a process to help reduce instructional casualties and identify students with specific learning disabilities. These mandates have placed a focus on the importance of using evidence-based instruction in both general and special education classrooms. Therefore, knowledge of what constitutes evidence-based instruction is essential for all educators and evaluators.

WHAT IS EVIDENCE-BASED INSTRUCTION?

Evidence-based instruction has been defined as "the integration of professional wisdom with the best available empirical evidence in making decisions about how to deliver instruction" (Whitehurst, 2002, slide 2). At its core, evidence-based instruction simply means that the program, methodology, and/or practice have records of success. In other words, reliable and valid evidence indicates that intervention works. Most educators agree that evidence of effectiveness should be objective, valid, reliable, systematic, and refereed. The No Child Left Behind Act of 2001 states that *scientifically based research* means research that involves the application of rigorous, systematic, and objective procedures to obtain reliable and valid knowledge relevant to educational activities and programs. However, the integration of practitioner expertise with the best available research evidence is the practical application of evidence-based instruction. The practitioner is ultimately responsible for determining whether or not the specific instruction or intervention is producing the desired results (Frederickson, 2002).

The search for effective pro-

DON'T FORGET

Although they have different definitions, the terms evidence-based, research-based, or scientifically based are often used interchangeably.

grams is not new. In the mid-1960s, the First Grade Studies were completed (Bond & Dykstra, 1967). These were a federally funded collection of 27 studies on reading instruction. The conclusion from this project was that no single approach or method was distinctly better in all situations than the others. More recently, the National Clearinghouse for Comprehensive School Reform (2001) concluded that ". . . no models had uniformly positive effects, and no models had uniformly negative or neutral effects. In other words, no model worked in every case and every situation" (p. 21). These findings are similar to the earlier conclusions of Monroe (1932), who found that one method did not work with all children: Different reading methodologies were needed for the different cases.

The International Reading Association (2002) recommends that teachers and administrators ask certain questions when reviewing materials. While the questions apply to selecting reading materials, the first two questions clearly provide guidance regarding how to select and implement evidence-based instruction irrespective of academic domain.

1. Does this program or instructional approach provide systematic and explicit instruction in the particular strategies that have been proven to relate to high rates of achievement in reading for the children I teach?

2. Does the program or instructional approach provide flexibility for use with the range of learners in the various classrooms where it will be used? Are there assessment tools that assist teachers in identifying individual learning needs? Are there a variety

CAUTION

Just because a program or practice is described as evidence-based, it does not ensure that it will work with all learners. Educators must still determine if the materials or instructional methods are a good match for each student.

of strategies and activities that are consistent with diverse learning needs?

3. Does the program or instructional approach provide a collection of high-quality literary materials that are diverse in level of difficulty, genre, topic, and cultural representation to meet the individual needs and interests of the children with whom it will be used?

With legal mandates to use evidence-based instruction, there is an increasing need to evaluate programs, products, practices, and policies to determine if reliable and valid evidence supports their efficacy. To address the need for information on effective practices, the United States Department of Education's Institute for Education Sciences established the What Works Clearinghouse website (www.ies.ed.gov/ncee/wwc/) to provide a central, independent, and trusted source of scientific evidence of what works in the field of education. Selected evidence-based programs, products, practices, and policies can be found in the current text in the chapters related to each academic area.

> **DON'T FORGET**
>
> Information regarding evidence-based instruction can be found at the What Works Clearinghouse website (www.ies.ed.gov/ncee/wwc/).

WHAT WORKS? EVIDENCE-BASED PRACTICES

The central goal of this book is to make the essentials of evidence-based instruction easily accessible. While research has not identified one *best* program or model of instruction that works for all students, examinations of best practices have led to highly consistent results. Many teachers are already incorporating research-based practices into their teaching and clearly these effective teachers do make a difference.

Teacher Effect

Teachers have a powerful influence on learners (Bond & Dykstra, 1967, 1997). In fact, knowledgeable teachers are the key to successful classrooms (Invernizzi & Hayes, 2004). Highly effective teachers incorporate certain instructional principles in their classrooms that enhance student learning. A number of instructional practices should be part of the instructional program in every classroom from primary level to graduate school. Rapid Reference 1.1 presents ten effective teaching principles suggested by Ellis, Worthington, and Larkin (1994). Effective teachers incorporate all of these principles into their planning and lesson design.

Both researchers and effective teachers have known for a long time that students' responses to instruction are indicators of the quality of the instruction they are receiving. Three variables relate to the quality of instruction: the amount of time on task; the student's level of success; and the content covered (Archer & Issacson, 1989). Effective teachers manage instruction in such a way that the students spend the majority of instructional time actively engaged in learning, working with high levels of success, and progressing through the curriculum. The following key principles of effective teaching are applicable to all achievement domains.

Prior Knowledge

The ease of new learning is influenced by the learner's existing knowledge. By activating prior knowledge, teachers help students become ready to assimilate new information. This cueing helps the learner associate new information with previously learned knowledge, thereby improving the chances of a successful learning experience and retention.

More is known about the science of learning and how our brains

Ten Effective Teaching Principles

1. Active engagement. Students learn more when they are actively engaged in an instructional task.

2. Build-in success. High and moderate success rates are correlated positively with student learning outcomes, whereas low success rates are correlated negatively with outcomes.

3. Opportunity to learn. Increased opportunity to learn content is correlated positively with increased student learning achievement; therefore, the more content covered, the greater the potential for learning.

4. Direct instruction. Students achieve more in classes in which they spend much of their time being directly taught or supervised by their teacher.

5. Scaffold instruction. Students can become independent, self-regulated learners through instruction that is deliberately and carefully scaffolded. (See page 9 for more information on scaffolding instruction.)

6. Address forms of knowledge. The critical forms of knowledge associated with strategic learning are: (a) declarative knowledge (i.e., knowing facts), (b) procedural knowledge (i.e., knowing how to use the knowledge in specific ways), and (c) conditional knowledge (i.e., knowing when and where to apply the knowledge). Each of these must be addressed if students are to become independent, self-regulated learners.

7. Organizing and activating knowledge. Learning is increased when teaching is presented in a manner that assists students in organizing, storing, and retrieving knowledge.

8. Teach strategically. Students can become more independent, self-regulated learners through strategic instruction.

9. Explicit instruction. Students can become independent, self-regulated learners through explicit instruction.

10. Teach sameness. By teaching students how things are alike both within and across subjects, teachers promote the ability of students to link new information to previously learned concepts (i.e., generalize and transfer knowledge).

work than ever before. The human brain seeks to construct meaning by connecting new information and concepts to information already present in the neural network. Information about a certain concept—the essential unit of human thought—is usually stored in various parts of the brain rather than in just one location. Concepts that do not have multiple links with how an individual thinks about the world are not likely to be remembered or useful. For example, in learning the concept of *tiger,* the color of the tiger may be stored in one part of the brain, the sound the tiger makes in a different location, and the semantic category of animal in yet another. These multiple links make the information more useful and memorable because thinking about *tiger* causes numerous neurons to fire together. The more neurons fire together, the more they wire together (Hebb, 1949), thereby improving the process of storing and retrieving information.

Active Engagement

Another key predictor of academic success is the amount of time the student is actively engaged in learning (Greenwood, Horton, & Utley, 2002). When the student is an active participant, he or she is thinking about the task, increasing attention and focus. Numerous ways exist to engage the learner actively, including: discovery-based learning, peer tutoring, reciprocal teaching, writing, and cooperative learning. Ensuring that the student is an active, not passive participant means that the student is doing the *work* of learning. Meaningful involvement aids learning and retention.

Young children can learn most readily when things are concrete and directly accessible to their senses. Hands-on learning activities that incorporate tangible objects that are explored through sight, sound, smell, movement, or touch actively engage the learner. All learners, irrespective of age, can benefit from concrete examples and illustrations when learning something new.

Explicit Instruction

Nothing is left to chance with explicit instruction. The task is clearly explained, modeled or demonstrated by the teacher, practiced by the learner with frequent feedback, and then practiced independently. With explicit instruction, the student knows exactly what to do—it has been explained, demonstrated, and practiced with guidance to ensure that the skill is being mastered.

Scaffolding Instruction

Scaffolding instruction is another important element of effective teaching because it provides a bridge between what the student knows and what the student is learning. When explicit instruction is delivered as intended, the teacher uses scaffolding. In the first stage, the teacher assumes most of the responsibility for the learning process by modeling or demonstrating the task. In the next stage—guided practice—the student and teacher share responsibility for completing the task. The student practices the skill and the teacher provides assistance and feedback, thus supporting the student's learning during this stage. In the final stage—independent practice—the student has responsibility for the task. Scaffolding and explicit instruction both provide feedback and guidance to ensure success.

Differentiated Instruction

Differentiated instruction, based on a compilation of theories and practices, provides a means for dealing with individual student differences within the same class. It provides multiple op-

DON'T FORGET

Systematic, explicit instruction does not mean that everyone is on the same page at the same time in the same workbook (Invernizzi & Hayes, 2004). Explicit instruction provides differentiated instruction to individual learners.

tions and opportunities for students to learn the information. This form of instruction requires teacher flexibility in implementing an instructional approach that recognizes that one size *does not* fit all. Three elements of instruction can be differentiated: the content (what is to be learned), the process (how it is to be learned), and the product (the way mastery is demonstrated). The focus of differentiating instruction is the *how* to teach, but the how is highly dependent upon knowledge of each student, development of a learning environment that works for each student, and the design of an appropriate curriculum (Tomlinson, 2006).

Although many aspects of differentiated instruction have evidence of effectiveness as a whole, empirical evidence is lacking (Hall, 2002). Differentiated instruction does incorporate proven concepts such as readiness for a task, actively engaging learners, teaching at the student's level, and grouping students for instructional purposes. In addition, implementation of different technologies can increase the opportunities to differentiate instruction. Essentially, differentiated instruction is a way of thinking about teaching and acknowledging that students differ in their learning abilities, and that teachers must attempt to teach all students, as well as the content (Tomlinson, 2006).

Strategy Instruction

The use of strategies can also facilitate learning. Strategies are like game plans for successful learning. Some students use strategies automatically, whereas others need to be taught how, when, where, and why to use specific strategies. Different types of strategies are applicable in different situations. Self-monitoring strategies have the students ask questions such as "Am I on task?" Metacognitive strategies encourage the use of questions such as "Do I understand the task?" In addition, task-specific strategies, such as using a first-letter mnemonic, can help with the recall of specific information. For example, HOMES is a mnemonic for recalling the names of the Great Lakes: *H*uron, *O*ntario, *M*ichigan, *E*rie, and *S*uperior.

The Center for Research and Learning at the University of Kansas is at the forefront of research in the development of

DON'T FORGET

Self-questioning, the primary self-monitoring strategy, is a powerful and necessary technique for learning (Polloway & Patton, 1993).

evidence-based learning strategies for students with learning disabilities. Not only have they designed effective learning strategies to assist students with acquiring, retaining, and using knowledge, but they have also developed a Learning Strategies Curriculum. The focus of the curriculum is on direct, explicit instruction to help students become strategic learners.

Advance Organizers

Advance organizers are ways to cue the learner to the task at hand by providing an overview of the *big picture*. Advance organizers make use of prior knowledge and actively engage the learner. Teachers may use metaphors or analogies to help learners connect new information to existing knowledge. Other advance organizers include student- or teacher-generated questions and graphic organizers. The K-W-L procedure (Ogle, 1986) is easy to use as an advance organizer. Typically, students are provided with a graphic or they divide a paper into three columns and write at the top of each: Know (K), Want to Know (W), and Learned (L). First, the students write what they already know about the topic in the first column (activating prior knowledge). Second, the students write what they would like to learn about the topic in the middle column (active engagement). After the lesson, the students write what they have learned in the third column (actively engaged in summarizing). A fourth column can be added to create the graphic

K-W-L-Plus. In this last column, students can record additional information they still want to learn about the topic.

Higher-Order Thinking Skills

Another important teaching principle is to help students think deeply about the information and go beyond simple memorization of facts. Deep thinking, or elaboration, actively engages the learner in the task. Unfortunately, teaching frequently focuses on students acquiring knowledge through rote recall. Findings from research have indicated that teachers engage students in activities requiring higher-order thinking skills less than 1% of the time (Goodlad, 1984). If students are expected to think critically and apply skills to novel situations, they must be given many opportunities to engage in this type of thinking.

Feedback

Still another important principle for successful learning is the provision of immediate, corrective feedback (Marzano, Pickering, & Pollock, 2001; Mathes & Babyak, 2001). Learning is enhanced when the learner has the opportunity to express ideas and get immediate, frequent, and relevant feedback from teachers or peers. Feedback that is provided long after the learner completes the task (e.g., 2 weeks later, at the end of the semester) is not beneficial. In addition, the learner needs the opportunity to reflect on the feedback, make adjustments, and then revise information or try the task again.

Expectations/Climate of Success

Success breeds more success. Learners who believe they can complete tasks make more progress than those who lack confidence in their capabilities. If faced with repeated failures, most students will give up.

Because ineffective instruction often leads to student failure (Engelmann & Carnine, 1982; Kame'enui & Simmons, 1990), teachers must create successful learning opportunities for all students. Tasks need to be chal-

> **DON'T FORGET**
> ....
> For optimal effectiveness, the student must experience a success rate of about 80 to 85% on instructional tasks.

lenging but possible to complete. For optimum effectiveness, the student must experience a success rate of about 80 to 85% (Greenleaf, 2005; Tomlinson, 2000). This is why scaffolding instruction and effective teaching practices are so critical. They help build-in success for each student.

In addition, students are sensitive to the expectations of others. Both the positive and negative expectations of parents, teachers, peers, and even the media can affect students' expectations and thus their learning behaviors. Negative messages can create a loss of self-confidence and inhibit their performance. For example, it is commonly believed that girls do not do as well as boys in science and math. If this negative expectation is reinforced, it can decrease a girl's confidence in her ability to succeed in such courses of study or in a career related to math or science.

Peer-Mediated Instruction

Peer-mediated instruction is another powerful influence on academic motivation and achievement (Light & Littleton, 1999; Steinberg, Dornbusch, & Brown, 1992; Wentzel, 1999). This type of instruction can also help students develop social skills (Fuchs, Fuchs, Mathes, & Martinez, 2002; Miller & Miller, 1995; Rohrbeck, Ginsburg-Block, Fantuzzo, & Miller, 2003). Students that are taught how to work cooperatively make greater progress than those who are not given any instruction on how to work together (Fuchs et al., 1997). The two major forms of peer-mediated instruction are peer tutoring and cooperative learning.

Peer tutoring

Peer tutoring pairs up two students, of similar or dissimilar abilities, to practice skills that have been presented earlier. The students help each other or, in some cases, a higher achieving student helps and monitors the performance of a lower achieving student (Maheady, Sacca, & Harper, 1988). Cross-age tutoring, peer-assisted learning strategies (PALS) (Fuchs & Fuchs, 1995), and reciprocal peer tutoring (RPT) (Fantuzzo & Ginsburg-Block, 1998) are all examples of peer-tutoring strategies. Rapid Reference 1.2 provides tips for organizing a peer tutoring lesson.

Rapid Reference 1.2

Tips for Organizing a Peer-Tutoring Lesson

- Design lessons to reinforce skills already taught to students.
- Identify a specific learning objective to be presented by the tutor.
- Teach students how to be tutors.
- Provide a script of prompts for the tutor.
- Provide necessary flash cards or lists of skills to the tutors.
- Provide a daily log to record the results of the tutoring session.

Cooperative learning

Cooperative learning involves groups of students, usually three or more of differing ability levels. The students work in small, heterogeneous groups on tasks they are expected to help each other learn (Slavin, 1983). The best outcomes are associated with cooperative learning groups that require individual accountability in order to earn the group reward. One side benefit of cooperative learning groups is the increased social acceptance of low achievers by high achievers, resulting in higher levels of self-esteem for the low achievers (Madden & Slavin, 1983).

≡ Rapid Reference 1.3

Nine Best Instructional Strategies

1. Identifying similarities and differences
2. Summarizing and note taking
3. Reinforcing effort and providing recognition
4. Providing appropriate homework and practice
5. Producing physical or mental images (nonlinguistic representations)
6. Having students engage in cooperative learning
7. Setting goals and providing feedback
8. Generating and testing hypotheses (apply knowledge to a new situation)
9. Providing activities to help students activate prior knowledge

Nine Best Instructional Strategies

Rapid Reference 1.3 presents the nine best instructional strategies identified by Marzano et al. (2001). The strategies are listed in descending order of effectiveness. All of the strategies require active involvement of the learner, which is one of the most effective, evidence-based teaching practices.

DON'T FORGET

Effective instructional practices are critical elements of lesson design and delivery.

CONCLUSION

Knowledge of what constitutes effective instruction is not new. For several decades, researchers and educators alike have known the principles of effective teaching as well as the characteristics of effective teachers. Research continues to affirm these effective techniques, methods, and characteristics, even as researchers seek to validate the effectiveness of specific curricula and materials. What is new is the legal requirement to use evidence-based instruction. Both NCLB and IDEA mandate that general and special educators use methods and materials that work and have a positive impact on student progress.

The reason for these laws stems from concern regarding the academic progress of students. Based on the results of the National Assessment of Educational Progress (2007), less than one third of fourth (31%) and eighth (29%) graders were proficient in reading. In math, 38% of fourth graders and 31% of eighth graders were at the proficient level. Sadly, almost equal percentages were found to be below the basic level in both reading and math. The hope is that the application of research to practice will result in significant improvements in student learning and achievement.

✍ TEST YOURSELF ✍

1. *Evidence-based* **means that reliable and valid evidence indicates that the instruction or program works for many students.** True or False?

2. **What are the primary reasons for the focus on evidence-based instruction? (Choose all that apply.)**

   (a) No Child Left Behind, 2001

   (b) Individuals with Disabilities Education Improvement Act, 2004

   (c) pressure from parents and media

   (d) teachers' unions

3. **Use of an evidence-based instructional program ensures success for all students.** True or False?

4. Which of the following are characteristics of effective teachers? (Choose all that apply.)

(a)   engage students actively in learning

(b)   provide homework every day

(c)   ensure that students in class demonstrate time on task

(d)   use one, specific teaching approach

(e)   scaffold instruction

5. Why is it so important to actively engage the student in learning?

(a)   It keeps the students in their seats.

(b)   It makes the student do the work.

(c)   It leaves nothing to chance.

(d)   All of the above.

(e)   None of the above.

6. Assessment is a tool to inform instruction. True or False?

7. Which of the following is a benefit of assessment?

(a)   promotes learning

(b)   identifies whether instructional approaches or materials are working

(c)   helps students monitor their own learning

(d)   provides a means of understanding individual differences

(e)   All of the above.

(f)   b and d

8. Which type of instruction leaves nothing to chance?

(a)   strategy

(b)   peer-mediated

(c)   explicit

(d)   All of the above.

(e)   None of the above.

(continued)

9. Activating prior knowledge is an effective teaching principle because

    (a) it connects new knowledge to what is already known.

    (b) it actively engages the learner.

    (c) it primes the learner.

    (d) All of the above.

    (e) a and c

10. What is the primary self-monitoring strategy?

Answers: 1. True; 2. a and b; 3. False; 4. a, c, and e; 5. b; 6. True; 7. e; 8. c; 9. d; 10. self-questioning

Two

PHONOLOGICAL AWARENESS AND BEGINNING PHONICS

PHONOLOGICAL AWARENESS

Phonological awareness is an oral language ability that provides the foundation for learning to apply phonics knowledge to reading and spelling. Although some people use the terms interchangeably, others distinguish between the terms of phonemic awareness and phonological awareness. *Phonemic awareness* is a narrow ability that refers to detecting and manipulating individual phonemes, whereas *phonological awareness* is a broader ability that encompasses all aspects of sounds, including activities, such as rhyming words or hearing syllables within a word. Thus, phonological awareness includes all types of activities that focus upon sounds at the phoneme, syllable, or word level. Rapid Reference 2.1 illustrates several common phonological awareness activities.

Sometimes teachers are confused between the terms of phonological awareness and phonics, thinking that they are one and the same. *Phonology* refers to the speech system, an aspect of oral language, whereas *phonics* refers to a particular type of reading approach in which individuals are taught speech sounds and their corresponding letters directly. A child may have beginning levels of phonological awareness but not know the ways that the letters represent sounds in printed words (Torgesen & Mathes, 2000).

≡ *Rapid Reference 2.1*

Types of Phonological Awareness Activities

- Recognizing rhymes: Do *man* and *fan* rhyme?
- Producing rhymes: Tell me a word that rhymes with *cat*.
- Blending sounds (pushing them together): Listen to these sounds /k//a//t/. What is the word?
- Segmenting sounds (pushing them apart): Tell me the sounds in the word *bag*.
- Analyzing initial, final, and medial sounds in words: What sound does *sun* begin with?
- Deleting sounds (taking sounds out of words): Say *trip* without the /r/ sound.
- Inserting sounds (adding sounds to words): Add /k/ to the front of *at*.
- Manipulating sounds (changing the position or order of sounds in a word): Say the sounds in the word *tip* /t//i//p/, in reverse order (*pit*).

DON'T FORGET

- Phonological awareness is a broad ability that includes phonemic awareness.
- Phonological awareness is an auditory skill and does not involve written letters.

Characteristics of Individuals Struggling with Phonological Awareness

Phonemic awareness is critical for developing reading and spelling skills (Adams, 1990) and is the best predictor of reading difficulties in kindergarten and first grade (Lyon, 1995). An early warning sign for individuals at risk for reading problems is difficulty with rhyming words. Individuals with weaknesses in phonological awareness typically have trouble with the acquisition, retention, and application of phonic skills. They have difficulty learning to read and spell because of weaknesses in distinguishing, memorizing, or retrieving the various speech sounds (phonemes) that are associated with the various letters and letter patterns (the graphemes).

Developmental Course

For most children, phonological awareness and knowledge of phoneme–grapheme correspondences develop naturally over the preschool and early elementary years, progressing from the skill of rhyming words to the ability to hear and manipulate the individual sounds within words. As general guidelines, many children in preschool and most students in kindergarten are able to rhyme words. The majority of first-grade students can count syllables, delete part of a compound word, and count and blend syllables (Smith, 1997). Most children are able to perform all phonological awareness tasks by the end of second grade. Rapid Reference 2.2 provides a summary of the developmental sequence of phonological skills. Anthony and Francis (2005) describe two overlapping developmental patterns: (a) children become increasingly sensitive to smaller and smaller parts of words as they grow older, and (b) children can first manipulate and detect syllables in words, then onsets and rimes, and finally phonemes.

Rapid Reference 2.2

Developmental Sequence for Phonological Awareness

- Rhyming: preschool and kindergarten
- Counting syllables: first grade
- Deleting part of a compound word: first grade
- Blending and segmenting syllables: first grade
- Blending, segmenting, and manipulating phonemes: second grade

The manipulation tasks that involve deleting, substituting, or inserting sounds are the most difficult. These types of tasks involve both working memory (juggling, visualizing, and re-ordering of the sounds) as well as phonological and phonemic awareness. To reduce the memory demands, magnetic letters or letter tiles can be used. In fact, phonemic awareness develops more quickly when it is tied to literacy instruction (Anthony & Francis, 2005). Many years ago, Perfetti, Beck, Bell, and Hughes (1987) described the reciprocal relationship between phonemic awareness and learning to read. As children learn the names and sounds of letters and begin to learn to read and spell, their phonemic awareness increases. Phonological awareness instruction when combined with instruction in letter knowledge leads to long-standing improvements in reading and spelling (Anthony & Francis, 2005).

Blending and Segmenting

The two most important phonological awareness abilities for reading and spelling are blending (e.g., if I say these sounds, what word am I saying? /f/ /i/ /sh/) and segmenting (e.g., tell me the three sounds that you hear in the word *fish*?) (Ehri, 2006). Instruction in blending and segmentation results in more improvement in reading than did programs that placed an emphasis on mastery of multiple skills (NRP, 2000). Blending is important for decoding or applying phonics skills to reading unfamiliar words.

Segmentation is primarily important to encoding (spelling) because a person must listen to the speech sounds in a word while recording the sounds in order with matching graphemes. Rapid Reference 2.3 describes easy procedures for teaching sound blending and segmentation.

DON'T FORGET

The two most important phonological awareness abilities for reading and spelling are blending (pushing the sounds together) and segmenting (pulling the sounds apart).

≡ Rapid Reference 2.3

Teaching Sound Blending

1. Begin with speech sounds that can be sustained, such as /s/ and /m/.
2. Progress from words with two speech sounds to three, and then to four.
3. Gradually increase the length of the pause between sounds from a one-fourth second pause to a half-second, to a full second.
4. Demonstrate, model, and practice the process with written words with regular phoneme–grapheme correspondence.

Teaching Segmentation

1. Begin with compound words (e.g., baseball), progress to syllables, then onset-rimes, and then phonemes.
2. Use manipulatives, such as tiles or blocks, to push apart the sounds.
3. Start with compound words with two parts (e.g., raincoat) and then progress to words with two syllables.
4. At the phoneme level, progress from words with two speech sounds, to three, and then to four.
5. Practice breaking apart the phonemes in words with regular phoneme–grapheme correspondence.

BEGINNING PHONICS

When first acquiring phonics, students must not only learn the connections between phonemes and graphemes, but they must also be able to put the sounds in a correct sequence. This can be difficult at first for children because sounds are co-articulated in a continuous stream when speaking, and not broken apart into phonemes. Thus, the child hears a word like *dog* as a single burst of sound, rather than as three individual phonemes; this makes speech fluent, but it also makes it hard for children to hear individual phonemes within words (Torgesen & Mathes, 2000).

English has from 40 to 44 speech sounds. The reason it is hard to count the number of phonemes accurately is that dialectical differences affect how certain sounds are pronounced in different regions in the country. For example, in certain regions of the country, speakers do not distinguish between the short /i/ sound in the word *pin* and the short /e/ sound in the word *pen*. The phoneme is the smallest unit of speech that signifies a difference in word meaning. The change of the vowel sound in the words *pin* and *pen*, for example, indicates two distinct words with different meanings.

The English speech sounds are represented by letters and groups of letters, referred to as *graphemes*. English has about 220 graphemes or written spelling patterns. English spelling is somewhat complicated because the same grapheme (e.g., c) can represent more than one phoneme (e.g., the first sound in *coin* and the first sound in *city*) and the same phoneme (e.g., /s/) can be spelled with different graphemes (e.g., the first letter in *city* and *safe*). Sometimes graphemes are spelled with more than one letter, such as the two letters "ph" representing the /f/ sound as in *phone,* or the letters "gh" representing the /f/ sound as in *rough*. Sometimes the number of phonemes and graphemes in a word is not the same. For example, the word *phone* has three speech sounds (/f/ /o/ /n/) but five letters, whereas the word *fox* has three letters but four speech sounds (/f/ /o/ /k/ /s/).

Understanding of the relationships between phonemes and graphemes is referred to as knowledge of the *alphabetic principle*. The major factor impeding development of the alphabetic principle is a lack of phonemic awareness. Without mastery of the alphabetic principle, a student's ability to read words is negatively impacted.

Graphemes then are part of the system of marks that make up printed language, which is called *orthography* (Wagner & Barker, 1994). Some languages, such as Finnish, have what is called a *shallow* or *transparent* orthography because the connections between the letters and speech sounds are consistent. Other languages, such as English and French, have what is referred to as *deep* orthography because the connections between the sounds and words are more complex and not always based on phoneme–grapheme correspondences. For example, the word *know* and the first syllable in *knowledge* have different sounds, but the spelling is kept to preserve the meaning (Henry, 2005).

Learning to read and spell English presents a particular challenge to English language learners whose primary language may be more transparent (e.g., Spanish). Furthermore, students who are learning English as a second language are likely to misperceive some English phonemes as they will categorize phonemes in their first language. These confusions will be most obvious in their spelling of unfamiliar words, such as a native Spanish speaker spelling /sh/ with the letters "ch" (NRP, 2000).

EFFECTIVE INSTRUCTION

Findings from the meta-analyses of the National Reading Panel (NRP, 2000) indicate that phonological awareness instruction is most effective when it is taught by having children manipulate letters, thus becoming phonics instruction. Rapid Reference 2.4 summarizes several of the main conclusions from the NRP (2000) regarding instruction in phonological awareness. Overall findings indicate that instruction in phonological awareness is effective for improving the reading and spelling skills of at-risk children, as well as the reading skills of older students with reading disabilities. One finding is that phonological awareness training does not improve the spelling of older students with reading disabilities. The likely reason for this finding is that correct spelling also involves knowledge of orthographic patterns (e.g., ight), as well as morphological rules (e.g., the past tense of *jump* is spelled with -ed, rather than with -t).

≡ *Rapid Reference 2.4*

National Reading Panel Findings on Phonological Awareness

- Phonological awareness training enhances reading and spelling development for most students.
- Individual children differ in the amount of training time needed.
- Instruction is most effective in small groups.
- Effective training time varies from 5 to 18 hours of total instructional time.
- The most effective programs teach children how to segment phonemes in words with letters.
- Phonological awareness training is ineffective for improving the spelling of older students with reading disabilities.

Reading Aloud

An effective way to develop a child's phonemic awareness and language ability is to read aloud to the child (Adams, 1990). Exposing the child to the sounds and rhythm of language helps develop the prerequisite skills needed for learning to read. In addition, reading aloud provides opportunities to interact with the child, thus building and expanding his or her language skills. Dialogic reading is one example of an interactive read-aloud approach. The acronym PEER is used to guide the adult in the interaction. PEER represents four steps; *P*rompt, *E*valuate, *E*xpand, and *R*epeat. Rapid Reference 2.5 illustrates the steps involved in dialogic reading.

Initial Phonics Instruction

Phonics instruction is systematic with clear, sequential instruction addressing all of the major letter–sound correspondences (Ehri, 2004).

≡ *Rapid Reference 2.5*

Using Dialogic Read Alouds

1. Select a book appropriate for the child's age and interests.
2. Read the story aloud to the child and use the PEER steps to interact.
3. PROMPT the child by asking a question about a picture or element of the story. For example, point to a picture of a fire truck and say, "What is this?"
4. EVALUATE the child's response by affirming or correcting as needed. For example, if the child said "truck," affirm by saying "Yes, that is a truck."
5. EXPAND the child's response by adding more description. For example, expand the truck response by saying "that is a red fire truck."
6. REPEAT—have the child repeat the expanded response. For example, say, "Can you say red fire truck?"

The essential components of phonics instruction involve teaching a student phoneme–grapheme relationships and how to blend sounds. Phonics instruction may begin with single phonemes and graphemes, often referred to as a *synthetic phonics approach,* or with common onset and rime patterns, sometimes described as an *analogy phonics approach* (NRP, 2000). The English syllable has essentially two parts: the beginning consonant letters (the onset) and then the common endings (the rimes), which begin with a vowel sound. All English words have a rime, but not necessarily an onset. Thus, in the word *meat,* the /m/ is the onset and the *eat* is the rime; whereas in the word *eat,* the syllable is only a rime. Rapid Reference 2.6 illustrates 37 common rimes that may be used to construct 500 primary level words (Wylie & Durrell, 1970).

☰ *Rapid Reference 2.6*

Set of 37 Rimes from Which 500 Primary Words Can Be Taught

ack	ain	ake	ale	all	ame	an
ank	ap	ash	at	ate	aw	ay
eat	ell	est	ice	ick	ide	ight
ill	in	ine	ing	ink	ip	ir
ock	oke	op	or	ore	uck	ug
					ump	unk

Teaching Phoneme–Grapheme Connections

Findings from the NRP Report indicate that the connections between the phonemes and graphemes must be taught explicitly and that children must practice applying phonological awareness skills in their reading and writing (NRP, 2000). Many of the methods that are used to help students make these connections between speech sounds and letters are based on the work of Elkonin, a Russian psychologist (1973). The use of Elkonin boxes and similar procedures are used in many programs. Rapid Reference 2.7 describes an adapted Elkonin procedure. Three programs that are based on research and

> **DON'T FORGET**
>
> A phoneme is a single speech sound and a grapheme is the written letter or a written letter pattern that represents that sound (e.g., tch).

> **DON'T FORGET**
>
> Phonological awareness is an aspect of oral language, whereas phonics is a reading method that teaches phoneme–grapheme correspondences directly.

≡ Rapid Reference 2.7

Adapted Elkonin Procedure

1. Select simple words that have regular phoneme–grapheme correspondence (the number of speech sounds and letters are the same and the sounds are the most common sounds of the letter).

2. Select simple pictures that depict the word (e.g., pig, frog, nest).

3. Draw boxes for the number of phonemes under the picture.

4. Ask the student to push forward a colored marker as he or she says each sound.

5. Color code the vowel sounds (e.g., consonants blue poker chips and vowels red).

6. After the student successfully segments three and four sounds, introduce letter tiles and have the student push forward each tile while making the sound of the letter.

7. Gradually introduce additional phonics elements, such as consonant blends and digraphs (which should be written in one box because they make one sound).

8. Dictate the words and have the student write the words while saying each sound.

research-based principles and that stress the transitions from phonemes to graphemes, as well as mastery of sound blending and sound–symbol connections, are *Road to the Code* (Blachman, Ball, Black, & Tangel, 2000), *Phonic Reading Lessons* (Kirk, Kirk, Minskoff, Mather, & Roberts, 2007; Roberts & Mather, 2007), and *Phoneme–Grapheme Mapping* (Grace, 2007). One research-based software program that has been especially effective for increasing phonological awareness and early reading ability is *Read, Write, and Type* (available from www.talkingfingers.com).

CONCLUSION

Training in phonemic awareness clearly does not constitute a complete reading program; phonological awareness is necessary but not sufficient for good reading (NRP, 2000; Torgesen & Mathes, 2000). Good reading also requires mastery of more complex phonic skills, automaticity with sight words, a robust vocabulary, reasoning abilities, and world knowledge. Training in phonological awareness when coupled with systematic instruction in letter–sound correspondences, however, will help children move along the pathway to the development of efficient reading skills.

✍ TEST YOURSELF ✍

1. **The best example of a phonological segmentation task would be:**
   (a) Tell me a word that rhymes with *cat.*
   (b) How many sounds do you hear in the word *cat?*
   (c) Tell me a word that begins with the same sound as the word *cat.*
   (d) What word is composed of these three sounds: /k/ /a/ /t/?
   (e) All of the above are examples of segmentation tasks.

2. **Which of the following is an example of an onset-rime?**
   (a) ba-by
   (b) on-ly
   (c) f-og
   (d) fro-m

3. **How many phonemes do you hear in the word *box?***
   (a) 2
   (b) 3
   (c) 4
   (d) 5

4. What is the difference between phonological awareness and phonemic awareness?

(a) Phonemic awareness refers to the ability to manipulate the smallest unit of speech—the phoneme—whereas phonological awareness is a broader term including tasks at the word and syllable level.

(b) The two terms mean the same things.

(c) Phonological awareness refers to the ability to rhyme and segment sounds, whereas phonemic awareness refers to the ability to blend the individual sounds in words together.

(d) Phonological awareness refers to the ability to break the words in sentences apart, whereas phonemic awareness refers to the ability to identify individual sounds in words.

5. Segmentation ability is particularly important for

(a) decoding.

(b) encoding.

(c) decoding and encoding.

(d) neither decoding nor encoding.

6. About how many phonemes and graphemes are in the English language?

7. Knowledge of the relationships and connections between phonemes and graphemes is referred to as

(a) alphabetic insight.

(b) alphabetic patterns.

(c) alphabetic knowledge.

(d) alphabetic principle.

8. Synthetic phonics approaches begin with

(a) onsets and rimes.

(b) syllables.

(c) single phonemes and graphemes.

(d) whole words.

(e) any of the above.

(continued)

9. The adapted Elkonin procedure

   (a) teaches segmentation.

   (b) stresses the differences between consonant and vowel sounds.

   (c) teaches connections between phonemes and graphemes.

   (d) addresses all of the above.

10. Results from the NRP Report indicate that phonemic awareness training does not appear to improve

   (a) the reading performance of first-grade students.

   (b) the spelling performance of first-grade students.

   (c) the reading performance of older students with reading disabilities.

   (d) the spelling performance of older students with reading disabilities.

Answers: 1. b; 2. c; 3. c; 4. a; 5. b; 6. English has from 40 to 44 phonemes and about 220 graphemes; 7. d; 8. c; 9. d; 10. d

Three

PHONICS AND SIGHT WORD INSTRUCTION

PHONICS

Some children just seem to intuit the principles of phonics from their reading and print experiences with little or no instruction, whereas other children do not seem to profit so readily from their repeated exposures to print. Students who do not learn and recall phoneme–grapheme relationships with ease require a more intensive, sequential approach to reading in order to master alphabetic knowledge. As a rule, these students have trouble reading and spelling phonically regular nonwords or pseudowords, such as *flib* or *roust*.

Phonics approaches focus on direct and explicit instruction in phoneme–grapheme relationships. These types of approaches have been used with people of all ages who have difficulty learning to pronounce and spell words. Readers need to have efficient and automatic word pronunciation skill so that all of their attention can be directed toward understanding, considering, critiquing, and enjoying what they read.

DON'T FORGET

Phonics instruction is just a means to help students achieve proficient reading and spelling competency.

SIGHT WORDS

As readers acquire phonics skills, they must also master sight words. The term *sight words* is used to refer to two different kinds of words (Ehri, 1998). One meaning refers to all high-frequency words—the words that are most commonly used in writing. They are called sight words because they are supposed to be recognized instantly and easily without an analysis of sounds. As noted by Ehri (1998), with sufficient practice, all words acquire the status of sight words.

Another meaning of *sight words* is words that contain one or more irregular elements and thus cannot be pronounced correctly through the application of phonics (e.g., once). These words are particularly problematic for spelling and are discussed in more depth in that chapter. Most phonics programs introduce high-frequency words and sight words in a systematic way, providing a lot of practice and repetition so that these common words become automatic.

Development of Automaticity with Words

How do competent readers gain such facility and ease with the recognition and pronunciation of so many words? To explain this phenomenon, Ehri (1998, 2000) describes the following four overlapping phases that underlie the development of efficient, quick reading skill: prealphabetic, partial alphabetic, full alphabetic, and consolidated alphabetic. These phases were based on the consensus of many research studies that addressed how young children develop and progress in reading skill.

During the prealphabetic phase, beginning readers recognize words by the visual features of the word, not through analysis of the grapheme–phoneme relationships. Many preschool children can "read" the McDonald's sign or the label on the Pepsi can. In the partial-alphabetic phase, readers begin to make connections between some of the letters and sounds in written words. Partial-phase readers tend to pay attention to beginning and ending consonant sounds but they confuse words with similar spellings and do not have all of the letters of a word stored in memory. They often misread vowel sounds. In the full-alphabetic phase, readers have developed complete connections between letters and sounds and they are able to pronounce words with accuracy that conform to phonics rules. They can pronounce nonsense words as well. In the consolidated-alphabetic phase, the reader has mastered letter patterns that occur across many words, including morphemes, syllables, and rimes. Recognition of these chunks or word parts makes it easier to decode longer words that have several syllables (Ehri, 2000). In regard to recognizing words quickly, readers cannot retain many sight words until they are fully alphabetic. In essence, developing readers must know phoneme–grapheme relationships before they can amass a substantial sight vocabulary. Thus, the most promising approaches to increasing word recognition skills seem to focus first on developing accuracy in word reading, and then they work on improving fluency and rate.

Characteristics of Individuals Struggling with Phonics or Sight Words

A number of cognitive correlates for basic reading skills have been identified by researchers, including phonemic awareness, associative memory, rapid naming, orthographic processing, perceptual speed, and working memory (e.g., Berninger, 2008; Swanson, Trainin, Necoechea, & Hammill, 2003). Students struggling with acquiring sound–symbol relationships often do so because of limited phonemic awareness. In addition, students often have difficulty storing and retrieving accurate representations of phoneme–grapheme relationships and words, implicating weaknesses in associative memory, working memory, and/or orthographic processing. Early warning signs include difficulty learning letter names and letter sounds. Some students will demonstrate pronounced problems with the phonological aspects of reading, whereas others will have more difficulty with the visual, or orthographic, aspects of reading.

Teacher Training

As with any area of instruction, teachers need to know how to teach phonics and monitor student progress. Some teachers have been trained in how to teach phonics, but others have not. Although not all

Rapid Reference 3.1

Common Phonics Terminology

- Alphabetic principle: knowledge of the connections between sounds and letters
- Consonant: a speech sound made in which the sound going through the vocal tract is obstructed by the lips, tongue, or teeth
- Consonant blend: two adjacent letters that maintain their own sounds
- Digraph: two adjacent consonant or vowel letters that make one new sound (e.g., ph, oa)
- Diphthong: two adjacent vowel sounds that are pronounced together with a slide (ou, ow, oi, and oy)
- Grapheme: a letter or letter string
- Morpheme: the smallest unit of meaning (e.g., affixes, root words)
- Phoneme: the smallest unit of speech sound
- Vowel: a speech sound made in which the sound goes through the vocal tract unobstructed

children need systematic phonics instruction to learn to read, many struggling readers do need this type of instruction. Intensive phonics instruction is usually provided by a special education or reading teacher in a small group or one-to-one instructional format. These teachers are familiar with phonics terminology and the scope and sequence of skills. Rapid Reference 3.1 contains several commonly used phonics terms.

EFFECTIVE INSTRUCTION

Most primary teachers would report that they provide some level of phonics instruction to their students. The question becomes, however, how systematic is the instruction and is it sufficient to ensure that all students have knowledge of the alphabetic principle (Stuebing, Barth, Cirino, Francis, & Fletcher, 2008)? Although teachers may deliver phonics instruction in a planned, systematic sequence without reliance on a specific program, effective phonics instruction is often facilitated through the use of carefully developed programs.

Commercial Phonics Programs

Many phonics programs exist and although many aspects may be similar, the programs vary regarding: the use of teacher scripts for instruction, the scope and sequence of the programs, the integration with decodable text, the size of the instructional group, the intensity of teacher training, and the application of these skills to reading and spelling. A variety of systematic phonics programs have been shown to be effective for students of differing ages, abilities, and socioeconomic backgrounds (NRP, 2000). Rapid Reference 3.2 provides examples of programs that provide systematic phonics instruction. The supporting materials that a teacher selects may vary depending upon teacher and student knowledge and skills (Stuebing et al., 2008).

≡ *Rapid Reference 3.2*

Examples of Systematic Phonics Approaches

- Corrective Reading (www.sraonline.com)
- Explode the Code (www.epsbooks.com)
- Fundations (www.wilsonlanguage.com)
- Glass Analysis (www.glassanalysis.com)
- Herman Method (www.sopriswest.com)
- Language! (www.teachlanguage.com)
- Phonics Reading Lessons (www.academictherapy.com)
- Primary Phonics (www.epsbooks.com)
- Spalding Method (www.spalding.org)
- S.P.I.R.E. (www.epsbooks.com)
- Touch Phonics (www.epsbooks.com)
- Wilson Reading System (www.wilsonlanguage.com)

Decodable Text

In conjunction with phonics instruction, the student practices reading with decodable text. *Decodable text* refers to reading books in which most of the selected words conform to common phoneme–grapheme relationships. By using a controlled vocabulary, these books provide readers with practice applying the phonics skills that they are learning in isolation. Typically, high-frequency words are introduced slowly and practiced within the stories. Many phonics programs

CAUTION

The purpose of decodable text is to practice application of phoneme–grapheme relationships, not to enhance vocabulary or increase reading comprehension. These types of readers are only for the practice of phonics skills. Remember that students also need to hear and discuss rich, authentic text.

come with a set of decodable books that match with the content of the lessons. The main limitation of decodable text is that the language content is reduced so that the sentences have limited content, the vocabulary is impoverished, and the stories lack meaning (e.g., The pig did a jig on a fig).

Pronunciation of Multisyllabic Words

Once students have learned how to apply phoneme–grapheme relationships, they need to be able to break words apart to pronounce larger units, such as syllables. This is the phase that Ehri (1998, 2000) refers to as the *consolidated-alphabetic phase*. The reader can easily pronounce multisyllabic words and has many of these word parts stored in memory as units (e.g., tion). Students who have trouble reading longer words require instruction in how to break words apart. Many programs teach the student how to recognize common affixes (prefixes and suffixes), as well as the root word. Rapid Reference 3.3 provides a list of programs that are designed to improve students' abilities to read longer, more complex words.

≡ Rapid Reference 3.3

Examples of Programs for Multisyllabic Word Reading

- Decoding Multisyllabic Words (www.scholastic.com)
- Glass Analysis (www.glassanalysis.com)
- Mega-words (www.epsbooks.com)
- Patterns for Success in Reading and Spelling (www.proedinc.com)
- WORDS (www.proedinc.com)
- REWARDS (www.rewardsreading.com)

Morphology

More advanced word recognition skills also involve an understanding of morphology. *Morphology* refers to the meaning units of language. Just as a phoneme refers to the smallest unit of sound, a morpheme refers to the smallest unit of meaning. For example, the word *girls* is composed of two morphemes—the meaning unit *girl* and the plural marker *s*. Understanding these individual units of meaning can also influence spelling development. For example, understanding that past tense is typically spelled with the letters -ed can help a person spell the word *jumped* correctly, even though it sounds like it ends with a /t/. Additional study can focus on prefixes and suffixes and learning the six syllable types, as well as the meanings and pronunciations of common Latin and Greek roots.

Prefixes and Suffixes

Instruction in multisyllabic words often begins with the teaching of common affixes. The first prefixes that are generally added to words are: in-, un-, mis-, dis-, fore-, de-, re-, and pre- (Henry, 2003). Children can practice reading these prefixes and adding them to base words, such as *like* and *read*. The first suffixes students learn are the inflectional endings that change the number, person, or tense of a base word, including -s, -ed-, -ing, -er, -es, and -est. Derivational endings are added to the word and often change the word to a different part of speech, including: -ly, -less, -ness, -ship, -fold, and -ment (Henry, 2003). Lists of the most common prefixes and suffixes and their meanings can be found on the Internet.

Six Syllable Types

Several programs, including the Wilson Reading System, teach the students how to recognize and pronounce the six basic syllable types in the

≡ *Rapid Reference 3.4*

The Six English Syllable Types

- Closed syllable: at, mat (VC or CVC with short vowel sound)
- Silent e: bike, shake (CVCe or CCVCe with a long vowel sound)
- Open syllable: motion (long vowel sound and the syllable ends with a vowel mo-)
- Consonant -le: turtle
- R-controlled vowel: car, burn
- Digraph and Diphthong syllable: boat, meat, out, coin

English language (closed syllables, syllables with a long vowel and silent e, open syllables, syllables ending in a consonant with -le, r-controlled syllables, and vowel team or digraph and diphthong syllables). In the elementary grades, the closed, open, and consonant -le syllables are the most common (Henry, 2003). Understanding of these syllables can (usually) help a struggling reader know how to pronounce the vowel sound. Examples of these six syllable types are provided in Rapid Reference 3.4.

In the Wilson Reading System, a simple syllable marking is used to code each of these syllable types. Using a left-to-right movement, the reader draws a curved or straight line under each syllable and then identifies the type of syllable, codes the vowels with a long or short marking, puts a slash through the e if it is a silent e or consonant -le syllable, and draws a circle around the vowels. Instruction in syllable types may also facilitate spelling, particularly mastery of words that end with a final silent e.

Latin and Greek Combining Forms

Upper elementary students will encounter many multisyllabic words and can benefit from instruction in Latin roots and Greek combining forms

(Henry, 2003). This type of instruction also helps with vocabulary development. Latin words are built from the addition of prefixes and suffixes to a root word. Examples of common Latin roots include: aud (to hear), dic (to say), cogn (to know), duc (to lead), port (to carry), rupt (to break), and spect (to see). Many Greek words are found within content-area reading, including science and mathematics. These words are usually compounded, such as in the word *photograph*. They are called *combining forms* because both parts contribute equally to the meaning of the word. Common examples of Greek combining forms include: bio (life), geo (earth), graph (written), morph (form), phon (sound), psych (mind), and scope (see). Henry (2003) provides a scope and sequence for teaching Latin and Greek word parts. In addition, comprehensive lists of Latin and Greek roots can be found on the Internet. Rapid Reference 3.5 provides an overview of a typical sequence for phonics instruction progressing from phonological awareness to advanced word study.

☰ *Rapid Reference 3.5*

Typical Sequence of Phonics Instruction

- Blending and segmentation
- Single consonants and short vowels in closed syllables
- CVCe syllables
- Consonant blends
- Consonant digraphs
- Open syllables
- Vowel digraphs and diphthongs (vowel team syllable)
- Silent letters
- Common prefixes and suffixes
- Additional syllable types (r-controlled and consonant -le)
- Latin and Greek roots

Sight Word Instruction

Instant words

One systematic way to practice high-frequency words is to use a carefully developed list of words, such as Edward Fry's list of 300 Instant Words (Fry, 1977). This list of words makes up about 65% of the words used in written material (see Table 3.1) and it may be used for both

Table 3.1. Fry's 300 Instant Words

FIRST HUNDRED WORDS (Approximately First Grade)			
Group 1a	Group 1b	Group 1c	Group 1d
the	he	go	who
a	I	see	an
is	they	then	their
you	one	us	she
to	good	no	new
and	me	him	said
we	about	by	did
that	had	was	boy
in	if	come	three
not	some	get	down
for	up	or	work
at	her	two	put
with	do	man	were
it	when	little	before

(continued)

Table 3.1 (Continued)

Group 1a	Group 1b	Group 1c	Group 1d
on	so	has	just
can	my	them	long
will	very	how	here
are	all	like	other
of	would	our	old
this	any	what	take
your	been	know	cat
as	out	make	again
but	there	which	give
be	from	much	after
have	day	his	many

SECOND HUNDRED WORDS
(Approximately Second Grade)

Group 2a	Group 2b	Group 2c	Group 2d
saw	big	may	ran
home	where	let	five
soon	am	use	read
stand	ball	these	over
box	morning	right	such
upon	live	present	way
first	four	tell	too
came	last	next	shall
girl	color	please	own
house	away	leave	most

Table 3.1 (Continued)

Group 2a	Group 2b	Group 2c	Group 2d
find	red	hand	sure
because	friend	more	thing
made	pretty	why	only
could	eat	better	near
book	want	under	than
look	year	while	open
mother	white	should	kind
run	got	never	must
school	play	each	high
people	found	best	far
night	left	another	both
into	men	seem	end
say	bring	tree	also
think	wish	name	until
back	black	dear	call

THIRD HUNDRED WORDS
(Approximately Third Grade)

Group 3a	Group 3b	Group 3c	Group 3d
ask	hat	off	fire
small	car	sister	ten
yellow	write	happy	order
show	try	once	part
goes	myself	didn't	early

(continued)

Table 3.1 (Continued)

Group 3a	Group 3b	Group 3c	Group 3d
clean	longer	set	fat
buy	those	round	third
thank	hold	dress	same
sleep	full	fell	love
letter	carry	wash	hear
jump	eight	start	yesterday
help	sing	always	eyes
fly	warm	anything	door
don't	sit	around	clothes
fast	dog	close	through
cold	ride	walk	o'clock
today	hot	money	second
does	grow	turn	water
face	cut	might	town
green	seven	hard	took
every	woman	along	pair
brown	funny	bed	now
coat	yes	fine	keep
six	ate	sat	head
gave	stop	hope	food

Note: From *Elementary Reading Instruction* (p. 73), by E. B. Fry, 1977, New York: McGraw-Hill Book Company. Copyright 1977 by Edward B. Fry. Reprinted with permission.

≡ *Rapid Reference 3.6*

Sample Rapid Word Recognition Chart

who	they	said	of	who	come
people	of	they	who	come	people
said	come	people	said	of	who
they	said	come	people	who	of
come	people	said	who	of	come

reading and spelling instruction. The first 100 words make up about 50% of words used in written materials. As an informal assessment, a student may attempt to read or spell the words starting at the beginning of the list and continuing until an error is made. Instruction can then begin at the point where the student does not immediately recognize or does not know how to spell a word. The student can continue working on the list until all 300 words have been mastered.

Rapid word recognition chart

Another simple way to improve speed of recognition for words with an irregular element is the use of a rapid word recognition chart (Carreker, 2005a). The chart is a matrix that contains five rows of six irregular words (e.g., who, said), with each row containing the same six words in a different order. After a brief review of the words and a warm up in which the teacher points randomly to eight to ten words on the chart, students are timed for 1 minute (or until they complete the chart) as they read each word in the squares aloud. Students can then count and record the number of words they read correctly. Rapid Reference 3.6 illustrates this type of chart. Additional methods for building speed of

≣ Rapid Reference 3.7

Examples of Websites with Information on Basic Reading Skills

- Cambridge Online Dictionary (http://dictionary.cambridge.org)
- Dolch Sight Words (www.createdbyteachers.com)
- Florida Center for Reading Research (www.fcrr.org)
- Fry Instant Words (www.literacyconnections.com)
- National Institute for Literacy (www.nifl.gov)
- National Right to Read Foundation (www.nrrf.org)
- Read Well (www.readwell.net)
- Read-Write-Think (www.readwritethink.org)
- Reading Rockets (www.readingrockets.org)
- Starfall (www.Starfall.com)
- Vaughn Gross Center for Reading and Language Arts (www.texasreading.org)

word perception and recognition are discussed in the chapter on Reading Fluency.

Web sites

Numerous web sites provide guidance, support, materials, and instructional practice for developing basic reading skills. A few examples are listed in Rapid Reference 3.7.

CONCLUSION

If a reader has poor basic reading skills, automatic word recognition and fluency are sacrificed and comprehension is compromised. Just as a house needs a foundation, accuracy with word reading provides the foundation for more advanced reading abilities. Research has identified effective ways to teach basic reading skills and several explicit, systematic, synthetic phonics programs exist that have been found to be highly effective with children struggling to learn to read.

Mastering basic reading skills represents a means to an end, not the end itself. The ultimate goal is to develop readers who can use reading as a tool for both learning and enjoyment. If children do not acquire these basic reading skills during the first 3 years of schooling, they will have a difficult time developing the levels of fluency, vocabulary, and comprehension necessary for effective reading in the upper grades. Depending upon the nature of their difficulties, different children will require a different amount of emphasis on the various components of reading.

🐊 TEST YOURSELF 🐊

1. **Which word(s) contains a consonant blend?**
   (a) phone
   (b) flip
   (c) catch
   (d) them
   (e) both phone and them

2. **Which word contains a diphthong?**
   (a) coin
   (b) seal
   (c) ocean
   (d) fork

(continued)

3. Which word(s) contain a consonant digraph?

(a) back

(b) snow

(c) thin

(d) both back and thin

4. Which word contains a short vowel sound?

(a) cave

(b) moan

(c) lid

(d) try

5. Which word contains a vowel digraph?

(a) toe

(b) bed

(c) fine

(d) boy

6. The purpose of decodable text is to

(a) learn high-frequency words.

(b) practice application of phoneme–grapheme relationships.

(c) increase reading vocabulary.

(d) increase reading fluency.

7. In Ehri's phases of word reading development, readers in the partial-alphabetic phase

(a) do not pay attention to all the letter details in a word and tend to rely on consonant sounds.

(b) do not use phoneme–grapheme associations but instead recognize the word through salient visual cues.

(c) have mastered all phoneme–grapheme relationships but have trouble pronouncing longer words.

(d) can break words into syllables but still read slowly.

8. Understanding the six syllable types can help a struggling reader

(a) learn the vowels and consonants.

(b) understand Latin roots.

(c) pronounce the vowel sounds correctly.

(d) recognize words more quickly.

9. Morphemes are the smallest

(a) sound units in words.

(b) prefixes in words.

(c) word endings.

(d) units of word meaning.

10. High-frequency words are

(a) words that have an irregular element.

(b) words that are not spelled the way they sound.

(c) the most common words found in reading and writing.

(d) the most difficult words to read and spell.

Answers: 1. b; 2. a; 3. d; 4. c; 5. a; 6. b; 7. a; 8. c; 9. d; 10. c

Four

READING FLUENCY

In the Orient, children bawl in concert over a book, imitating their fellows or their teacher until they come to know what the page says and to read it for themselves.

—*Huey, 1968*

Fluency is often described as forming the link or the bridge between word analysis and comprehension (Carnine, Silbert, Kame'enui, & Tarver, 2004; Chard, Vaughn, & Tyler, 2002; Pikulski & Chard, 2005; Wolf et al., 2003). Reading fluency encompasses the speed or rate of reading, as well as the ability to read materials with ease and expression. Fluency has been defined as "the ability to read connected text rapidly, smoothly, effortlessly, and automatically with little conscious attention to the mechanics of reading, such as decoding" (Meyer & Felton, 1999, p. 284). Readers are judged to be successful with decoding when their ability to identify words is fast and nearly effortless or automatic. To be fluent, words must be read with automaticity. In fact, this ability to read words by sight automatically has been described as the key to skilled reading (Ehri, 1998). Readers are judged to be less skilled when their reading is slow and marked by hesitations, repetitions, and mispronunciations. Rapid Reference 4.1 describes several central ways that slow reading can affect performance, as summarized by Mastropieri, Leinart, and Scruggs (1999).

Two theories have been proposed that relate to the development of fluent word reading: automaticity theory (LaBerge & Samuels, 1974) and verbal efficiency theory (Perfetti, 1985). These theorists maintain that beginning readers first must focus on accuracy of reading and as their skills develop shift more attention to understanding what they read. Thus, fluent reading facilitates comprehension (e.g., Fuchs, Fuchs, Hosp, & Jenkins, 2001). When readers allocate too much attention to lower-level processes, such as trying to decode words, insufficient attentional resources are left to accomplish the higher-order linguistic pro-

Rapid Reference 4.1

How Slow Reading Affects Reading Performance

- Students read less text and have less time to remember, review, or comprehend the text
- Students expend more cognitive energy than peers trying to identify individual words
- Students have trouble retaining parts of text in their memories and are then less likely to integrate those segments with other parts

cessing involved in comprehension (LaBerge & Samuels, 1974; Perfetti & Hogaboam, 1975). When readers are fluent, reading is effortless and the reader is free to focus on meaning rather than word decoding (Chard et al., 2002).

As older students or adults, struggling readers become overwhelmed by lengthy reading assignments because of their slower reading rates (Wolf, 2007). In fact, secondary students that are not yet fluent readers find reading so laborious that they may avoid reading altogether (Rasinski et al., 2005). Thus, older children with reading difficulties do not have

CAUTION

Automatic word reading does not equal reading fluency. It is necessary, but insufficient for reading fluency. Fluency requires an appropriate rate, high accuracy, and expression.

> **DON'T FORGET**
> ....
> Skilled reading is characterized by automaticity of word reading.

sufficient practice reading and it becomes increasingly more difficult to close the gap in fluency. Outside the school setting, a child at the 90th percentile may read as many words in 2 days as the child at the 10th percentile reads in an entire year (Torgesen, 2007).

Characteristics of Individuals Struggling with Reading Fluency

Some children have developed accurate word pronunciation skills but they read slowly and their decoding is neither automatic nor fluent. Reading is word-by-word with limited expression. A student who lacks expression when reading may be described as having *limited prosody*, or trouble modulating his or her voice with proper stress and intonation. For example, the student will ignore punctuation marks, such as not pausing at periods or raising the tone of voice for a question mark. Readers who do not divide sentences into meaningful phrases will have trouble comprehending written text (Therrien, 2004). Poor prosody can lead to inappropriate expression or meaningless groupings of words, instead of meaningful phrases, whereas good prosody enhances reading comprehension of the reader, as well as listening comprehension of the listener (Hudson, Lane, & Pullen, 2005). Rapid Reference 4.2 describes elements of good oral reading prosody. Due to subjectivity, assessing prosody may be the most challenging aspect of evaluating reading fluency. Rasinski (2004) developed the following four-point expressiveness rubric to help evaluate prosody:

1. expression and speaking (volume)
2. phrasing
3. smoothness
4. pace

The core cognitive correlates of reading fluency appear to involve rapid automatic naming (RAN), orthographic processing, working memory and attention, and lexical retrieval (Fletcher, Lyon, Fuchs, & Barnes, 2007).

The rapid naming of colors, objects, digits, and letters appears to be related to the later development of reading fluency. Both naming speed and reading involve multiple perceptual, lexical, and motoric processes; thus, the speed of naming letters is a good predictor of the efficiency of later processes involved in fluency and provides an early approximation of a student's later reading speed for words (Wolf et al., 2003). In kindergarten and first grade, these early naming speed deficits are good predictors of who will struggle with fluency later in school (Wolf, 2007). In a longitudinal study of the development of word reading fluency in German, Landerl and Wimmer (2008) found that early naming speed was the strongest predictor of later reading fluency. They concluded that for a language like German that has relatively consistent phoneme–grapheme relationships, reading development depends more upon adequate naming speed than on phonological awareness.

Orthographic processing problems cause some students to have trouble developing accurate high-quality mental representations of word patterns and spellings, and thus these students have problems acquiring a sight vocabulary (Carlisle & Rice, 2002). These students are slow to recognize common syllable units and word parts easily and thus

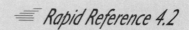

Rapid Reference 4.2

Elements of Oral Prosody

- Vocal emphasis is placed on appropriate words
- Voice tone rises and falls at appropriate places in test
- Voice tone rises at the end of a question
- Vocal tone represents character's feelings and emotions
- Appropriate pauses are made at phrase boundaries, using punctuation, prepositional phrases, subject-verb divisions, and conjunctions

fail to develop automaticity with word recognition.

Working memory and attention also play a role in reading fluency. Clearly, readers have to pay attention to the appearance of words to develop accurate orthographic representations. LaBerge and Samuels (1974) indicate that slow word recognition results in a working memory bottleneck that then uses up attentional resources and affects reading comprehension. If a reader's attention is drained by decoding words, little energy is left for the demanding process of comprehension (Pikulski & Chard, 2005).

Lexical retrieval, the ability to retrieve verbal labels from memory quickly, is another factor that can impede the development of reading fluency (Carlisle & Rice, 2002). Slow speed in producing labels can also be the reason for a low RAN score. Ehri (1998) explains how fluent reading also depends upon familiarity with the syntactical and meaning aspects of the word. Thus, fluency also depends on a person's vocabulary knowledge and ability to associate words with their meanings.

Determining a Student's Reading Rate and Accuracy Level

Reading rate can be calculated by dividing the number of words read correctly by the total amount of reading time. For example, a teacher can count out 100 words in a passage and then time students as they read the passage. If a student reads 92 words correctly out of the 100 in 1.5 minutes, the words correct per minute (wcpm) would be 61. Another way to determine rate is to have the student read a text for 1 minute. Count the total number of words read, minus the number of errors, to obtain the number of wcpm. While self-corrections are not counted as errors, they do impact reading rate.

To determine the student's accuracy level (percentage of words read correctly), divide the number of words read correctly by the total number of words attempted. For example, if the student reads 110 words correctly out of a total of 120 words, the accuracy rate is 92% (110 wcpm/120 wpm = .916 or 92%). Knowing the student's accuracy level ensures that materials for building reading fluency will be at an appropriate instructional level for that student. In general, the student should have an accuracy rate of 90 to 94% on the material used for reading fluency instruction. To help determine if instruction should focus on building accuracy or fluency, Simmons and Kame'enui (1998) suggest the following guidelines: (a) If a student is making more than one error for every ten words read, instruction should focus on building accuracy; (b) if the student is making fewer errors, for example one error in every 15 to 20 words, but has slow speed, then instruction should focus on building fluency. Hasbrouck and Tindal (2005) completed an extensive study of oral reading fluency in 2004, which is published in a technical report entitled, "Oral Reading Fluency: 90 Years of Measurement." The report and norms are available on the University of Oregon's web site at: brt.uoregon.edu/tech_reports.htm.

Adjusting Reading Rate

Most people have a constant rate when reading. This rate is the fastest pace at which a person can understand complete thoughts in successive sentences of relatively easy material. As long as the material is relatively easy to read, a person's rate stays the same. For different types of tasks, however, readers often alter their rates. Students with slow reading rates are often not aware that good readers adjust their rates depending on the purpose of reading. Making these types of adjustments is particularly important for studying or completing assigned readings because a student with poor reading skills otherwise struggles to complete lengthy reading assignments.

Carver (1990) uses the analogy of adjusting reading speed to the shifting of gears in a car. First and second gears are the slowest, most powerful gears. First gear is used to memorize materials, whereas second gear is used to learn material. Third gear is the typical reading rate. The fourth gear, skimming, and the fifth gear, scanning, are the fastest but least powerful gears. The fastest gears are useful when one is trying to locate a specific piece of information or trying to get the general sense of a passage without reading every word.

Skilled readers know how to adjust the gears of their reading rates based upon their purposes for reading. If a student is trying to memorize material for a test, the reading pace should be slow and reflective, characterized by stopping and reviewing what has been read. If the student is reading a novel for pleasure, the pace should be steady and fluent. If one is searching for information in a catalog, the pace is rapid.

Some children have not learned how to adjust their reading rates and they attempt to read information in an encyclopedia at the same rate that they would read a novel. The teacher can model for the students how to change their rate of reading for different types of materials. They can practice skimming through a chapter to get a general sense of the information and then move through the chapter more slowly to study for a quiz.

EFFECTIVE INSTRUCTION

Unfortunately, dysfluent reading appears to be a highly stable characteristic that is hard to remediate (Landerl & Wimmer, 2008; Torgesen, 2007). In summarizing the consistent findings from their intervention research, Torgesen (2007) explains that performance in phonemic decoding, reading accuracy, and comprehension can be substantially improved; but for children with moderate and severe impairments in reading, the gap in fluency remains. Thus, it is important to ensure that all children have sufficient practice reading in the early elementary years.

The purpose of fluency instruction is to increase ease and automaticity with reading so that a reader can devote all of his or her attention to understanding the material. In discussing the purpose, Wolf et al. (2003) state:

> The goal of working toward reading fluency has only a little to do with fluency instruction itself. Just like decoding accuracy, fluency is a bridge toward comprehension and the desire to read more, which will ultimately enable deeper comprehension. Fluency, therefore, is a means—just like decoding—to a higher end than itself. For the end of all our efforts is a child who reads accurately enough and fluently enough to understand what she reads and to reach for more. (p. 373)

In general, students who benefit from methods to increase reading fluency have acquired some proficiency in decoding skill, but their reading level is lower than their oral language abilities. Most of the fluency procedures involve repeated exposures to words with material at the student's instructional reading level (Fletcher et al., 2007). Chard and Osborn (1999) suggest that a beginning reading program should provide opportunities for partner reading, practice reading difficult words prior to reading the text, timings for accuracy and rate, opportunities to hear books read, and opportunities to read to others.

Chard et al. (2002) reviewed the results of 24 studies that investigated the application of reading fluency interventions for students with reading disabilities. Their findings indicate that effective fluency interventions include: (a) provision of an explicit model of fluent reading, (b) multiple readings of text with corrective feedback on missed words, and (c) established performance criteria for increasing the difficulty level of the text. In addition, instruction and practice recognizing larger orthographic units quickly enhance fluency. Many of the fluency intervention procedures described in the next section include these components.

CAUTION

Students should first become accurate readers before an emphasis is placed on speed of reading.

DON'T FORGET

Students who read and reread passages orally with guidance and/or feedback increase their reading skills (Armbruster, Lehr, & Olsen, 2001).

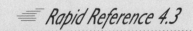

Rapid Reference 4.3

Word Reading Rate for 1-Minute Timings

- 30 correct wpm for first- and second-grade children
- 40 correct wpm for third-grade children
- 60 correct wpm for mid–third-grade children
- 80 wpm for students in fourth grade and higher

Speed Drills

To conduct a speed drill, the student reads a list of words for 1 minute as someone records the number of errors. The list may be a high-frequency word list or the sample speed drills provided in a program like *Concept Phonics*, where lists are provided for 1-minute timings. The purpose of these drills is to help students develop automatic sight recognition of words. The general guidelines for reading lists of words at the desired rate are presented in Rapid Reference 4.3.

Choral Reading or Neurological Impress Method

The neurological impress method (Heckelman, 1969, 1986) is a method for choral or concert reading. In this method, you read aloud together with a student for 10 to 15 minutes daily. To begin, select a high-interest book or a content-area textbook from the classroom. Sit next to the student and read aloud as you point to the words with your index finger. Read at a slightly faster pace than the student and encourage him or her to try and keep up with you.

When necessary, remind the student to keep his or her eyes on the words. Successful decoding requires the reader to connect the flow of spoken language with the flow of text (Carreker, 2005a). Reading aloud with students can help them to practice phrasing and improve oral reading prosody. Echo reading is an easy way to introduce unison reading. For this procedure, the teacher reads a sentence and the student then reads it back. Therrien (2004) indicates that three other fluency strategies evolved out of the Neurological Impress Method: assisted reading and reading while listening, using audiotapes or CDs, and paired reading, where students read along with a model until they feel ready to read alone. Rapid Reference 4.4 lists the common elements involved in the use of choral reading methods or taped books.

Repeated Reading

The repeated reading technique is designed for children who read slowly despite adequate word recognition (Samuels, 1979). This method has an extensive research base (Therrien, 2004). For example, research suggests that repeatedly practicing oral reading of instructional-level text with a model and feedback supports growth in oral reading fluency (Denton, Fletcher, Anthony, & Francis, 2006). Both oral and silent repeated readings have been found to be effective for increasing reading fluency and improving

Rapid Reference 4.4

Common Elements in Choral Reading Methods

- Students listen to text as they follow along with the book
- Students follow along with the print using their fingers as guides
- Reading materials can be used that students would be unable to read independently
- Procedures are done 10 to 15 minutes daily
- More advanced readers provide feedback and assistance
- Comprehension activities can be added before and after reading

comprehension (e.g., Fuchs et al., 2001; NRP, 2000; Perfetti, 1986; Shankweiler, Lundquist, Dreyer, & Dickinson, 1996). In a review of the effectiveness of repeated reading, Meyer and Felton (1999) concluded that the method of repeated reading improves reading speed for a wide variety of readers. Rapid Reference 4.5 summarizes recommendations for helping students to improve fluency through repeated reading (Meyer & Felton, 1999; Stahl, 2004; Therrien, 2004; Torgesen, Alexander et al., 2001). It is important to keep in mind, however, that repeated reading does not address the rapid processing of other subcomponents of reading, as well as the development of the syntactic and semantic systems (Wolf et al., 2003).

When using the repeated reading procedure, the child reads the same passage over and over again until a desired level of fluency is attained. To begin, the teacher may select an interesting passage that is 50 to 100

≡ Rapid Reference 4.5

Recommendations for Increasing Fluency

- Select interesting passages
- Ensure active engagement
- Have students engage in multiple readings (three or four times)
- Use instructional-level text
- Use decodable text with struggling readers
- Read passages aloud to an adult
- Provide extra practice with trained tutors
- Provide corrective feedback on word errors
- Establish a performance goal or criterion of the number of words per minute
- Provide short, frequent periods of fluency practice
- Provide concrete measures of progress using charts and graphs

words long from a book that is slightly above the student's independent reading level. The teacher has the student read the selection orally while he or she times the reading and counts the

DON'T FORGET

Explicit modeling of fluent reading is a critical component of effective instruction.

number of words that are pronounced incorrectly. The teacher then records the reading time and the number of words pronounced incorrectly. If desired, the teacher and student can set a realistic goal for speed and number of errors.

The teacher may use two different color pencils for recording time and errors, or a circle to indicate points on the line for time and an X or a square to indicate points on the line for errors. When the student is ready, he or she rereads the same passage. Once again, the teacher times the reading and records the time and number of errors. The student repeatedly practices reading the selection as the teacher charts progress after each trial until a predetermined goal is reached or until the student is able to read the passage fluently with few mistakes.

Teaching monitoring is essential for this technique to be effective (Stahl, 2004). Between timings, the teacher may ask the student to look over the selection, reread it, practice it with a peer, or review words that caused difficulty in the initial reading. The amount of teacher guidance and feedback is based on each individual's characteristics. With students with poor reading skills, modeling and practicing of words between readings improve student performance and reduce frustration. In fact, corrective feedback on word errors and reading speed is a critical instructional component for these students (Stahl, 2004). Error correction can be immediate after a student mispronounces or hesitates on a word for over 3 seconds, or delayed, when corrective feedback is provided at the completion of the reading and before the next reading. The correction procedure can be as simple as providing the word and asking the student to repeat it (Therrien & Kubina, 2006).

DON'T FORGET

Corrective feedback is necessary for maximal reading gains.

CAUTION

Having children reread or relisten to text repeatedly without explicit teaching or monitoring is likely to be ineffective. For maximum gains in reading, students need active monitoring and guidance (Stahl, 2004).

Use other genres

To provide practice in accuracy, automaticity, prosody, and comprehension, a teacher can select other types of text genre besides fiction and nonfiction material that are meant to be performed and lend themselves to oral interpretive reading, such as: poetry, song lyrics, chants, plays (Readers Theater), monologues, and dialogues (Rasinski, 2006). Rasinki observes that this type of repeated reading results in both growth and enjoyment in reading because the emphasis is placed on expressive, meaning-filled reading, not on speed.

Partner or paired reading

Before allowing students to use this technique independently, the teacher must teach it explicitly including modeling and guided practice. In addition, the teacher must guide the students in the error correction procedure that will be used during partner reading. Rapid Reference 4.6 summarizes one error correction procedure that might be taught (Carnine et al., 2004). After explicit instruction in the procedures, students are assigned a partner for reading. There are different ways to partner students. For example, proficient readers can be paired with less proficient readers, or readers with similar interests can be partnered. The basic routine for partners involves one partner reading a paragraph first as the other partner follows along. Then the partners reverse roles. After both partners have read the paragraph, they discuss what they read by retelling or identifying the main points. This

≡ *Rapid Reference 4.6*

Example of an Error Correction Procedure for Partner Reading

- If a student makes an error on a word (reads it incorrectly, skips it, does not know it), the partner points to the word and asks, "What is this word?"
- If the student then reads the word correctly, the partner says, "Yes, that word is _____. What is the word? Please reread the sentence."
- If the student still does not know the word, the partner says, "That word is _____. What is the word? Please reread the sentence."

continues paragraph by paragraph until the passage has been completed.

Classwide peer tutoring

Repeated reading has also been used as a component of classwide peer tutoring (Mathes & Fuchs, 1993). In a study of this intervention, pairs of students in one group read continuously over a 10-minute period, whereas pairs of students in the other group read a passage together three times before going on. Although both experimental conditions produced higher results than the typical reading instruction, no difference existed between the procedures, suggesting that the main benefit of the intervention is the student reading involvement and the increased time spent in reading (Mastropieri et al., 1999). One also must consider, however, who is conducting the intervention. Results from a meta-analysis demonstrated that repeated reading interventions were three times more effective when conducted by adults or well-trained peer tutors (Therrien, 2004).

CAUTION

Instruction should not just focus on reading faster for the sake of reading faster without giving commensurate attention to comprehension—the ultimate goal of reading instruction (Rasinski, 2006).

DON'T FORGET

The repeated reading of text is effective for increasing reading fluency.

Reread to meet a performance criterion

Another important instructional component is to have students reread passages until a performance criterion is reached (Therrien & Kubina, 2006). Carnine et al. (2004) suggest that for rate-building exercises using repeated readings, the first step is to determine a target-rereading rate for a 100-word passage. This rate is set at 40% higher than the student's current reading rate. If a student reads at a rate of 50 words per minute, the target rate would be set at 70 words per minute (50 + [40% of 50 = 20] = 70). The student then practices reading the excerpt independently or with a peer, until the passage can be read in the specified time with no more than two errors. Carnine et al. indicate that by fourth grade students should be able to read at least 135 words per minute on the initial reading and that exercises to build reading rate should continue until this goal is met.

Monitor progress

Research on repeated reading suggests that fluency can be improved as long as students are provided with specific instructions and procedures are used to monitor their progress (Mastropieri et al., 1999). An easy way to monitor student performance is for the teacher to keep a log of the dated charts. To control for a similar readability level, the teacher may select the passages to read from the same book. As performance improves, the time to perform the initial reading should decrease.

Previewing

Previewing is a technique similar to repeated reading but it involves reviewing the materials before they are formally read (Rose, 1984). For this type of procedure, a student can preview the material silently, or you may read the passage aloud as the student follows along, or the student may first listen to the recorded passage on tape. Rose and Sherry (1984) found that both silent previewing and teacher-directed previewing were more effective than no previewing.

Taped Books and Technology

Another way to help students practice reading is to use taped books. The student can listen to the tape or CD while following along with an unabridged copy of the book. Most public libraries provide a wide selection of recorded books for loan; however, some commercial readings go too fast for slow readers. In addition, because younger and struggling readers lose their place quite frequently, it is important to have a procedure for relocating the place at the top of each page. Many teachers prefer to make their own recordings of books so that they can select materials that are of high interest to students and control the rate of delivery.

In some studies, assisted approaches, such as listening while reading, were more effective than nonassisted approaches, such as repeated reading. In fact, in a review of studies comparing repeated readings of a small number of texts and nonrepetitive readings of a larger set of texts, both procedures were effective (Kuhn & Stahl, 2003).

Recording for the Blind & Dyslexic (RFB&D)

If a student has been identified as having a reading disability or dyslexia, tapes and CDs are available from *Recording for the*

DON'T FORGET

The amount of time spent orally reading connected text leads to improvements in fluency and comprehension.

Blind & Dyslexic (RFB&D). This national, nonprofit organization provides textbooks for individuals who are unable to read standard print because of visual, physical, or reading disabilities. The extensive tape library has educational books that range from upper-elementary to postgraduate level. If a book is unavailable, an individual may request that it be recorded and it will be, as long as it fits within the scope of the collection.

Kurzweil 3000

Kurzweil 3000™ provides software that can access virtually any type of information—printed, electronic, or on the Internet. Because Kurzweil 3000 can be used with all types of reading materials, it can be used with any curriculum. After the material has been scanned, the program then highlights and reads aloud each word to the student. Kurzweil 3000 provides a digital means of engaging with text that can help students access the general education curriculum, increase reading speed, and improve abilities to learn and study independently.

CAUTION

Remember that when students are listening to text, they must follow along with the print or their reading will not improve.

Soliloquy Reading Assistant

This program allows the student to read, record, and reread passages and keep track of the number of words read per minute. When students skip or misread words the program goes back to the word so the reader can correct it. Immediate, corrective feedback is provided. The program keeps track of missed words, marking them in the text and instructing students to review their pronunciation and meanings prior to rereading the text. The program also promotes vocabulary development, as well as comprehension. Science and social studies text are provided for older readers.

Carbo method

Carbo (1989) developed procedures for recording books to achieve maximum gains in fluency. Rapid Reference 4.7 provides a brief description of her recommendations for recording books. As general guidelines, record 5 to 15 minutes at a typical pace for instructional level material and have the student listen to the tape once. For difficult material, record no more than 2 minutes at a slow pace with good expression and have the student listen to the passage two or three times. After listening to the passage several times, have the student read the passage aloud.

≡ Rapid Reference 4.7

Carbo's Recommendations for Recording Books

- Choose which pages will be recorded on each cassette side.
- Let the tape run for about 5 seconds before starting to record.
- Speak into the microphone from a distance of approximately 6 to 8 inches.
- Use expression when reading.
- Begin by reading the story title, providing a brief introduction, pausing, and then telling the student which page to turn to.
- Pause long enough so that the reader has enough time to turn the pages and look at pictures.
- Tell the student when to turn the page and soften your voice slightly when stating a page number.
- Read the story in logical phrases, slowly enough so that most students can follow along but not so slowly that they become bored.
- End each tape with, "Please rewind the tape for the next listener. This ends this recording."

Prosody

The use of taped books and CDs can also improve oral reading prosody through modeling of expressive reading. Other effective ways for improving prosody are: cueing phrase boundaries, repeated reading practice of plays and dialogues, and radio reading, which adds sound effects to a performance (Hudson et al., 2005). Hudson and colleagues describe how the concept of phrase boundaries can be taught by putting slashes after phrases throughout the text, with double slashes for longer pauses. In addition, a teacher can draw scoops underneath phrases while reading to illustrate where the reader should pause to emphasize the meaning.

Fluency and Comprehension

Numerous researchers investigated the role of reading fluency on comprehension (e.g., Allington, 1983; Cunningham & Stanovich, 1998; Fuchs et al., 2001; Fuchs, Fuchs, & Maxwell, 1988; Hasbrouck, Ihnot, & Rogers, 1999; Jenkins & Jewell, 1993; Mastropieri et al., 1999; Sindelar, Monda, & O'Shea, 1990). Some believe that readers cannot be considered to be fluent unless they understand what they read (Pikulski & Chard, 2005; Wolf & Katzir-Cohen, 2001). Pikulski and Chard indicate that fluency includes at least two activities—word identification and comprehension, or the construction of meaning from text.

Research has not, however, always demonstrated that interventions designed to increase fluency also enhance comprehension abilities. Fluency makes it more likely that a reader will understand a text, but it does not guarantee that they will (Carlisle & Rice, 2002). More complex interventions with multiple components appear more effective for gains in both fluency and comprehension. Reading instruction that integrates teaching of the alphabetic principle, applying these skills in context, and reading the same words repeatedly in different contexts may increase

reading fluency in a way that improves reading comprehension
(Berninger, Abbott, Vermeulen,
& Fulton, 2006). In addition,
combining the repeated reading
procedures with comprehension
activities appears to enhance

> ## CAUTION
> ....
> Accurate and fluent reading can
> facilitate comprehension, but it
> does not guarantee it.

both fluency and comprehension (Chard et al., 2002). Flood, Lapp, and
Fisher (2005) found that combining the Neurological Impress Method
with a comprehension component improved oral and silent reading
fluency as well as comprehension with struggling readers in upper-
elementary school. After the choral reading, the students were asked to
retell the text and answer six comprehension questions. The researchers
found that the addition of comprehension activities using authentic
children's literature motivated students to read more. In addition, simply
asking students to read a passage three to four times and with a focus
on both fluency and comprehension improves speed and understanding
(Therrien, 2004).

Commercial Programs

Several commercial programs are available for increasing reading fluency. Two widely used fluency-based reading programs that meet the
criteria for effective practices are *Great Leaps©* (Campbell, 1998, 2005;
Mercer & Campbell, 1998) and *Read Naturally©* (Ihnot, Mastoff, Gavin,
& Hendrickson, 2001). Rapid Reference 4.8 provides information on
resources for improving fluency.

Great Leaps

Great Leaps (Campbell, 1998, 2005) was designed to help students improve several components of reading, including reading speed. *Great
Leaps* spans reading levels K through 8 with interest levels through

≡ Rapid Reference 4.8

Reading Fluency Programs and Related Web Sites

- Concept Phonics (Speed Drills) (http://www.oxtonhouse.com/concept_phonics.html)
- Great Leaps (www.greatleaps.com)
- Kurzweil 3000 (www.kurzweiledu.com)
- OKAPI! (used to create curriculum-based measurement probes) (http://www.interventioncentral.org/htmdocs/tools/okapi/okapi.php)
- One Minute Reader (www.oneminutereader.com)
- Online Leveled Reading Library K–6 (http://www.raz-kids.com/)
- QuickReads (www.QuickReads.org)
- RAVE-O (http://ase.tufts.edu/crlr/raveo.html)
- Read Naturally (www.readnaturally.com)
- Read Well (www.readwell.net)
- Reader's Theatre Scripts (http://www.teachingheart.net/readers theater.htm)
- Recordings for the Blind & the Dyslexic (www.rfbd.org)
- Six-Minute Solution (http://store.cambiumlearning.com)
- Soliloquy Reading Assistant (http://www.soliloquylearning.com)

adulthood. A K through 2 version of this program provides a phonological awareness instruction component (Mercer & Campbell, 1998). The program uses 1-minute timings on three types of stimuli: phonics, sight phrases, and short stories. Before beginning this program, teachers assess the students' present reading levels. Instruction begins at the level within the program for which reading speed is slow and the student makes several errors.

After the reading, the teacher reviews the errors with the student and discusses strategies that they can use to improve performance. Performance is charted on graphs so that both students and teachers can keep track of progress. The program takes approximately 10 minutes per day. In one study, daily application of this program with middle school students who had reading difficulties contributed to growth in reading and an improvement in reading rate (Mercer, Campbell, Miller, Mercer, & Lane, 2000).

Read Naturally

Another program designed to build fluency in students from mid-first through sixth grade is called *Read Naturally*. Instruction is individualized and involves three main steps: (a) reading along with an audiotape of a story that provides a model of fluent reading; (b) intensive, repeated practicing to build speed and accuracy; and (c) monitoring and evaluating performance through graphing. To use the program, students are placed into an appropriate level on the basis of their oral reading fluency. In addition, the lower level materials have been translated into Spanish. Passages range from pre-K to 8th grade levels. The *Read Naturally* program combines three evidence-based strategies to develop reading fluency: reading from a model, repeated readings, and progress monitoring. Research documents the effectiveness of the *Read Naturally* program at both the elementary and the secondary levels (Denton et al., 2006; Hasbrouck et al., 1999; NRP, 2000; Onken, 2002; Wahl, 2006).

The One Minute Reader is another component of this program. Students read a story while listening to an audio CD. After reading along, the students read the story independently several times. They then graph their times before and after they read along and read alone.

QuickReads

QuickReads were designed to increase fluency, automaticity, and comprehension in students Grades 2 through 6. These are short, meaningful social studies and science texts that are designed to be read quickly. The program has six levels with 90 texts per level. These texts support automaticity with the high-frequency words and phonics/syllabic patterns needed to be a successful reader at a particular grade level.

Six-Minute Solution

The *Six-Minute Solution* (Adams & Brown, 2003) is based on the repeated readings of 1-minute nonfiction passages with a peer-monitoring and feedback system. Students read together in pairs and do 1-minute timings on nonfiction passages. One student reads while the other student counts the number of words read correctly. Three program levels are available: primary, intermediate, and secondary.

RAVE-O

A new promising approach is the Retrieval, Automaticity, Vocabulary, Elaboration, Orthography (*RAVE-O*) program, described as a multi-component approach to increasing fluency (Wolf, Miller, & Donnelly, 2000; Wolf et al., 2003). Although the program is not being widely distributed at this time, its availability will likely increase in coming years. With the use of computerized games and a variety of manipulative materials, the program is designed to help develop and increase accuracy and automaticity at both the sublexical and the lexical levels by helping young readers develop explicit and rapid connections among the phonological, orthographic, syntactic, semantic, and morphological systems (Wolf et al., 2003). For example, students practice daily the rapid recognition of the most frequent orthographic letter patterns in English. When used as an intervention, *RAVE-O* is supplemented with a program that teaches phonological awareness and blending.

The program was developed from a strong research and theoretical base, and preliminary research results support its effectiveness (Lovett, Lacerenza, & Borden, 2000). The curriculum was originally designed to assist struggling second and third graders; however, successful results have been obtained with fourth-grade children (Wolf et al., 2003). Although *RAVE-O* is described as a reading fluency intervention, its goal is improvement in comprehension through use of a comprehensive, engaging, developmental approach (Wolf et al., 2003).

CONCLUSION

Fluency interventions are designed to help readers increase their reading rates and automaticity. Methods to increase rate are particularly beneficial for students who have strong oral language abilities but slow decoding abilities. The repeated reading of words and text provides students with numerous exposures that can help facilitate word mastery and automaticity and improve their ability to comprehend. These types of methods are just one part of an effective reading program, along with instruction in phonological awareness and decoding in the younger grades, and vocabulary and comprehension in all grades (Stahl, 2004). In essence, fluency instruction can foster growth in many facets of reading, but this type of instruction should begin as soon as accuracy is developed.

 TEST YOURSELF

I. Prosody in oral reading refers to

  (a) reading with natural expression.

  (b) reading with accuracy.

  (c) reading with speed.

  (d) reading as fast as possible.

(continued)

2. **Carnine et al. (2004) suggest that by fourth grade students should be able to read at least ____ words per minute on the initial reading.**

    (a) 110

    (b) 120

    (c) 135

    (d) 160

3. **What are two ways that the Neurological Impress Method differs from the repeated reading procedure?**

4. **What type of reader will benefit from a fluency method?**

5. **What are the effective components of fluency instruction?**

6. **Fluency is often described as a bridge between _____ and _____.**

7. **Lack of fluency inhibits understanding because**

    (a) attention is focused at the word level.

    (b) a bottleneck is formed in working memory.

    (c) cognitive resources needed for understanding are unavailable.

    (d) all of the above

8. **Dysfluent reading is a highly stable characteristic and easy to remediate.** True or False?

9. **The student's accuracy level should be _____ on materials used for fluency instruction.**

    (a) 95–99%

    (b) 90–94%

    (c) 85–89%

    (d) 80–84%

10. **A naming speed deficit in Kindergarten is a good predictor of later difficulty with reading fluency.** True or False?

Answers: 1. a; 2. c; 3. text is only read one time; the reading is not timed; reading is done in unison; 4. a slow, word-by-word reader whose oral language abilities are higher than their word recognition skills; 5. repeated readings of text; feedback on errors from adults or trained tutors; charting and monitoring of progress; modeling of reading with expression; 6. word identification and comprehension; 7. d; 8. False; 9. b; 10. True

Five

VOCABULARY AND READING COMPREHENSION

What learners are able to learn is dependent to a large extent upon what they already know.

—*Reid, 1988*

R eading comprehension is a complex task that requires the reader to identify words in text, know the meaning of the words, connect the ideas to prior knowledge, and retain information long enough to understand what is being read. More simply, comprehension results from an integration of decoding skills with language comprehension skills (Snow, Burns, & Griffin, 1998). Fluent word identification, or *decoding automaticity,* underlies comprehension (Chall, 1996; Ehri, 1995). If a reader cannot quickly decode or recognize the words in the text, then comprehension will suffer. In addition, vocabulary, or *word knowledge,* is a key element of comprehension (Baker, Simmons, & Kame'enui, 1995). If a reader can decode words but does not know what they mean, then comprehension is compromised. Prior knowledge also plays a key role in comprehension (Anderson & Pearson, 1984). If the reader cannot connect the ideas presented in the text with existing knowledge, then comprehension is difficult. Although each of these skills plays a necessary role in comprehension, none guarantee that comprehension will occur (Pressley, 2000). Thus, comprehension relies on the integration of multiple linguistic factors and difficulty in any one can affect the understanding of text.

The various factors that impact reading comprehension must be considered when planning an appropriate instructional program for an individual. For example, some individuals experience difficulty with comprehension because of poor decoding skills or a slow reading rate. Intervention would then be directed toward improving basic reading skills. Chapters 2, 3, and 4 of this text address the foundational skills of phonemic awareness, phonics, and fluency. Other individuals have difficulty with comprehension because of limitations in reasoning, language, or experience. These types of students need specific instruction in two additional facets of reading performance: vocabulary and reading comprehension.

VOCABULARY

Children come to school with varying levels of word knowledge, which leads to varying degrees of readiness for successful learning. Factors such as exposure to literacy and language activities, the educational level of the parents, as well as the socioeconomic level of the family impact the child's acquisition of language (Hart & Risley, 1995). Based on socioeconomic level alone, Hart and Risley found an enormous gap in the volume of words children were exposed to in their homes. Children from homes at or near the poverty level were exposed to about one fourth the volume of words that children from professional level families were exposed to. By the end of second grade, a 4,000 word difference exists between children in the highest vocabulary quartile and children in the lowest, which is mostly a reflection of differences in experience (Biemiller, 2004). Thus, some young children enter school with thousands of hours of exposure to rich oral language experiences, whereas others begin school with very limited knowledge of word meanings (Coyne, Simmons, & Kame'enui, 2004). These gaps in both word knowledge and world knowledge affect reading development.

It is often said that children learn to read during Grades 1 to 3 and then read to learn after that. Research indicates that students struggling with reading during the first 3 years will have difficulty developing sufficient vocabulary (Cunningham & Stanovich, 1998), using adequate comprehension strategies (Brown, Palincsar, & Purcell, 1986), and acquiring adequate fluency (Torgesen, Rashotte, & Alexander, 2001). In fact, children with a limited oral vocabulary will struggle with nearly all aspects of academics. Even if these children can decode words, their difficulty recognizing the meanings of words in a text will create a bottleneck in comprehension (Perfetti, Landi, & Oakhill, 2007).

After Grade 3, when decoding skills are typically in place, students use reading as the primary means of acquiring new vocabulary (Nagy & Anderson, 1984). Children struggling with reading due to either limited decoding skill or limited word knowledge are not exposed to the same vocabulary as their classmates with good reading skills. If students with reading disabilities have good oral language, they tend to expand their vocabulary through conversation and listening, not reading (Carlisle & Rice, 2002). Although reading and listening comprehension abilities are related throughout the life span, substantial asymmetries can develop because of poor word identification skill (Perfetti et al., 2007).

Even as early as kindergarten, vocabulary size is an effective predictor of later reading comprehension (Scarborough, 1998). The effect of limited vocabulary knowledge continues to impact learning throughout the school years. For example, a student's oral vocabulary level at the end of Grade 1 is a significant predictor of reading comprehension 10 years later (Cunningham & Stanovich, 1997). Also, a limited vocabulary by Grade 3 has been linked to declining comprehension scores in the later elementary years (Chall, Jacobs, & Baldwin, 1990). Adequate read-

DON'T FORGET

Vocabulary has a strong influence on reading comprehension and young children with limited word knowledge are at high risk for experiencing reading difficulties.

DON'T FORGET

Language development serves as the foundation for vocabulary development. Children must have rich and varied language experiences to develop an adequate vocabulary.

ing comprehension depends on a person already knowing 90 to 95% of the words in a text (Nagy & Scott, 2000). By the end of third grade, children are expected to recognize and know the meaning of well over 80,000 different words (Adams, 1990).

Reading comprehension becomes increasingly vulnerable to differences in both word and world knowledge as children advance in school. Thus, for readers at all skill levels, the causal relationship between reading comprehension and vocabulary appears to be reciprocal; vocabulary knowledge contributes to improved reading comprehension; and word knowledge increases through reading experiences (Ackerman, Weir, Metzler, & Dykman, 1996; Cunningham & Stanovich, 1991; Perfetti et al., 2007).

CHARACTERISTICS OF INDIVIDUALS STRUGGLING WITH VOCABULARY DEVELOPMENT

Early signs of children with vocabulary deficits include difficulty comprehending oral language and trouble remembering and retrieving words. These children may have limited word choice and exhibit errors when speaking, reading, or writing. They may have difficulty repeating sentences or learning new words. All academic learning will be impacted for these individuals, with problems most apparent in reading comprehension and written expression, although the language of math may also cause problems.

The cognitive ability most related to reading vocabulary is *crystallized intelligence,* or verbal ability. This ability is often referred to as a store of acquired knowledge that has a strong relationship with reading across the life span (Evans, Floyd, McGrew, & Leforgee, 2002). This knowledge develops through multiple sources, including both spoken and written communication, and it grows indefinitely (Perfetti et al., 2007). Without adequate vocabulary and prior knowledge, students will have difficulty learning.

CAUTION

It is important to remember that some students with extensive lexical knowledge of word meanings do not recognize words they know when reading. Their oral language abilities are much more advanced than their reading skills.

EFFECTIVE INSTRUCTION

Enriching the language and life experiences of children must begin as early as possible due to the detrimental effects of limited word and world knowledge on learning. Before a child can read, most vocabulary words are learned incidentally through the development of oral language abilities or through listening to

DON'T FORGET

An individual's oral vocabulary is a good indicator of his or her expected reading vocabulary. Determining if the individual's reading vocabulary is commensurate with his or her oral vocabulary can help identify the possible reasons for learning difficulties and lead to appropriate instructional planning.

stories. Once a child is a reader, the amount of time spent reading dictates the quantity of incidental word learning that occurs. Reading for different purposes and at different levels of difficulty exposes the student to new words that would never be encountered in oral language alone (NRP, 2000). Rapid Reference 5.1 indicates the findings of the National Reading Panel that relate to vocabulary.

The overall goal of a vocabulary program is to expand both receptive and expressive vocabularies, and to move more words from the receptive level (e.g., I understand the word when I hear it or read it) to the expressive level (e.g., I understand the word when I use it in conversa-

Rapid Reference 5.1

National Reading Panel Findings Related to Vocabulary

- Vocabulary should be taught directly and indirectly
- Words must be seen multiple times and in multiple contexts
- Language-rich environments foster incidental learning of vocabulary
- Technology helps develop vocabulary
- No one single method works best all of the time for teaching vocabulary

tion or write it) (Blachowicz, Fisher, & Watts-Taffe, 2005). Knowledge of vocabulary does not break into the categories of known and unknown words. When considering vocabulary knowledge, a student may have: (a) no understanding, (b) minimal understanding, (c) some understanding, or (d) thorough understanding of a word. For words to be used accurately and precisely in expressive vocabulary, a complete understanding of a word's meaning or meanings is necessary.

DON'T FORGET

Interventions for building vocabulary are essentially the same whether the problem is oral vocabulary or reading vocabulary. Oral vocabulary is the basis for understanding words that are read.

CAUTION

Simply teaching words and their definitions is insufficient for ensuring increases in the breadth and depth of vocabulary.

Incidental Word Learning

Although most vocabulary is acquired incidentally, teachers and parents can play an important role in influencing the child's incidental word learning. One component of effective vocabulary instruction is that the teacher is an active, enthusiastic vocabulary learner who, in addition to providing direct instruction, pays frequent, impromptu

DON'T FORGET

Most vocabulary is acquired incidentally, primarily through listening, reading, writing, and discussing.

attention to new and interesting word meanings (McKeown & Beck, 2004). There are four primary avenues for learning words incidentally: listening, reading, discussing, and writing (Graves, 2006). A conscious decision to expose children to different words during any of these four activities helps incidental word learning. For example, a teacher or parent who uses a variety of words when speaking (e.g., "be persistent" instead of "keep trying") will help broaden the vocabulary of the child. Additional elements important to incidental word learning include maintaining a variety of children's books at home or in the school library and providing time to read inside and outside of the classroom.

Read aloud

Reading aloud to a child is an easy and effective way to enrich the child's vocabulary, world knowledge, and sense of language and story structure (Adams, 1990). It is most effective when the reader interacts with the child and the text. One such approach, Dialogic Reading, is described in Chapter 2 of this text. Another interactive approach is Text Talk (Beck & McKeown, 2001), which engages students and teachers in vocabulary instruction tied to comprehension. Text Talk incorporates teacher read alouds, with active talking between the teacher and students (questioning, following up, word explanations, use of background knowledge), and explicit instruction on target words. *Bringing Words to Life* (Beck, McKeown, & Kucan, 2002) and *Text Talk* (Beck & McKeown, 2005) are two commercially available

DON'T FORGET

Reading stories aloud and discussing word meanings is a powerful way to build vocabulary for students of all ages.

research-based programs that develop comprehension through meaningful vocabulary instruction. When books are read aloud to children several times with typically eight to ten words a day being explained, most children acquire two to three new words a day (Biemiller, 2004). Thus, the explicit teaching of word meanings during story reading is an effective procedure for decreasing the vocabulary differences among children in the primary grades (Coyne et al., 2004).

Books on tape

Listening to books on tape is an effective strategy for developing vocabulary. This method exposes individuals with reading difficulties to words, language, and story structures that cannot be accessed through reading. Books are available from a number of sources, including Recording for the Blind and Dyslexic (RFB&D) (www.rfbd.org) and Books on Tape (http://school.booksontape.com). Individuals with a documented reading disability are eligible for a membership with RFB&D. In addition, public libraries often have a wide selection of recorded books.

Word consciousness

Word consciousness is the knowledge of and interest in words. Word-conscious students enjoy learning new words and engaging in word play, such as Hink-Pinks (a clue "obese feline" that results in two rhyming words: "fat cat"), puns, board games, charades, or limericks (Blachowicz & Fisher, 2004). Blachowicz and Fisher indicate that word play is grounded in four research-based principles: (a) increases motivation; (b) encourages metacognitive reflection on words, word parts, and context; (c) requires active learning and social construction of meaning; and (d) engages students in practice and rehearsal of word meanings. Promoting word consciousness helps develop word knowledge (Anderson & Nagy, 1992; Graves & Watts-Taffe, 2002; Nagy & Scott, 2000). Teachers must help students understand how written language is different from everyday conversation by making them aware of the distinctive characteristics of written language. For example, reading and discussing two versions of the same story, one with rich language and one with less interesting language, can promote word consciousness in younger students. Older students can be asked to identify examples of effective language use from their reading and then share their examples with the class.

In their research, McKeown and Beck (2004) used a Word Wizard Chart, in which students are asked to find challenging words outside of the classroom and then bring in an explanation of how the word was used. Words were then recorded on a large classroom chart and students earned points and then certificates (e.g., Word Wizard, Word Wildcat, Word Watcher) for achieving a certain amount of points. Figure 5.1 illustrates one type of Word Wizard chart.

This type of engaging activity increases student motivation and interest in word learning and encourages students to increase responsibility for their own learning.

Intentional Explicit Word Instruction

Vocabulary can also be developed through explicit instruction, which is essential for students with limited word knowledge. The intentional, direct teaching of specific words and word-learning strategies will improve vocabulary as well as increase comprehension of passages including those words. Effective, rich instructional activities get students to use, think about, and become involved with the words they are learning (McKeown & Beck, 2004). In a review of four effective vocabulary

Figure 5.1. Example of a Word Wizard Chart

Words to Notice	Heard the word (1 pt)	Read the word (1 pt)	Wrote the word (1 pt)	Spoke the word (1 pt)
crucial	Bobby Sarah	Missy	Juan Sarah	Alex
fragile	Juan	Bobby	Missy	Sarah Juan
imitate	Alex	Sarah Juan	Bobby Alex	Missy
Add more lines as you add additional interesting words for students to notice.				

programs, Foorman, Seals, Anthony, and Pollard-Durodola (2003) found that the programs employed the following consistent instructional principles: (a) introduction of approximately three words per day with no more than 12 to 15 words per week; (b) selection of words that could be extended derivationally and conceptually through discussion; (c) location and discussion of words in engaging text; (d) provision of contextualized definitions with practice opportunities in new and multiple contexts; and (e) introduction of words in a sensible sequence with an attempt to determine which words should be learned next.

STAR

Blachowicz (2005) describes a general framework for vocabulary instruction, using the mnemonic STAR: Select, Teach, Activate/Analyze/Apply, and Revisit. The teacher's first task is to select the words most relevant for instruction. Words should be chosen that are useful and that students are likely to encounter often (McKeown & Beck, 2004). Teaching is done before, during, and after reading. The teacher can provide a definition, provide examples, and en-

> **DON'T FORGET**
> ....
> Multiple exposures to words in varying contexts are essential for increasing vocabulary.

courage students to use the words in sentences. In the third step, Activate, students work on understanding the word. Students can work in pairs to locate words in reading and discuss the author's use of the words. In the last step, Revisit, students can review word meanings through games and activities, the creation of semantic maps, practice applying words in new contexts, and making associations with related words.

Synonyms, antonyms, multiple-meaning words

Teaching synonyms, antonyms, and multiple-meaning words is an effective way to build vocabulary (Graves, Juel, & Graves, 2004; NRP, 2000). For example, using word pairs can be an effective means of helping students see how words are alike or different as well as explore the relationships between the words (Stahl & Kapinus, 2001). Deep thinking is required when determining similarities, differences, and relationships—a key ingredient for effective learning (Marzano et al., 2001). A word-pair chart presents the word pairs in the left-hand column and then offers three additional columns labeled "similar," "different," and "no relation." The students think about the word pair and place an X in the column that best describes the relationship between the words in the pair. Students with limited vocabularies, or English Language Learners (ELLs), often find multiple-meaning words difficult. Sometimes the meaning of a word changes depending on the subject area. Even simple words can cause confusion because they are used to mean very different things.

Semantic feature analysis

Semantic feature analysis helps increase vocabulary by exploring similarities, differences, and connections between words and concepts (Anders & Bos, 1986; Pittelman, Heimlich, Berglund, & French, 1991). In this approach, the teacher creates a grid by listing the target vocabulary words vertically and then listing the features or ideas related to the words horizontally. Next the teacher asks the students to evaluate each target word with each feature and place a + or – in each cell of the grid depending on whether the word does or does not have the feature listed. Finally, similarities, differences, connections, and patterns among the target words are discussed. As skill increases, students can be involved in brainstorming the features or related ideas for the target words.

Semantic maps, word webs, graphic organizers

Using semantic maps, word webs, or other graphic organizers provides a visual tool to help students acquire new vocabulary and concepts (Heimlich & Pittelman, 1986). Semantic maps help students organize their prior knowledge in relationship to the new word or concept and can be used before or after reading. A word web expands word knowledge by asking the student to think of related words, or synonyms, for a target word. The target word is placed in the center of the web and related words or synonyms radiate on lines from the center.

Preteaching vocabulary words

Preteaching key vocabulary words and concepts prior to a reading assignment not only develops the student's vocabulary, but it also aids comprehension. Explicit instruction on specific vocabulary words should focus on important, useful, or difficult words (Armbruster et al., 2001). This is sometimes referred to as teaching the *big idea* words, which are words that directly relate to what is being read (Feldman & Kinsella, 2004). Words should not be too difficult and beyond the child's ability or too easy, but rather they should be just right, or what Stahl and Stahl (2004) refer to as "Goldilocks" words (p. 65). Students must be actively engaged in learning the words and repeated exposures are required for effective learning.

Examples and nonexamples

Providing, or generating, examples and nonexamples of a word can help students clarify the meaning of the target word (Baumann & Kame'enui, 1991; Blachowicz & Fisher, 2000). This approach provides more context for the new word, allowing the student to connect new information to prior knowledge, and thereby deepening the student's conceptual understanding. The Frayer Model (Frayer, Frederick, & Klausmeier, 1969) is a graphic organizer that provides a framework for organizing examples and nonexamples of words. A paper is divided into four quadrants with the target word in the center. Each of the four quadrants has one of the following labels: definition, characteristics, examples, and nonexamples. An even simpler organizer lists the target word or concept at the top of a paper and divides the page into two columns. Examples that are related to the word or concept are listed in one column, and nonexamples are listed in the other.

> **CAUTION**
>
> Do not spend time teaching words that students are unlikely to encounter frequently in their reading or use in their speaking or writing.

> **DON'T FORGET**
>
> English Language Learners (ELLs) benefit from instruction that highlights the relationships between words: especially synonyms, antonyms, or word families (Echevarria, Vogt, & Short, 2004; Grognet, Jameson, Franco, & Derrick-Mescua, 2000).

Keyword method

The keyword method (Mastropieri, 1988) was designed to help students recall more difficult vocabulary through the creation of visual images. The method involves associating new words with visual images to help students recall word meanings and learn new vocabulary.

Three steps are used: recoding, relating, and retrieving. For recoding, students change the new vocabulary word into a known word that has a similar sound and is easily pictured. For relating, students associate the key word with the definition of the new vocabulary word through a mental image or a sentence. For retrieving, students think of the key word, remember the association, and then retrieve the definition. Research findings indicate that the keyword mnemonic strategy increases vocabulary knowledge as well as facilitates recall of words over time (Jitendra, Edwards, Sacks, & Jacobsen, 2004). Rapid Reference 5.2 reviews the steps of this technique. Although the keyword method has been used effectively in content area courses with middle-school and secondary students, this technique is likely to be less effective with younger students (Carlisle & Rice, 2002).

A similar technique is used in *Vocabulary Cartoons I* and *II* (Burchers, 1997, 2000). Each page of the book contains five elements: the word to be learned and its definition, the link word, a caption, a cartoon linking the word in a visual mnemonic, and sample sentences in different contexts. For example, to learn the word *appease,* the link word is peas. The cartoon depicts a young boy eating peas with his parents' encouragement and the sentence "To APPEASE his parents, Johnny ate his PEAS" (Burchers, 2000, p. 149).

=== *Rapid Reference 5.2*

Steps for Using the Mnemonic Keyword Strategy

1. The teacher defines and discusses the meaning of the new word with students.
2. The teacher and students think of a related key word. The word may rhyme or evoke specific visual imagery.
3. The teacher and students create a mental image or picture that makes a link between the keyword and the word's definition.
4. Students study the association until they can easily recall the meaning of the word.

Independent Word-Learning Strategies

Explicit instruction in the identification and use of context clues, use of dictionary and other reference tools, as well as direct instruction in morphology can also help students develop vocabulary and comprehension (Armbruster et al., 2001; Baumann, Kame'enui, & Ash, 2003; Blachowicz & Fisher, 2000; Graves, 2000; NRP, 2000). Rapid Reference 5.3 summarizes several word-learning strategies.

Contextual analysis

Context clues provide hints to the reader about what a word means. Instruction focuses on teaching students strategies to use as well as things to look for in their reading (see Rapid Reference 5.3). Simple context clue

---

≣ *Rapid Reference 5.3*

Teach Independent Word-Learning Strategies

Use Context Clues	Teacher models how to do it and what to look for: • a dash or comma preceding the definition • a detailed description that defines the word • a contrast or synonym
Use Morphology	
Affixes (prefixes/suffixes)	Common prefixes: un-, re-, in-, dis- Common suffixes: -able, -en, -er, -less
Root words	Common Greek or Latin roots
Use Reference Tools	Teach how to use a dictionary, glossary, thesaurus, or online tools

CAUTION

Teachers often instruct students to use context clues for determining the meaning of an unknown word. While helpful, encouraging sole reliance on context clues is ineffective for vocabulary instruction because this strategy does not always work and the context does not always give strong clues about a word's meaning (Beck et al., 2002; Edwards, Font, Baumann, & Boland, 2004; McKeown & Beck, 2004).

DON'T FORGET

Most vocabulary is acquired indirectly through oral language interactions, being read to, or reading on your own. Some vocabulary is acquired directly through explicit instruction in word meanings and word-learning strategies.

strategies include rereading the sentence that contains the unknown word, rereading the sentences before and after the sentence with the unknown word, making a guess about the meaning of the unknown word based on the clues, and inserting the guess in the sentence to see if it makes sense. Some context clues should be taught explicitly such as recognizing when the author provides the definition, a synonym, an antonym, or an example (Baumann, Font, Edwards, & Boland, 2005). Teachers must model how to use context clues while reading and then provide guided practice for the students.

Resources

Independent learning may be facilitated by teaching students how to use dictionaries, glossaries, thesauruses, and online reference tools. The dictionary is a valuable tool that will assist students with locating the spelling, meaning, and pronunciation of words. All students will benefit from instruction in how to use a dictionary, but it will be especially helpful to those struggling with language, including ELL students. Keep in mind, however, that dictionary entries are most useful to students who already have a good sense of the meaning of the word they are looking up (Carlisle & Rice, 2002). Sometimes the words that are used to define the word are also unfamiliar to the reader and do not clarify the meaning. Portable electronic dictionaries (PEDs), such as those available from Franklin (www.Franklin.com), can be invaluable to students. Instruction in using a thesaurus will help students expand their vocabularies for speaking, reading, and writing. The Internet has numerous sources that can provide assistance to the learner and foster independence. Rapid Reference 5.4 provides a sampling of web sites that support independent word learning.

≡ *Rapid Reference 5.4*

Web sites Providing Tools for Independent Word Learning (in alphabetical order)

- Dictionary.com (www.dictionary.com)
- Encarta (http://encarta.msn.com)
- Kids Online Resources (www.kidsolr.com/reference/)
- Latin and Greek Roots (www.wordexplorations.com)
- Merriam-Webster Online (www.merriam-webster.com)
- Rhyming (http://rhyme.lycos.com)
- Roget's II: The New Thesaurus (www.bartleby.com)
- The Free Dictionary (www.thefreedictionary.com)
- Thesaurus.com (www.thesaurus.com)
- Thinkmap Visual Thesaurus (www.visualthesaurus.com)
- Vocabulary (www.vocabulary.com)
- Wikipedia (www.wikipedia.org)
- Word Central (www.wordcentral.com)
- Wordsmith (www.wordsmith.org)
- Wordsmyth (www.wordsmyth.net)

> ## CAUTION
>
> Students must have adequate vocabulary knowledge to use a thesaurus effectively. They must have some familiarity with the meanings of the listed synonyms.

Morphemic analysis

Instruction in morphology, the meaningful units of language, focuses on teaching affixes (prefixes and suffixes), base words (words that can stand alone), and word roots (word parts that have meaning but cannot stand alone). The goal of morphemic analysis is to teach students how to analyze words into meaningful parts. This type of instruction can assist the student in multiple ways, including figuring out what words mean as well as how to pronounce and spell them. Edwards et al. (2004) suggest that the following four basic principles should be included when teaching students how to use morphemic analysis: (1) teach students how to break apart words into roots and affixes and learn how the parts work together for meaning; (2) use word families that include a root word and its derived forms (e.g., friend: friendship, friendly, befriend); (3) promote independent use of morphemic analysis; and (4) remind students that morphemic analysis does not always work.

Instruction can begin with prefixes because their meanings are more consistent than suffixes. Prefixes are especially worth teaching for the following reasons: (a) a small number of prefixes are used in a large amount of words; (b) they occur at the front of words and have consistent spelling; (c) they are easy to identify; and (d) they have a clear lexical meaning (Graves, 2004). White, Power, and White (1989) found that only 20 prefixes make up 97% of the words with prefixes that are typically encountered in school and that the three most common prefixes un-, re-, and in- account for 51% of words with prefixes. A list of the most common prefixes, ordered by frequency, is presented in Rapid Reference 5.5. In contrast, suffixes vary in meaning so teaching their

≣ *Rapid Reference 5.5*

20 Most Common Prefixes

un-	pre-
re-	inter-
in- (im-, ir-, il-) (not)	fore-
dis-	de-
en-, em-	trans-
non-	super-
in-, im- (in or into)	semi-
over-	anti-
mis-	mid-
sub-	under-

Source: Graves, 2004; White et al., 1989

definitions has limited value. Providing students with repeated exposure and experience with words with suffixes may be the better instructional approach (Stahl, 1999).

A word part analysis chart may be beneficial in helping students learn word parts. One example of a word analysis chart is the Word Part Clue Evaluation Chart (Diamond & Gutlohn, 2006). The teacher identifies words from a reading or content area text that the student will encounter and then lists them in the left-hand column of the chart. Other columns on the chart are labeled: (a) no prefix and root word; (b) prefix and

CAUTION

Teachers often assume secondary students know all about prefixes, suffixes, and root words. This is frequently not the case for students struggling with reading.

≡ *Rapid Reference 5.6*

Prefix Removal Strategy

1. Remove the prefix.
2. Check to see if you have a real word. If you do, it is a prefix.
3. Analyze the meanings of the prefix and root word.
4. Combine the meanings and attempt to infer the meaning of the unknown word.
5. Try out the word in the sentence and see if it makes sense.

Source: Graves, 2004

CAUTION

Although methods that work well for English-only students also work well for ELL students, the strategies may need to be adapted to the strengths and needs of the individual (Calderón et al., 2005). Also, ELL students may require specific instruction in more basic words that most English-only students already know.

root word; (c) prefix + root = meaning; and (d) prefix + root ≠ meaning. The teacher uses explicit instruction and modeling to demonstrate how to use the chart. This approach helps students build understanding of words as they think about the word parts. Rapid Reference 5.6 describes a similar strategy for determining the meaning of unknown words with prefixes (Graves, 2004).

Instruction in word roots—especially the Latin or Greek roots, which account for approximately 60% of all English words—is important for students struggling with decoding or word meaning. In addition, English Language Learners (ELLs) may benefit from instruction in words with a Latin or Greek root. August and colleagues (2005) suggest using the student's first language if it shares cognates with English to help teach vocabulary. *Cognates* are words that exist in different languages but look and sound similar and have similar meanings. For example, the word *telescopio* in Spanish and the word *telescope* in English share cognates.

COMPREHENSION

Comprehension has been described as "intentional thinking during which meaning is constructed through interactions between text and reader" (Durkin, 1993, p. 76). It has also been described as a process in which readers construct meaning by interacting with text through the combination of prior knowledge and previous experience, information in the text, and the stance the reader takes in relationship to the ideas presented in the text (Pardo, 2004). No matter how one defines comprehension, understanding and grasping the meaning of the text are required in the definition.

DON'T FORGET

Although vocabulary knowledge can contribute to poor comprehension, comprehension difficulties can still occur when the vocabulary is familiar to the reader (Nation, 2007).

Characteristics of Good Readers

Good readers exhibit certain behaviors that contribute to their reading performance, such as continually monitoring and evaluating their understanding of what they are reading. Rapid Reference 5.7 lists the characteristics of good readers. In addition, good readers use a variety of strategies to facilitate comprehension such as predicting, questioning, summarizing, and visualizing (Duke & Pearson, 2002; Keene & Zimmermann, 1997; NRP, 2000). Rapid Reference 5.8 summarizes these strategies. The goal of instruction is to get struggling readers to employ these same strategies.

Characteristics of Individuals Struggling with Reading Comprehension

In a research synthesis on reading comprehension instruction for students with learning disabilities, Gersten and Baker (1999) identified a

≡ Rapid Reference 5.7

Characteristics of Good Readers

1. Reads actively (thinks about what is being read).
2. Reads for a purpose (goal-oriented).
3. Previews text (structure, relevant sections).
4. Predicts while reading.
5. Reads selectively (focusing on what is important).
6. Constructs, revises, and questions meanings while reading.
7. Determines meaning of unfamiliar words and concepts.
8. Uses prior knowledge to help understand the text.
9. Monitors understanding.
10. Adjusts reading rate and approach based on genre.

≡ Rapid Reference 5.8

Strategies Used by Good Readers

- Relating new information with prior knowledge
- Figuring out the main ideas
- Questioning (generating and answering)
- Using knowledge of text structure (genre)
- Constructing mental images of the meaning conveyed by the text
- Making inferences beyond the information given in the text
- Monitoring comprehension (self-regulation, think aloud)
- Summarizing and paraphrasing important information
- Seeking clarification when the meaning is confusing

number of characteristics of students who were struggling with reading comprehension. Many students struggled with comprehension because of language-based problems, such as limited vocabulary or knowledge gaps that interfered with their ability to understand material they read. In addition, students with reading comprehension problems lacked persistence—giving up too easily when the reading becomes too difficult. This is especially problematic on expository texts where persistence is required of the reader, even a good reader. Further, these students did not monitor their reading or pay attention to how well they understood what they were reading. As a result, they did not recall what they read, could not identify important information, and had difficulty differentiating relevant from irrelevant information. Poor readers tended to read all texts in the same manner, rather than adjusting their reading based on the type of text or the purpose for reading.

Some students appear to read fluently but, in fact, do not comprehend what they read. This is especially true for older students who have difficulty: (a) relating information to prior knowledge; (b) monitoring their understanding; (c) making inferences; and (d) applying comprehension strategies (Biancarosa & Snow, 2004; Carlisle & Rice, 2002; Nation, 2007; Snow, 2002). The most commonly cited factors that cause students to experience difficulty with expository text are: (a) limited knowledge of text structures; (b) low vocabulary knowledge; (c) insufficient prior knowledge; (d) the complexity of the ideas expressed (conceptual density); (e) difficulties in making inferences; and (f) limited familiarity with the content (Carlisle & Rice, 2002; Mather & Urso, 2008).

Cognitive abilities most related to reading comprehension include verbal ability and listen-

> ### CAUTION
>
> Poor readers tend to read all texts in the same manner, rather than adjusting their reading based on the type of text or the purpose for reading.

CAUTION

Students can appear to be fluent readers but still not understand or remember what they are reading. These students will require instruction that builds vocabulary and background knowledge.

DON'T FORGET

The oral language abilities of individuals with reading disabilities often exceed their reading and writing abilities.

ing comprehension, reasoning, and working memory. Students with good decoding but poor reading comprehension do not have an impairment that is specific to reading, but rather the difficulties are usually related to a more general impairment in language comprehension involving the processing and storage of verbal material (Nation, 2007). Working memory can also affect comprehension of a text. Readers have to remember words, retrieve information, and understand the preceding text (Perfetti et al., 2007). Children with a history of language delays, weaknesses in working memory, and limited exposure to the vocabulary and syntax in grade-level text will likely have difficulty understanding sentences (Carlisle & Rice, 2002).

Individuals who have impairments affecting the acquisition of decoding skills may also have comprehension difficulties as a result. It is important to consider the impact of word decoding skill (fluency and automaticity) on comprehension as attention may also need to be directed toward improving these skills in order to improve comprehension.

EFFECTIVE INSTRUCTION

Comprehension instruction should include explicit instruction in specific comprehension strategies, as well as plenty of time and opportunity for actual reading, writing, and discussing text. In other words, comprehension instruction should be balanced between teaching and practicing. Additionally, comprehension instruction should not wait until students master decoding, but rather should be emphasized from the very beginning of reading instruction (Armbruster et al., 2001). Students need to understand that there is a purpose for reading, and that the purpose is comprehension. Beyond reading instruction, ample opportunities to read real texts for real purposes must be provided. Wide and varied reading exposes students to different genres and vocabulary (e.g., Anderson, 1996). Instruction should occur in a supportive classroom environment that fosters high-quality teacher-to-student and student-to-student dialogues and interactions about texts. Opportunities to write make use of the connection between reading and writing and help students develop both abilities. Rapid Reference 5.9 lists the findings of the National Reading Panel (2000) related to reading comprehension.

≡ Rapid Reference 5.9

National Reading Panel Findings Related to Reading Comprehension

Vocabulary instruction is required to develop word knowledge.

A combination of comprehension strategies is most effective.

The seven most effective strategies are:

1. Comprehension monitoring
2. Cooperative learning
3. Graphic and semantic organizers
4. Question answering
5. Question generating
6. Story structures
7. Summarization

> **DON'T FORGET**
> ....
> "Comprehension strategies are specific, learned procedures that foster active, competent, self-regulated, and intentional reading" (Trabasso & Bouchard, 2002, p. 177).

Teachers need training in how to teach comprehension strategies. In a meta-analysis of reading instruction, Swanson (1999, 2001) identifies teaching methods and instruction components that are most effective in developing the reading comprehension skills of children and adolescents with learning disabilities. The most effective approach includes a combination of direct and strategy instruction. Rapid Reference 5.10 summarizes these findings.

Strategy Instruction

An important finding in the reading research is that good comprehension requires using a variety of strategies. Good readers use strategies automatically but struggling readers require explicit strategy instruction that includes how, when, where, and why to use each strategy. As with all explicit instruction, the teacher models the strategy using a think-aloud approach. Then the student practices under supervision with immediate corrective feedback before attempting independent practice.

Some general strategies can be taught that will help readers improve their understanding of a text. For example, before reading, the student can learn how to preview a text to identify difficult vocabulary and necessary background knowledge, as well as make predictions about the content of the text. During reading, the reader must learn how to monitor understanding. After reading, the reader must learn how to summarize and evaluate the ideas. Rapid Reference 5.11 summarizes these general strategies (Flood & Lapp, 1991). Essentially, instruction must

≡ *Rapid Reference 5.10*

Most Effective Teaching Methods and Instruction Components for Reading Comprehension

Instruction Component	Activity or Technique
Directed response/questioning	Teacher asks questions, encourages students to ask questions, teacher-student dialogue
Control difficulty of processing demands of task	Teacher provides assistance as needed, gives simplified demonstration, sequences steps from easy to difficult and presents in that order, allows student to control level of difficulty, keeps activities short
Elaboration	Activities provide students with additional information and explanation about skills/steps, use redundant text or repetition within text
Modeling of steps by teacher	Teacher demonstrates the steps students are to follow
Group instruction	Instruction or interaction between teacher and students occurs in small groups with 6 or fewer students
Strategy cues	Teacher reminds students to use strategies or steps, explains steps or procedures, uses a think-aloud model, identifies benefits of strategy use

≡ Rapid Reference 5.11

Strategies for Reading a Text

Before Reading	Preview the text, make predictions, build necessary vocabulary and background knowledge, set purpose for reading
During Reading	Check understanding, monitor comprehension, integrate new concepts
After Reading	Summarize, evaluate ideas, apply knowledge

help the struggling reader develop metacognitive strategies that encourage active engagement and thinking about the text.

Strategies for reading a text

A number of techniques are available that guide the reader through the steps illustrated in Rapid Reference 5.11. Examples of four of these techniques are: DR-TA, K-W-L, SQ3R, and MULTIPASS. The Directed Reading-Thinking Activity (DR-TA) (Stauffer, 1969) is a technique that encourages students to make predictions before, during, and after reading. DR-TA also helps students set a purpose for reading and monitor their comprehension when reading both narrative and expository texts. The steps in DR-TA involve activating the student's prior knowledge before reading, making predictions about what they will be reading, reading a passage or section, stopping and confirming or revising predictions (teacher predetermines these stopping points), making new predictions, and continuing to read the text. This process is repeated throughout the text, at the points predetermined by the teacher.

K-W-L is another instructional strategy that guides students through an expository passage (Ogle, 1986). When using K-W-L, a paper is divided into three columns: K for what is already Known, W for what the student Wants to learn, and L for what the student did Learn. Before reading, prior knowledge is activated by brainstorming what students already *know* about the topic. This information is recorded in the K column. Then, the purpose for reading is set as students establish what they *want* to know about the topic and record this in the W column. Finally, the students summarize what they *learned* by recording that information in the L column. Students then can use this information in the L column to write a summary of what they learned.

The SQ3R strategy guides the students through surveying, questions, reading, reciting, and reviewing an expository text. Students begin by surveying (S) the text. As they survey, they question (Q) the text by making questions about the title, headings, and introductory sentences. Then the students read (1R) the text, looking for the answers to those questions. After reading, students recite (2R) the answers to their questions out loud. Finally, the students review (3R) their questions and answers. The review occurs at multiple points: immediately after reading, 1 day after reading, 1 week after reading, and, if there is to be an exam on the material, then a review is done right before the exam.

MULTIPASS is an example of a content-area textbook study strategy that was developed by researchers at the University of Kansas (Schumaker, Deshler, Alley, Warner, & Denton, 1982). The teacher explains the steps and rationale, demonstrates the strategy by thinking aloud, and then students verbally rehearse the strategy. The student uses the following three steps: survey, size up, and sort-out, and never reads the passage in its entirety.

In the first step, Survey, the student reads the chapter title, introductory paragraph, the table of contents (in order to understand the relationship of the chapter to others in the text), subtitles, illustrations, diagrams, and summary paragraphs. The student then paraphrases all the information gained from the first pass. For the size-up step the student reads the questions at the end of the chapter and then checks off the ones for which the answer is known. The student then looks through the text for headings and parts of the text that are in italics, bold, or colored print in order to identify cues. The student turns each of these cues into a question and skims the text to find the answer. At the end of the chapter, the student paraphrases all remembered facts and ideas. In the final step, sort-out, the student sorts out by reading the questions at the end of the chapter and marking those questions that cannot be answered immediately. If a question cannot be answered, the student attempts to locate the answer by skimming the text. This strategy is particularly effective for use with content-area textbooks and management of lengthy reading assignments.

Predicting

Another effective comprehension strategy is making predictions that involve activating prior knowledge related to the text and then previewing the text. After the predictions are made, the reader then reads to determine whether or not the predictions were correct. The goal is to make use of existing knowledge to facilitate understanding of what will come next. Checking the accuracy of the predictions further enhances comprehension. Rapid Reference 5.12 summarizes the steps for teaching students how to use the strategy of making predictions (Duke & Pearson, 2002). Explicit instruction with modeling and thinking aloud is used at every step except during independent practice.

DON'T FORGET

Activating and reviewing prior knowledge relevant to the reading content enhances comprehension.

Think aloud

Use of either teacher or student think-aloud approaches can also improve comprehension. Thinking aloud is an important part of explicit instruction as illustrated in Rapid Reference 5.12. The most effective strategy instruction leaves very little for students to figure out on their own (Raphael, Wonnacott, & Pearson, 1983). Comprehension and

Comprehension Strategy: Making Predictions

1. Teacher provides a clear description of the strategy and when and how to use it.

   a. Teacher explains that predicting is like making guesses.

   b. Teacher explains that readers should make guesses about their reading.

   c. Teacher tells students they should stop and make a prediction after reading a section (or after every page or two).

2. Teacher models the strategy in action.

   a. Teacher thinks aloud about the process and the book, starting with the cover and the title.

   b. Teacher describes cover art and thinks aloud about what it might mean and why.

   c. Teacher reads the title and thinks aloud about what the story may be about and why.

   d. Teacher indicates that reading will begin now.

3. Collaborative use of the strategy.

   a. Teacher invites the students to make their own predictions by asking them to stop and think about what might happen next.

   b. Teacher asks students to tell what they think and why.

4. Guided practice using the strategy.

   a. Teacher reminds students that they will be making predictions about the story.

   b. Teacher asks students to stop and make a prediction after every few pages.

   c. Teacher asks students to share their predictions.

   d. Teacher tells students to continue reading to see if their predictions were correct.

5. Independent use of the strategy.

   a. Teacher reminds the students that they will be making predictions during silent reading.

   b. Teacher reminds the students to make predictions every few pages.

   c. Teacher tells students to ask themselves why they made each prediction.

   d. Teacher tells students to check as they read to see if predictions were correct.

summarization skills are improved when students are asked to think aloud while reading (Bereiter & Bird, 1985; Silven & Vauras, 1992).

Visualization

When a reader visualizes while reading, his or her comprehension is improved. Visualizing requires active engagement by the reader as well as deep thinking about the content. It is sometimes referred to as "making a movie in your head." Some students may require explicit instruction in how to visualize or how to make use of mental imagery while reading. For example, the teacher may need to ask specific questions about how something looks, smells, tastes, sounds, or feels. Then the students may be guided to apply this at a sentence level, responding to questions about which specific words in the sentence triggered an image. For longer passages, the teacher models how to use imagery through a think-aloud process. Pictures can be drawn to illustrate what the reader is visualizing.

Text structures

Knowing the structure of a text helps organize the reader's thinking and enhances understanding and recall of the information (Gallagher & Pearson, 1989). Good readers use their knowledge of text structure to activate prior knowledge, preview the text, and understand the purpose of the text, thus facilitating comprehension. The two broad categories of text structure are narrative and expository.

Frequently, various types of graphic organizers are used as a means of teaching text structure. Use of a graphic organizer provides a visual, concrete representation of information that helps to connect new information to prior knowledge, thereby enhancing comprehension. When completing a graphic organizer, the student is actively engaged in seeing and remembering patterns and relationships. Graphic organizers may be used before, during, or after reading. When teaching narrative structures, for example, the teacher might make use of a story map, or story grammar. A story map helps students identify four key elements of a narrative: (1) important characters and their personalities and motivation, (2) main problem and significant plot developments, (3) characters' attempts to solve problems, and (4) the overarching theme and conclusion.

A variety of expository text structures exist and multiple structures can occur within one text, which can make expository text more difficult to understand than narrative text. When working with expository texts, one organizer may focus on main ideas and supporting details, whereas other organizers focus on sequence, comparing and contrasting, drawing conclusions, cause and effect, or categorization.

> **DON'T FORGET**
> ....
> Explicit teaching of text structures and how to recognize them is particularly important for students who are English Language Learners and for students with learning disabilities (Dickson, Simmons, & Kame'enui, 1998).

> **DON'T FORGET**
> ....
> The comprehension of students with learning difficulties improves when they are taught to use graphic organizers (Kim, Vaughn, Wanzek, & Wei, 2004).

In addition to using graphic organizers with expository text, students can learn how to locate signal words or cohesive ties in the text. Cohesive ties help clarify the relationships between the ideas presented in the text. For example, temporal words such as *after, before,* or *following* help the student identify the sequence, or chronological order in a text; whereas cause-effect words include *if, then, consequently, accordingly,* or *therefore.*

Summarizing

One of the most effective instructional strategies is summarization (Marzano et al., 2001). Summarization can be taught via step-by-step procedures or in a more holistic manner. Rapid Reference 5.13 illustrates an example of a step-by-step, or rule-governed, approach (Mc-

Comprehension Strategy: Step-by-Step Summarization

Step 1: Delete unnecessary material.

Step 2: Delete redundant material.

Step 3: Compose a word to replace a list of items.

Step 4: Compose a word to replace individual parts of an action.

Step 5: Select a topic sentence.

Step 6: Invent a topic sentence if one is not available.

Neil & Donant, 1982). Again, explicit instruction is used to teach the student how to summarize. An example of a holistic approach is the GIST procedure (Cunningham, 1982). Students are asked to write a summary using 15 or fewer words. First, they summarize a single sentence. Eventually, they summarize a complete paragraph. Instruction progresses from the entire class, to small groups, to individuals. The Get the Gist strategy (Klingner, Vaughn, & Schumm, 1998) helps students understand the concept of *main idea*. The strategy has the following three primary steps: (1) identify *who* or *what* the paragraph is about; (2) determine what is the most important information about the *who* or *what* in the paragraph; and (3) say it in a main idea statement of 10 words or less. It is sometimes helpful to teach the strategy using a picture or cartoon first, rather than using a text. As with all strategy instruction, teaching needs to be explicit and include modeling, application, and practice of the strategy.

Questioning

Generating and answering questions also leads to improved comprehension (NRP, 2000; Rosenshine, Meister, & Chapman, 1996; Yopp, 1988). The type of question used tends to influence the reader's focus. For example, if literal questions are asked frequently, the reader will focus on facts and details. If the teacher wishes to work on drawing inferences, then inferential questions are used. When students generate inferential questions about their reading of expository texts, their understanding of the concepts presented improves (Taboada & Guthrie, 2006).

One technique in particular, *Question-Answer-Relationships (QAR)* (Raphael, 1986), helps students differentiate the types of questions they can ask. The technique identifies three types of questions: (1) Right There (explicitly stated in the text); (2) Think and Search (answers in text but require making inferences); and (3) On My Own (answer drawn from reader's prior knowledge). This technique has been updated and is known as *QAR now* (Raphael, Highland, & Au, 2006).

Another comprehension technique, *Questioning the Author* (Beck, Hamilton, Kucan, & McKeown, 1997), is an interactive teaching strategy that encourages the reader to construct meaning by thinking about what the author is trying to say in the text. A series of questions guide the reader through the process of questioning the author. Rapid Reference 5.14 lists examples of initiating and follow-up questions to guide the reading.

Monitoring comprehension

Good readers are aware while they are reading whether or not the text is making sense. Struggling readers do not monitor their reading and require explicit instruction in how to accomplish

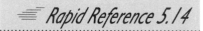

Rapid Reference 5.14

Questioning the Author

Examples of Initiating Questions

- What is the author trying to say? What is the author's message?
- What do you think the author wants us to know from this?

Examples of Follow-Up Questions

- Does the author explain that clearly?
- That is what the author says, but what does the author mean?
- What did the author say to make (Name) think of that?

DON'T FORGET

Asking readers to generate questions during reading had the strongest scientific evidence of effectiveness for comprehension instruction (NRP, 2000).

this important strategy. At a very basic level, monitoring is as simple as asking oneself while reading "Does this make sense?" Then, if the text does not make sense, the student needs to implement fix-up or repair strategies, like rereading the text.

The Interactive Notation to Effective Reading and Thinking (IN-SERT) (IRA/NCTE, 2003) strategy was designed to help students monitor their thinking and learning while reading. Students are taught to reflect on their reading, connect to prior knowledge, and insert one of four symbols as they think about their reading. Rapid Reference 5.15 illustrates the four symbols used to code the text, what the code means, and what the student should be thinking.

Additional techniques

Three additional techniques that are effective for improving reading comprehension include: repeated readings, retelling, and the reader's workshop. While repeated reading is often mentioned as a means of improving fluency, it is also an effective way to increase comprehension. When students have the opportunity to read material more than once, their comprehension is enhanced (Gersten, Fuchs, Williams, &

≡ Rapid Reference 5.15

Monitoring Comprehension Strategy: INSERT

✓ Confirms what you already knew: "I knew that."
− Contradicts what you thought: "I thought differently."
? Confuses you: "I don't understand this."
+ Something new: "I didn't know that!"

Baker, 2001). Retelling is an effective comprehension strategy that increases the student's understanding of story structure, oral language development, and reading comprehension (Benson & Cummins, 2000). Students learn to identify, clarify, and organize their thinking. A reading workshop is a framework for organizing many classroom learning experiences that engage students in reading and sharing with other students. Mini-lessons are used as needed to provide explicit instruction on specific topics. Additional information can be found at www.readersworkshop.org.

Methods of Effective Instruction

Explicit instruction is required for students who are struggling to learn. The methods found to be most effective for improving reading comprehension incorporate explicit instruction: teacher modeling of the skill, guided practice with feedback, and independent practice. Four effective instructional methods that incorporate these principles are: Reciprocal Teaching, Collaborative Strategic Reading (CSR), Students Achieve Independent Learning (SAIL), and Peer-Assisted Learning Strategies (PALS).

Reciprocal teaching
This method of instruction gradually shifts the responsibility from the teacher to the student. It incorporates elements of explicit instruction, such as teacher modeling and guided practice. When used for teaching comprehension, reciprocal teaching focuses on four comprehension strategies: predicting, questioning, seeking clarification, and summarizing (Palincsar & Brown, 1984). First, the teacher models the strategy and then the student models the strategy. As the student moves through the steps of the strategy, the teacher provides feedback and prompts as needed. Reciprocal teaching effectively improves comprehension (Rosenshine & Meister, 1994; Weedman & Weedman, 2001).

Collaborative strategic reading (CSR)

One adaptation of reciprocal teaching is Collaborative Strategic Reading (Klingner & Vaughn, 1996, 1998). This approach has been found to be effective in improving comprehension across a wide age range (elementary to secondary) and with various populations (e.g., individuals with learning disabilities, ELLs). CSR combines reciprocal teaching with cooperative learning (Johnson & Johnson, 1987), or student pairing. It focuses on four comprehension strategies that students learn to apply before, during, and after reading in small cooperative groups: (1) preview (before reading); (2) click and clunk (during reading); (3) get the gist (during reading); and (4) wrap up (after reading). Rapid Reference 5.16 summarizes the steps in CSR. This instructional method works well in mixed-ability classrooms and may also be used in subject areas such as science or social studies. Additional information about CSR can be found at (www.texas-reading.org) or in *Collaborative Strategic Reading: Strategies for Improving Comprehension* (Klingner, Vaughn, Dimino, Schumm, & Bryant, 2001).

Students achieving independent learning (SAIL)

Strategies emphasized in SAIL include predicting, visualizing, questioning, clarifying, making associations using prior knowledge, and summarizing (Pressley et al., 1994). SAIL makes use of explicit instruction and teacher think-alouds and is similar to the self-talk strategies or private speech found effective in the cognitive strategy research. Students are encouraged to verbalize what the strategies are and how to use them as well as discuss with other students when they are and are not appropriate to use.

Peer-Assisted Learning Strategies (PALS)

Peer-Assisted Learning Strategies (PALS) was originally designed for students in Grades 2 through 6 (Fuchs, Fuchs, Mathes, & Simmons, 1997) and has since expanded to separate programs for kindergarten, first grade, and high school. A strong research base exists for the effi-

≡ Rapid Reference 5.16

Implementing Collaborative Strategic Reading (CSR)

1. Teach the 4 strategies explicitly (teacher-led teaching).

   a. Preview (brainstorm and predict).

   b. Click and clunk (self-monitoring strategy, use fix-up strategies).

   c. Get the gist (identify main ideas and restate in own words).

   d. Wrap up (generate questions and review).

2. Cooperative learning group, or student pairing.

   a. Set the stage (teacher assigns roles to students in each group).

     i. Roles may include leader, clunk expert, gist expert, announcer.

     ii. Roles should be rotated.

   b. Whole class instruction (teacher introduces topic, vocabulary, etc.).

   c. Cooperative group activity (each student has a role).

   d. Whole class wrap up (review reading, answer questions, share information).

3. Possible fix-up strategies (can be placed on cue cards).

   a. Reread the sentence without the word. Think about the information that is provided and how it might help you understand the meaning of the word.

   b. Reread the sentence with the clunk and the sentences before and after the clunk. Look for clues.

   c. Look for a prefix or suffix in the word.

   d. Break the word apart. Look for parts you know.

DON'T FORGET

Strategy instruction using peer-mediated approaches is effective in improving reading comprehension even with secondary students.

cacy of PALS. Fuchs, Fuchs, and Kazdan (1999) studied the effects of PALS on high-school students struggling with reading comprehension. Comprehension improved when three collaborative activities were included: (a) reading aloud with partner modeling and coaching; (b) asking and answering questions about each paragraph to formulate a general understanding; and (c) making predictions and checking the accuracy of those predictions.

Commercial Products

Several programs have been identified as having potentially positive effects for teaching reading comprehension (see the What Works Clearinghouse web site). Rapid Reference 5.17 provides a summary of those

≡ Rapid Reference 5.17

Commercially Available Programs (with potentially positive effects)

Accelerated Reader/Reading Renaissance (www.renlearn.com)

Early Intervention in Reading (www.earlyinterventioninreading.com)

Failure Free Reading (www.failurefreereading.com)

Kaplan SpellRead (www.kaplank12.com)

Peer-Assisted Learning Strategies (http://kc.vanderbilt.edu/pals/)

Reading Recovery (www.readingrecovery.org)

Start Making a Reader Today (www.getsmartoregon.org)

materials. For ELLs, eight programs were found to have potentially positive effects on reading achievement. As examples, four of those programs were Success for All (www.successforall.net), Reading Mastery (www.sraonline.com), Read Well (http://store.cambiumlearning.com), and Peer-Assisted Learning Strategies (see Rapid Reference 5.17).

CONCLUSION

Reading research indicates that children who get off to a poor start in reading in first grade typically continue on this trajectory and do not catch up (Francis, Shaywitz, Stuebing, Shaywitz, & Fletcher, 1996; Torgesen & Burgess, 1998). The consequences of a slow start in reading have been described as the Matthew Effect (Stanovich, 1986; Walberg & Tsai, 1983). This is a biblical reference to a verse from the Gospel of Matthew (25:29) that, in essence, states that the rich get richer and the poor get poorer. As it applies to reading, students with good reading skills accrue many benefits such as increased vocabulary and enhanced knowledge (the rich get richer), while those who struggle with reading fail to achieve similar linguistic benefits (the poor get poorer). Reading is a gateway skill that provides access to learning, opportunity, and knowledge.

Reading comprehension is a complex process requiring the integration of numerous cognitive and metacognitive processes, relying upon many different kinds of information, and resulting in complex mental representations (Block & Pressley, 2002; Kintsch & Rawson, 2007). Difficulty in any one area can impede comprehension. Therefore, a thorough understanding of the sources of an individual's reading comprehension problems is necessary for planning an appropriate instructional program.

☚ TEST YOURSELF ☛

....

1. **A child's level of oral vocabulary is usually a good predictor of his or her reading vocabulary.** True or False?

2. **Most vocabulary is learned through explicit instruction.** True or False?

3. **Which of the following impacts a child's incidental word learning?**

    (a) socioeconomic level of family

    (b) being read to

    (c) playing with words

    (d) All of the above.

    (e) None of the above.

4. **List three examples of activities for intentional explicit word instruction.**

5. **Which of the following is not an independent word-learning strategy?**

    (a) using a dictionary

    (b) using semantic feature analysis

    (c) using context clues

    (d) using word parts

6. **Fluent decoding results in good comprehension.** True or False?

7. **List three effective reading comprehension strategies.**

8. **Graphic organizers are effective in improving comprehension because they**

    (a) provide a visual framework for connecting new information to prior knowledge.

    (b) actively engage the reader.

    (c) remind the reader of the text structure.

    (d) All of the above.

    (e) a and c

9. Reading comprehension may be affected by

   (a) limited vocabulary.

   (b) limited decoding skill.

   (c) limited fluency.

   (d) limited attention.

   (e) Any of the above.

10. Effective reading comprehension instruction

   (a) teaches decoding first.

   (b) uses explicit instruction to teach a variety of strategies.

   (c) teaches students to ask and answer questions about their reading.

   (d) All of the above.

   (e) b and c

Answers: 1. True; 2. False; 3. d; 4. Three of the following: teaching synonyms, antonyms, multiple-meaning words; preteaching vocabulary; using semantic feature analysis or semantic maps or word webs; using examples and nonexamples of words; teaching independent word-learning strategies including context clues, use of reference tools, morphology; 5. b; 6. False; 7. Three of the following: predicting, questioning, summarizing, comprehension monitoring, cooperative learning, using graphic and semantic organizers, using text structures, visualizing, thinking aloud; 8. d; 9. e; 10. e

Six

SPELLING

SPELLING DEVELOPMENT

Similar linguistic processes are involved in pronouncing and spelling words, but spelling is much more difficult. Reading a word requires only recognition, whereas spelling requires the complete recall of every letter in the correct sequence. Thus, individuals may have adequate reading abilities, but poor spelling. This is particularly true of individuals with specific reading disabilities whose spelling abilities often lag behind their reading skills. A decade of research from the University of Washington has demonstrated that long after children with reading disabilities have learned to read, they continue to have ongoing spelling problems (Berninger, 2008). In fact, at times, spelling problems are the only remaining indication of dyslexia in adulthood (Romani, Olson, & Di Betta, 2007).

Characteristics of Individuals Struggling with Spelling

A weakness in phonemic awareness is often found in poor spellers in the early grades. However, in the later grades, the primary characteristics of a poor speller include difficulty understanding spelling rules, word structure, and letter patterns. Poor spellers are thought to have a visual memory problem specific to letters and words. This specific problem is referred to as *orthographic memory* because the individual's visual memory for other material may be intact.

Although spelling is not listed as one of the eight areas of achievement in IDEA 2004, it is a foundational skill of written expression, which is listed. In addition, poor spelling performance is a common characteristic of dyslexia. Many times, reading and spelling problems coexist. Also, instruction in one can help improve the other, although instruction in spelling tends to influence reading more than reading instruction influences spelling. For many students, a phonological deficit underlies their problems with decoding and encoding (Cunningham & Cunningham, 1992). This has led researchers to predict that poor spellers will have a higher percentage of errors that are nonphonetic in nature (Bruck, 1988), but this has not always been the case (Moats, 1983). Other linguistic factors can contribute to spelling difficulties as well. For example, individuals with spelling-related learning difficulties tend to have more difficulty with morphological elements than do others (Carlisle, 1987).

Language Components

As with decoding, spelling involves several different types of linguistic abilities, including phonology, orthography, morphology, and vocabulary. Knowledge of speech sounds (phonology) forms the basis for discriminating and sequencing the sounds in words. To spell, one must convert phonemes into the representative graphemes. Knowledge of the spelling patterns (orthography) is required for quick production of common letter strings and letter patterns (e.g., -ight, -tion). Skilled spellers appear to have more precise word-specific spelling knowledge than do individuals who struggle with spelling (Figueredo & Varnhagen, 2004; Holmes & Castles, 2001). Thus, memory of orthographic letter patterns and representations is a key component of accurate spelling. In fact, problems in phonology or orthography are two different impairments that can affect one's ability to learn to spell (Romani et al., 2007).

Knowledge of the meaning units (morphology) is necessary for forming plurals, recording the correct verb tense, and adding affixes to root

DON'T FORGET

....

Phonological processing is needed to put the sounds of a word in order, whereas adequate orthographic representations are needed for the spelling of irregular words.

words. English spelling is described as *morpho-phonemic* as the spellings of word derivatives are often designed to preserve meaning, rather than sound-symbol correspondence (e.g., sign and signal, muscle and muscular). Knowledge of word meanings (vocabulary) is needed for spelling homophones (words that sound the same but are spelled differently) correctly and choosing the correct spelling of a word within the context of writing. For example, to spell the word *it's* correctly, one must know that *it's* stands for *it is* and is not a possessive form. Essentially, the elements of English orthography involve sounds, patterns, and meanings.

Regular Words

Regular words are ones that conform to the most common English spelling patterns and rules. Most regular words are spelled the way that they sound, so if a student segments and writes the sounds in order, the word will be spelled correctly. As noted in the section on phonological awareness, the most important phonological skill underlying spelling is segmentation. The students must be able to break a word down into each of its phonemes and then record each of these sounds in order. Students should be able to spell regular words correctly before their attention is directed to common, but irregular, spelling patterns (e.g., ight).

Irregular or Exception Words

Words that are referred to as *irregular* or *exception words* are ones in which one or more elements of the word do not conform to common English spelling patterns or rules. As noted in Chapter 3 (phonics), these words are sometimes referred to as *sight words.* In many irregular words, the irregular element is the vowel sound. For example, in the word *said,* the "ai" is considered to be irregular because it does not represent the sound of long a; but the /s/ and /d/ are regular. Students must memorize the unique features of these words to spell them correctly. Some people can spell regular words accurately because of their knowledge of phoneme–grapheme correspondences, but they have trouble spelling irregular words, most likely due to poor lexical representations (Romani et al., 2007). The errors that they make tend to involve spelling irregular word elements as if they were regular (e.g., thay for they, sed for said). These errors reveal that the writer is using sounds to spell but is not retaining the orthographic representations.

CAUTION

Teachers must ensure that students have learned and can write all of the letter–sound correspondences that are necessary for spelling the specific words on spelling tests.

DON'T FORGET

If a student cannot segment the phonemes in words accurately, spelling instruction should begin with teaching the student how to segment words into phonemes, and then how to match these phonemes with graphemes.

Developmental Stages

As with the development of word recognition skill, several researchers documented a developmental progression in spelling skills. Read (1971) analyzed the spellings of preschool children and found that their attempted spellings provided important information about their developing word knowledge. Over the next decades, Henderson and his colleagues at the University of Virginia corroborated and extended Read's findings to develop a comprehensive model of spelling development (Bear, Invernizzi, Templeton, & Johnston, 2008). Although the names of the phases or stages of orthographic knowledge have differed slightly from author to author, the description of the developmental trajectory is similar. Effective teaching requires consideration of children's developmental levels.

Emergent or prephonemic (preschool to kindergarten)

At this phase of development the child understands that letters communicate meaning and may be written, but he or she does not have knowledge of sound–letter relationships. The child may even write "stories" that consist of random strings of letters and numbers in several rows. The child does not yet understand the alphabetic principle, which is the basic concept that letters represent segments of speech (Moats, 2000). In the beginning stage, instruction in phonemic awareness is coupled with teaching the relationships among easy to hear letters and sounds, and encouraging invented spelling (listening to the speech sounds).

Early letter name/semiphonetic (kindergarten to middle second grade)

At this phase, the child has discovered the alphabetic principle and has developed some knowledge of sound–letter relationships. The child tends to rely on letter names as cues for the sounds they represent (Bear et al., 2008; Read, 1971) and will often write the most salient sounds in the word, particularly the beginning and ending consonants. The child often omits the vowel sounds from words, as well as the second sound from consonant blends. At this stage, instruction focuses on listening to

DON'T FORGET
....
Children's early spelling attempts provide a window into their developing understandings of sound–letter relationships.

and recording each speech sound and studying consonant blends and digraphs.

Middle to late letter name/phonetic (early first to late second grade)

In this phase, the child represents both consonant and vowel sounds in words but usually writes one letter for each sound. Short vowel sounds are confused, and long vowels appear but without silent letters. In addition, the child will often omit less distinct speech sounds, such as the nasal sound before an ending consonant (e.g., spelling *jump* as *jup*). Instruction at this stage focuses on helping the child identify and record each discrete phoneme, spell consonant blends and digraphs, and choose the correct vowel spellings.

Within word pattern spelling/transitional (first to fourth grade)

At the beginning of this phase, the child has mastered most digraphs, consonant blends, and includes preconsonantal nasals (e.g., jump). Each syllable contains a vowel sound. At this point, the child has internalized awareness of the sounds and corresponding letters and becomes more aware of orthographic patterns (Moats, 2000). The child no longer relies on a sound-by-sound approach and begins to use common spelling patterns and long vowel spellings correctly. The child pays more attention to the visual features of words and instruction focuses on the spellings of common letter patterns and more complex consonant units, such as -dge.

Syllables and affixes spelling (upper elementary to middle school)

During this phase, students must spell multisyllabic words. The student makes errors where syllables are joined or affixes are added (e.g., *hopefull* for *hopeful*). By the end of this stage, the student can spell most two- and three-syllable words correctly, common prefixes and suffixes, and less common vowel patterns (Abbott, 2001). At this stage, the instruction focuses on root words and the addition of morphemes, including affixes.

Derivational relations spelling (middle school to adulthood)

At this stage the student spells most words correctly but still lacks some knowledge of word derivations. Errors are still made on words involving a *schwa* sound, the addition of affixes, or changing adjectives to nouns (Bear et al., 2008). Instruction focuses on the study of the relationships among word structures, word origins, and word meanings. Students can explore word etymologies, as well as the spellings of words from other languages.

Error Analysis

Unless an evaluator analyzes the quality of a student's spelling errors from year to year, it is often difficult to demonstrate spelling growth and progress based solely on the results of standardized tests because the words on spelling tests are scored as correct or incorrect. A student may earn the same total score on a test, but when his or her prior spellings are compared to the most recent spellings, one can see marked improvement in spelling skill. At the beginning of third grade, Ivan

≡ Rapid Reference 6.1

Questions to Ask When Analyzing Spelling Errors

Does the student:

1. Put the sounds of words in the correct sequence?
2. Add or omit certain sounds from words?
3. Spell the irregular elements of words correctly?
4. Have vowels in every syllable?
5. Spell homophones correctly?
6. Spell common affixes correctly?
7. Understand how to form plurals and change verb tenses?

spelled the word *house* as *hs*. Two months later, it was spelled as *hows*. Several months later, it was spelled as *hous*. Although none of these spellings are correct, it is easy to see that Ivan's spellings of the word are progressing to a more accurate phonetic and orthographic representation. Curriculum-based measurements of spelling are much more sensitive to growth, as points are given for each letter written in a correct sequence. Rapid Reference 6.1 provides several questions to consider when doing a qualitative analysis of spelling errors.

DON'T FORGET

Remember, after administering tests, to analyze the student's attempted spellings. This analysis can provide valuable information for instructional planning.

CAUTION

Keep in mind that ELLs may use knowledge of the spelling system in their first language to help spell words in their second language.

EFFECTIVE INSTRUCTION

Depending upon an individual's developmental level, a variety of procedures can be used to increase spelling competence. Spelling instruction should engage students in active, reflective thinking about the reliable patterns and rules, and not be focused on copying and memorizing lists of individual words (Carreker, 2005b). In addition, explicit code instruction facilitates spelling development (Berninger & Amtmann, 2003). Several commercial spelling programs are designed for this

CAUTION

Rather than naming specific programs in IEPs, it is often best to describe the type of intervention or training that the student needs. In this way, the intervention is not restricted to just one program or methodology.

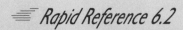

Rapid Reference 6.2

Elements of Effective Spelling Instruction

Provide instruction in:

- Segmenting spoken words into their sounds
- Matching the sounds to the letter correspondences
- Spelling common orthographic patterns
- Learning and practicing common spelling rules
- Spelling irregular words with emphasis on the irregular parts
- Adding affixes to words
- Spelling different syllable types
- Spelling word derivatives
- Learning about word origins

purpose (see Rapid Reference 6.6). Rapid Reference 6.2 provides a developmental overview of the elements of effective spelling instruction.

Model to Guide Instruction

In discussing the evolution of English orthography, Henderson and Templeton (1986) explain that the English spelling system involves a systematic layering of alphabet, pattern, and meaning. As examples, the alphabet layer includes beginning and ending consonants, short vowels, and consonant digraphs and blends. The pattern layer includes long vowel sounds, vowel teams and diphthongs, and complex consonant clusters. The meaning layer includes common affixes, as well as Latin and Greek root words and combining forms. Once students are proficient with the alphabet layer, instruction should address the pattern layer, and then the meaning layer.

Word Sorts

One easy way to help children acquire knowledge of spelling patterns is to have them engage in word sorts. Children can be given a group of words to sort and then asked to figure out various spelling patterns.

For example, a sort may include the following words: cow, found, plow, how, couch, shout, hound, wow. By sorting the words into two piles, the child can see that the *ou* sound is usually spelled with *ow* at the end of a word. Later, the child can learn that /ou/ is spelled with ow in a

> **DON'T FORGET**
>
> Students first need to be able to analyze the sounds in words and then write the letter or letters that represent the sounds. Knowledge of phonology precedes knowledge of orthography and morphology.

one-syllable word before a final /l/ or /n/ (e.g., down, owl) and before /er/ as in shower (Carreker, 2005b). Bear et al. (2008) describe how to use a variety of word sorts as a component of word study. Examples include: picture sorts to compare and contrast initial and final consonant sounds, picture sorts to compare and contrast single consonants with consonant blends, sorts to compare short vowel sounds, and picture sorts of long and short vowel sounds. Word sorts for alternative spellings of the same phoneme are also effective (Berninger, 2008). More advanced sorts can involve different syllable types, common affixes, or sorting words into Greek or Latin origins. The study of word features must match the student's developmental level of word knowledge (Bear et al., 2008). Word sorts can start with a focus on words in isolation and then progress to word searches that involve looking for similar words in connected text (Invernizzi & Hayes, 2004).

Spelling Rules

Although exceptions exist, knowledge of a few spelling rules can help children understand how to add suffixes and when a letter should be dropped, added, or changed. Children should be taught how to apply five major English spelling rules. Carreker (2005b) summarizes the major features of each rule:

1. *The rule for doubling the final consonant (the Floss rule).* In a one-syllable word that ends in f, l, or s and has a short vowel sound, the final consonant is doubled. (Floss is a mnemonic to help students remember the three sounds.) (Note: For one-syllable words that end in z, the final consonant is also doubled.)

2. *The rule for doubling the medial consonant (the Rabbit rule).* In a two-syllable base word with one medial consonant sound after a short vowel, the medial consonant is doubled (e.g., rabbit).

3. *The doubling rule.* The final consonant of a word is doubled when there is: (a) one vowel in the last syllable, (b) one consonant after the vowel, (c) the last syllable is accented, and (d) a vowel suffix is added (e.g., running, hopped). However, the following seven letters in English rarely or never double: h, j, k, v, w, x, and y.

4. *The dropping rule.* When the base word ends in an e and a vowel suffix is being added, the final e is dropped (hope becomes hoping).

5. *The changing rule.* When a base word ends in a consonant-y, and a suffix that does not begin with an "i" is added, the final -y changes to an i (e.g., fly-flies). If the base word has a vowel before the final -y, the y does not change to i (e.g., played).

Carreker explains that visual discovery is used to teach these spelling rules because the individual must distinguish and retain the visual features of the spelling rule, not the sounds of the words.

Spelling Tests

Students who struggle with spelling should not be required to memorize lists of unrelated words for a weekly spelling test. This type of testing is ineffective and, even if the word is spelled correctly on the test, the likelihood of retention is poor. Instead, the weekly spelling test should be based upon the spelling patterns that have been taught.

For students who are still struggling with recording sounds in the correct order, the spelling list should include only regular words and the student should be encouraged to say the word slowly while writing each sound. A variety of instructional activities, such as having students build words by placing letter tiles in the correct sequence, can help them improve their ability to sequence sounds correctly. Once the students can spell words the way they sound, lists can be developed that focus upon the mastery of common spelling patterns (e.g., ight).

Spelling flow lists

Students who struggle with spelling need a considerable amount of practice and review to master the spellings of words. Some research suggests that daily spelling tests are more effective than weekly spelling tests for these students. The procedure for keeping track of words has been referred to as a *spelling flow list,* or *add-a-word list.* This type of procedure provides students with sufficient repetition and review. Rapid Reference 6.3 provides an overview of the flow list procedure.

≡ *Rapid Reference 6.3*

Spelling Flow List Procedure

1. Create a graph on which words may be written down the left side of the paper, and the days of several weeks Monday (M) to Friday (F) are recorded across the top of the paper. Place a short list of words on the chart. These words may be words misspelled in a student's writings or words designed to teach a spelling pattern.

2. Do daily testing of the words, placing a plus (+) under each day the word is correct and a 0 in the box if a word is incorrect.

3. When the word is spelled correctly 3 days in a row, remove the word from the list, place it in a word box, and add a new word to the list.

4. Review the word in the word box 1 week later. If misspelled, add it back on the list. If correct, return it to the word box.

CAUTION

On written drafts or content-area exams, ensure that students are not penalized for misspellings.

Accommodations

Students with poor spelling will require an individualized approach to spelling instruction. Lists of words may be based upon specific spelling rules, specific spelling patterns, or a few common high-frequency words that the student misspells when writing. In addition, a teacher may need to make several adjustments on spelling tests, such as reducing the number of words, adjusting the difficulty level of the words, and increasing the amount of time and study for mastering the words.

Spelling Irregular Words

Words with irregular elements must be taught to students directly and practiced systematically. Teachers can draw extra attention to the irregular element by circling it or writing the irregular word part in a different color. Some teachers post lists of common irregular words on the wall so that the spellings are readily available to all students. In addition, individual students can have personalized spelling dictionaries in which they can easily access specific words they find to be problematic, such as *people* and *because*.

Some students benefit from a multisensory approach when learning how to spell irregular words. Many of the commonly used spelling interventions for struggling students are based on adaptations of the Fernald (1943) method. This method involves tracing the word (if needed), saying the word, and then writing the word from memory. Rapid Reference 6.4 provides an example of this type of procedure for practicing the spellings of words with irregular elements. Carreker (2005b) describes a similar procedure for learning to spell words with irregular spellings. Rapid Reference 6.5 reviews the steps of this procedure. In

≡ *Rapid Reference 6.4*

Fernald Multisensory Spelling Method

1. Write the word on a chalkboard or piece of paper.

2. Say the word clearly and ask the student to look at the word and pronounce it clearly.

3. Ask the student to study the word and try to develop a visual image of the word. The student may try to picture the word; may say the word; and/or may trace the word with the index finger. The student studies the word until he or she can make a mental picture.

4. When the student indicates that he/she knows how to spell the word, erase the word and then have the student attempt to write the word from memory.

5. Erase the word or turn the paper over and ask the student to write the word two more times correctly from memory.

≡ *Rapid Reference 6.5*

Carreker Multisensory Spelling Method

1. Write the word in large letters and have the student circle the irregular part of the word.

2. Have the student trace the word three times, saying the word and naming the letters while tracing.

3. Have the student write the word three times with the word in view, naming each letter while writing.

4. With eyes closed, have the student spell the word, then check the model. Repeat this step three times.

5. Remove the model, have the student say the word, then write the word three times, naming the letters while writing.

general these procedures add in a multisensory component for practicing words, require the person to write the word several times from memory, and place emphasis on the accurate recall of letter sequences. Having students write words from memory is far more effective than asking students to copy words several times.

CAUTION

Remember that effective use of a spell checker requires spelling competence and that this technology is not a substitute for systematic, explicit spelling instruction.

Technology

Although students should be encouraged to use the spelling checker option in word-processing programs, they must first develop a degree of spelling competence or the spell checker will not be able to recognize the word. The student must be able to spell the word the way it sounds and also be able to distinguish among several options that may be quite

≣ Rapid Reference 6.6

Examples of Commercial Programs for Explicit Spelling Instruction

- Phoneme-Grapheme Mapping (Sopris West)
- Scholastic Spelling (Scholastic)
- Sitton Spelling (Educators Publishing Service)
- Spellbound and the Spell of Words (Educators Publishing Service)
- Spellography (Sopris West)
- Spelling Mastery (SRA McGraw Hill)
- Spelling with Morphographs (SRA McGraw Hill)
- Spellwell (Educators Publishing Service)

similar in appearance. In addition, spelling checkers often do not detect spelling errors on homophones or errors that turn the word into another real word. Despite the limitations, a reasonable goal for students with poor spelling is to increase their spelling skills to the level at which they can use spelling checkers effectively and independently (Berninger & Amtmann, 2003).

Commercial Programs and Spelling-Related Websites

Programs for explicit, systematic spelling instruction are listed in Rapid Reference 6.6. Rapid Reference 6.7 lists a variety of spelling-related

≡ Rapid Reference 6.7

Spelling-Related Web Sites

Student Activities/Games/Tools
- www.wordcentral.com (online dictionary, thesaurus, games)
- www.spellingcity.com (educational site to help children improve their spelling)
- www.gamequarium.com/spelling
- www.funbrain.com/spellroo
- www.kidsspell.com

Teacher Resources
- www.readwritethink.org (IRA and NCTE)
- www.everydayspelling.com (Pearson Education)
- www.eduplace.com (Houghton-Mifflin)

Products
- Kurzweil (www.kurzweiledu.com)
- Read, Write, & Type (www.readwritetype.com)

web sites. Some provide practice and instruction for students, often using a game format. Others provide guidance to teachers, including lesson plans and activities to foster spelling. Also listed are web sites that provide support, such as online dictionaries, and ones related to products that will assist students with spelling difficulties.

CONCLUSION

Some children learn to spell relatively easily and are able to recall orthographic patterns and irregular word spellings in the early elementary years. These students seem to pick up the spellings of words from having just a few encounters in print. Other students, particularly those with reading disabilities, tend to struggle with spelling into adulthood. Even after numerous exposures to words, they have trouble recalling the correct spellings. In addition, some students develop adequate reading ability but still have compromised spelling. For students with specific reading and spelling disabilities, explicit, systematic instruction delivered by a skilled teacher is critical.

🪶 TEST YOURSELF 🪶

1. **Irregular words are difficult to spell because**

   (a) the word does not conform to predictable phoneme–grapheme correspondences.

   (b) a part of the word does not conform to standard English spelling patterns and rules.

   (c) they always derive from other languages.

   (d) they are rarely seen in print.

   (e) both b and d.

2. Morphology is important to spelling because

(a) some words are spelled the way they sound.

(b) some words have irregular elements that need to be memorized.

(c) some words are not spelled like they sound because the spellings preserve word meanings.

(d) some words are derived from foreign languages and their spellings do not conform to English spelling rules.

3. What stage of development do spellings such as *lk* for *like* and *bbl* for *baseball* represent?

(a) emergent

(b) early letter name

(c) late letter name

(d) within word pattern

4. What phase of development do spellings such as *runing* for *running*, *doller* for *dollar*, and *imobile* for *immobile* represent?

(a) late letter name

(b) within word pattern

(c) syllable and affixes

(d) derivational relations

5. If a student spells words exactly as they sound, his or her difficulties are most likely related to

(a) imprecise orthographic representations.

(b) poor phonological awareness.

(c) poor executive functioning.

(d) inaccurate phonetic transcriptions.

6. In one-syllable words with short vowel sounds, what final consonants are usually doubled?

7. When the base word ends in an e and a vowel suffix is being added, what happens to the final e?

8. A spelling flow list

(a) is similar to a weekly spelling test.

(b) uses words from the basal spelling program.

(c) provides daily testing on a few words.

(d) promotes mastery of the spelling of words.

(e) both c and d.

9. A person may be a good reader, but still struggle with spelling. True or False?

10. Young children rely mainly on rote visual memorization to spell words. True or False?

Answers: 1. b; 2. c; 3. b; 4. c; 5. a; 6. f, l, and s (Floss mnemonic); 7. the final e is dropped; 8. e; 9. True; 10. False (young children produce spellings based on their knowledge of sounds)

Seven

HANDWRITING AND WRITTEN EXPRESSION

Writing today is not a frill for the few, but an essential skill for the many.

—*The Neglected R, National Commission on Writing in America's Schools and Colleges, 2003*

Writing is a complex task that requires the integration of multiple cognitive, linguistic, and motor abilities. In fact, writing may be the most complex task students are asked to perform in school because it requires the integration of so many different skills. For example, good oral language and background knowledge underlie good writing; but this is not enough. Many students with writing difficulties can formulate clear, coherent ideas, but they then have trouble translating these thoughts into written form. The process of integrating the various language demands with the memory and motor demands can easily overload a student's ability to attend and concentrate, and, thus, the written output suffers. A problem in any one aspect of writing, including spelling or handwriting, can have a detrimental effect on the quality of written expression.

General agreement exists among researchers that writing involves both low-level transcription skills (handwriting, spelling, punctuation, capitalization, and grammar), as well as high-level composition skills (planning, content, organization, and revision) (Graham & Harris, 2005). Berninger and Abbott (2003) indicate that at least three distinct language levels are involved in writing: letter formation (handwriting); word formation (spelling or keyboarding); and text formation (composition). The first two levels, handwriting and spelling, are often viewed as foundational or low-level transcription skills, whereas the third level, composition, encompasses the high-level skills. Juel (1988) found that one third of fourth graders with writing difficulties had trouble with low-level skills; one third had trouble with the high-level skills; and the final one third had difficulty in both. This chapter addresses two aspects of writing skill: (1) handwriting and (2) written expression or composing. Chapter 6 of this text provides information on spelling.

HANDWRITING

One may question who cares about handwriting, especially in our modern world. Computers, word processing, e-mail, and text messaging dominate written communication. While technology certainly is used for a large portion of writing, the need for legible handwriting has not disappeared. When students are first learning to write, handwriting is the primary means for their composing. Even today there are many times that signatures, handwritten notes, or manual completion of forms are required. Illegible writing often leads to miscommunications, which can be frustrating, costly, or even deadly. For example, shipments fail to reach their destination because no one can read the label; refunds cannot be sent because the return address is illegible; and unclear medical prescriptions lead to adverse reactions, or even death. It is estimated that 60% of medication errors result from illegible handwriting or transcription errors (Shamliyan, Duval, Du, & Kane, 2008).

Over the past several decades, there has been decreasing em-

CAUTION

It is estimated that 60% of medication errors result from illegible handwriting or transcription errors.

phasis on handwriting instruction and competence. A recent study by Steve Graham indicates that only 12% of teachers have even taken a course in how to teach handwriting (Kelley, 2007). The importance of handwriting, however, is well documented in the research and evidence is growing that fluent handwriting is a fundamental building block of writing competence. For example, handwriting has been identified as an important predictor of the quality of written expression (Berninger et al., 1997) and fluent, automatic handwriting has been linked to the quality of compositions (Graham, Berninger, Abbott, Abbott, & Whitaker, 1997; Jones, 2004; Sheffield, 1996). If a student has to think about letter formation and production, the quality of the written expression will suffer because cognitive resources are focused on *how* to write rather than *what* to write. Graham indicates this is especially true for children in kindergarten through fourth grade because they think and write at the same time (Kelley, 2007). Only later do students begin thinking about their writing apart from their handwriting. In addition, learning to write has a reciprocal relationship with learning to read (Ehri, 2000) and the two are best learned in an integrated manner (Clay, 1982). The abilities to write and name letters are highly related in 4-year-olds (Molfese, Beswick, Molnar, & Jacobi-Vessels, 2006), providing further evidence of the reciprocity between writing and reading development. Finally, early intervention for students at risk for handwriting or spelling difficulties can prevent more serious writing disabilities later in school (Berninger & Amtmann, 2003; Graham, Harris, & Fink, 2000).

Handwriting is language by hand (Berninger & Graham, 1998), so it is more than just a fine-motor task. While handwriting may be considered a low-level transcription skill, it is a foundational skill for written expression. Legible handwriting results in clear communication. Figure 7.1 illustrates a handwriting sample from a fifth-grade student with legible handwriting but poor spelling. The quality of this student's handwriting makes it easier to overlook the poor spelling. A fourth grader's

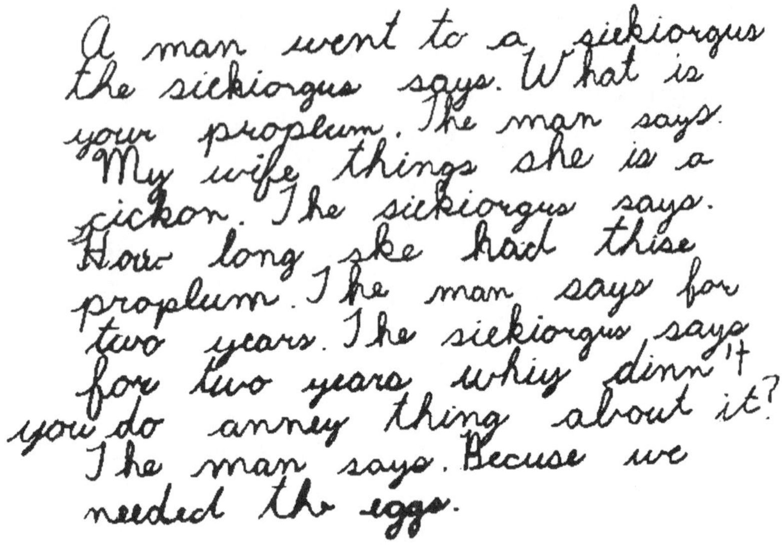

Figure 7.1. Grade 5 Legible Handwriting Example

Transcription
A man went to a psychiatrist the psychiatrist says. What is your problem. The man says. My wife thinks she is a chicken. The psychiatrist says. How long she had this problem. The man says for two years. The psychiatrist says for two years why didn't you do anything about it? The man says. Because we needed the eggs.

handwriting sample is shown in Figure 7.2. In this example, the handwriting is illegible, making communication virtually impossible.

Characteristics of Individuals Struggling with Handwriting

Difficulties in printing and cursive writing can be caused by poor motor abilities or coordination problems, memory of letter forms, or weaknesses in orthographic processing (Fletcher et al., 2007). Orthographic processing or coding involves associative memory because of the need to store and retrieve sound–symbol associations. Poor handwriting is an early warning sign of students at risk for problems with

Figure 7.2. Grade 4 Illegible Handwriting Example

Transcription
Mom and Dad are going crazy ....
Candy send me my game boy and game.

written expression. Automatic letter writing has been found to be the best predictor of composition length and quality from elementary school through college, providing further evidence of the importance of handwriting (Connelly, Campbell, MacLean, & Barnes, 2006; Graham et al., 1997; Jones, 2004).

> **DON'T FORGET**
> ....
> Handwriting is an important predictor of the quality of written expression.

EFFECTIVE INSTRUCTION

Formal handwriting instruction is absent from many classrooms. As mentioned previously in this chapter, there are compelling reasons to teach handwriting. Berninger and Richards (2002) found that explicit methods were most effective in teaching handwriting. The lessons should be short, 5 to 10 minutes, and followed by an opportunity to use handwriting in a meaningful manner.

Letter Formation

Children should be taught letter formation and then practice forming letters to develop automaticity of letter production. Improvements in both letter formation and fluency lead to improved handwriting and composition (Jones & Christensen, 1999). An effective program for teaching letter formation is based upon the following four principles: (1) overlearning letters in isolation and then applying them in a written context; (2) forming letters with external cues, such as verbalizing and tracing the letter forms until they become automatic; (3) encouraging students to evaluate their own handwriting; and (4) providing students with feedback and assistance in maintaining a consistent and legible writing style (Graham & Madan, 1981).

In a summary of their studies from the University of Washington that investigated the performance of students struggling with handwriting, Berninger (2008) reported that the most effective methods for practicing letter formation included: (a) practicing each letter by studying number arrow cues; (b) covering the letter and then writing it from memory; and (c) practicing writing letters within words and compositions. These methods improved automaticity of legible letter writing.

Writing aids
Some children will benefit from using a writing aid, such as a pencil grip or weight, or raised-line paper. These writing aids are available from stores or web sites offering educational or rehabilitation supplies (e.g., www.thepencilgrip.com, www.sammonspreston.com, www.theraproducts.com).

Commercial programs

Handwriting Without Tears is a developmentally based, flexible curriculum for teaching handwriting to children in preschool through Grade 5. It has a proven track record of success in making children's handwriting legible, fluent, and automatic. More information about this curriculum can be found at www.hwtears.com.

Keyboarding and Technology

Keyboarding skills should also be taught to children beginning in first grade, especially those children who struggle with handwriting. Children who struggle with the graphomotor aspects of writing may

≡ *Rapid Reference 7.1*

Software or Technology Tools to Support Keyboarding Skills

- Mavis Beacon Teaches Typing (ages 8+) (www.broderbund.com)
- Disney's Adventures in Typing with Timon and Pumbaa (ages 6+) (various sources)
- Typing Instructor (all ages) Individual Software
- Read, Write, and Type (ages 6–8) (www.talkingfingers.com)
- Typing Time (ages 11–14) Thomson Learning
- Neo or Neo2 Portable Word Processors (www.alphasmart.com)
- Laser PC6—Notetaker and Digital Notebook (www.perfectsolutions.com)
- Dragon Naturally Speaking (speech recognition software) (www.nuance.com/naturallyspeaking/standard)
- Fonts 4 Teachers (www.fonts4teachers.com)
- Startwrite (www.startwrite.com)

find keyboarding easier than handwriting. Different software programs designed to teach keyboarding skills are available. One program that has received numerous awards from teacher and parent groups is *Mavis Beacon Teaches Typing*. Once a student has keyboarding skills, a portable word processor, like Neo or Neo2 from Alpha-Smart, may be useful. Some students may require even more support and will benefit from using speech recognition software, such as *Dragon Naturally Speaking*, which translates speech into text. Both *Fonts 4 Teachers* and Start*write* allow teachers to create customized practice sheets and offer manuscript, cursive, and D'Nealian-style fonts for learning handwriting. In addition, the teacher can control the size of the font, and present letters as dots or with directional arrows. Rapid Reference 7.1 lists examples of these technology products.

WRITTEN EXPRESSION

The achievement domain of written language has not received the same intensity of focus from researchers, educators, or legislators as has reading, or even mathematics for that matter. In fact, writing has been called the "Neglected R" (National Commission on Writing in America's Schools and Colleges, 2003). This may help explain why a significant number of students do not demonstrate proficient writing skills (National Assessment of Educational Progress [NAEP], 2007). Although many children do learn to write, the quality of their writing is often lacking and many do not have the writing skills needed to meet the demands of higher education or of the workplace (e.g., National Commission on Writing in America's Schools and Colleges, 2004). It is estimated that states spend one quarter of a billion dollars annually to remediate employees' writing difficulties (*USA Today*, 2005, July 4).

Characteristics of Individuals Struggling with Written Expression

Poor writers lack awareness of what good writing is and do not know how to produce it. In addition, they lack knowledge of text structures (genres) and content, do not plan before or during writing, do not monitor their own performance, and show poor attention and concentration (Troia, 2002; Troia & Graham, 2003).

Limited language skills (vocabulary, syntax, morphology) and a lack of procedural and declarative knowledge have a negative impact on writing. Berninger and Winn (2006), in their not-so-simple view of writing, suggest that the text generation process (supported by transcription and executive functions) occurs in working memory. Working memory has links to short-term memory as well as stored knowledge and it consists of a three word-form storage system (phonological, morphological, and orthographic), a time-sensitive phonological loop, and executive functions (Berninger et al., 2006). Common characteristics of students with a disability in written expression are ineffective strategy use, minimal output, limited revising, and weak basic skills. Rapid Reference 7.2 provides examples of how various difficulties can impact a student's ability to express ideas in writing.

Many times, students struggling with writing have coexisting difficulties in other areas. For example, writing problems frequently are present in students with attention problems, possibly due to the number of elements that must be integrated and attended to when writing. Additionally, students with reading difficulties often exhibit difficulties in writing because of the common perceptual and linguistic demands required by both tasks.

DON'T FORGET

Students struggling with writing frequently have coexisting difficulties in other areas.

≡ *Rapid Reference 7.2*

Examples of How Various Difficulties Impact Writing Performance

Weakness	Impact on Writing Performance
Graphomotor	Slow writing, difficulty forming letters, awkward pencil grip, limited output on writing tasks
Attention	Distractibility, difficulty initiating writing tasks, careless errors, inconsistent legibility, poor planning
Spatial	Poor use of lines on paper, uneven spacing, organizational problems, misspellings
Memory	Poor vocabulary, misspellings, frequent errors in transcription skills
Language	Difficulty with sentence structure and word order, poor vocabulary, poor spelling

DON'T FORGET

A connection exists between reading and writing. The fact that when we *write* a word, we *read* it to see if we *spelled* it correctly illustrates this connection at a basic level.

Often times a student's writing difficulties are not noticed until about fourth grade because it is at this point that writing demands increase from minimal-level (providing single word responses or filling in blanks) to higher-level demands (composing). Instruction must focus on integrating low-level transcription skills with the high-level composing skills and teaching genre-specific writing. As these students progress in school, they will need to focus on time management, as well as use of technology.

EFFECTIVE INSTRUCTION

As with all effective instruction, the teacher plays a critical role. When students have writing difficulties, many teachers view them negatively, set low expectations for them, and then limit interactions with them (Graham & Harris, 1997). The quality of instruction students receive has a major impact on writing achievement (Graham & Harris, 2002), but the quality of instruction varies drastically from one classroom to the next. Some teachers focus primarily on the foundational skills of handwriting and spelling, whereas others provide time for writing but do not provide instruction on writing skills. Still others provide little or no time for writing instruction.

Unfortunately, many teachers may lack the knowledge of how to teach writing and some even feel it is not their responsibility. In 2004, the National Council of Teachers of English (NCTE) published their beliefs about teaching writing. Several of the statements are grounded in the research including those noting the relationship between reading and writing, that writing can be taught, and that practice in writing helps develop writing. Specific, effective instructional approaches, however, are not mentioned. Rapid Reference 7.3 summarizes the NCTE beliefs about teaching writing.

Writing Process

In the 1990s writing began to be viewed as a multistep process rather than a product. Although the steps in the writing process are logical and appear sequential, they are actually more fluid and recursive. Work done in one step

DON'T FORGET

The National Writing Project, designed for teachers of writing at all grades, is a professional development network that strives to improve student achievement by improving the teaching of writing. For more information see www.nwp.org.

≣ *Rapid Reference 7.3*

NCTE Beliefs about the Teaching of Writing

1. Everyone has the capacity to write, writing can be taught, and teachers can help students become better writers.
2. People learn to write by writing.
3. Writing is a process.
4. Writing is a tool for thinking.
5. Writing grows out of many different purposes.
6. Conventions of finished and edited texts are important to readers and therefore to writers.
7. Writing and reading are related.
8. Writing has a complex relationship to talk.
9. Literate practices are embedded in complicated social relationships.
10. Composing occurs in different modalities and technologies.
11. Assessment of writing involves complex, informed, human judgment.

may require revisiting a previously completed step. Proponents of teaching writing as a process believe writing should occur on a daily basis. Many educators use the instructional model of the Writers Workshop (see later in this chapter) to accomplish daily writing practice. The essential stages in the writing process are summarized in Rapid Reference 7.4. Although research provides some support that the process writing approach is effective (Graham & Perin, 2007), process writing instruction is not an evidence-based approach (Berninger, 2008). Many of the steps and instructional procedures that are taught at each stage, however, are supported. These methods are discussed next.

Explicit Instruction

Students who struggle with writing require intense, explicit instruction. In a meta-analysis of research-based instructional approaches for teaching written expression to students with learning disabilities, the following three elements emerge as most effective in improving student outcomes (Gersten & Baker, 1999): (1) adhering to a basic framework of planning, writing, and revision; (2) explicitly teaching critical steps in the writing process; and (3) providing feedback guided by the information explicitly taught. Rapid Reference 7.5 provides further information about each of these elements. Instruction that incorporated these three elements had a positive impact on students' self-efficacy as well. Other researchers document the importance of self-efficacy (e.g., Graham, Harris, & Troia, 2000; Pintrich & De Groot, 1990), also finding that students need both the *will* and the *skill* to succeed on written expression tasks and that a successful writing program must build positive attitudes toward writing.

In another meta-analysis of the writing intervention literature for

---

≡ Rapid Reference 7.4

Stages in the Writing Process

- Prewriting (get ideas—research, brainstorm, dialogue, graphic organizers)
- Writing/Drafting (get ideas down on paper—write a draft)
- Revising (clarify and improve writing)
- Editing (check spelling, punctuation, capitalization, grammar)
- Publishing (complete final revised, edited copy)

DON'T FORGET

How students view their writing capabilities greatly influences their achievement. Successful learning experiences have a positive impact on a student's self-efficacy.

≡ Rapid Reference 7.5

Three Effective Elements for Improving Written Expression (Gersten & Baker, 1999)

Use a framework of planning, writing, and revising

1. Teach each step explicitly, using examples.
2. Use a think sheet, a prompt card, or mnemonic for support.
3. Planning: Use a semantic map, verbalize the steps, use a planning think sheet that presents a series of structured prompts such as "Who am I writing for?" "Why am I writing?" "What do I know about the topic?"
4. Writing: create a first draft using the plan created.
5. Revising: peer editing, teacher-student conferences.

Explicitly teach critical steps in the writing process

1. Teach text structures (genres).
2. Use explicit models, prompts, mnemonics.

Provide relevant feedback on what is taught

1. Provide relevant and frequent feedback.
2. Engage in dialogues between teacher and student.
3. Help students develop metacognitive skills.

students in Grades 4 to 12, Graham and Perin (2007) found that a variety of instructional procedures improved the quality of writing. Based upon the largest effect size, Graham and Perin presented ten instructional recommendations, which are summarized in Rapid Reference 7.6, for teaching upper-elementary students and adolescents how to write.

DON'T FORGET

Explicit instruction that includes frequent, timely, and relevant feedback is essential to improving student performance.

≡ Rapid Reference 7.6

Ten Recommendations for Improving Writing (Graham & Perin, 2007)

1. Teach strategies for planning, revising, and editing compositions.
2. Teach strategies for summarizing reading material because this ability transfers to presenting information concisely in writing.
3. Use collaborative activities that have students work together to plan, draft, revise, and edit their compositions.
4. Set clear and specific goals for each writing product.
5. Encourage the use of word processors.
6. Teach students how to write more complex sentences using methods like sentence combining, in which simpler sentences are combined into more sophisticated ones.
7. Provide teachers with professional development in how to implement the process writing approach.
8. Select writing activities that involve inquiry and analysis.
9. Engage students in prewriting activities that help them collect and organize information before writing a first draft.
10. Provide students with good models of each type of writing and encourage them to imitate the critical elements.

Strategy Instruction

Self-regulated strategy development (SRSD)—a writing strategy approach developed over the past 2 decades by Karen Harris, Steve Graham, and colleagues—is a supplemental method designed to help students learn, use, and adopt the strategies of a skilled writer. Over 40 studies involving students from the elementary grades through high school demonstrate that SRSD results in improvement in four main aspects of student writing performance: (1) the quality of writing,

(2) knowledge of writing, (3) approach to writing, and (4) self-efficacy (Harris, Graham, Mason, & Friedlander, 2008). SRSD involves explicit teaching of strategies, interactive learning between the teacher and the student, individualized instruction based on the student's needs, self-pacing based on mastery of criterion, continuous introductions of new strategies, and instruction in new ways to use previously learned strategies. The SRSD approach can be used with entire classrooms, small groups, and individual students (Harris et al., 2008). Mnemonics are explicitly taught as part of SRSD. Examples of these mnemonic strategies include:

1. *TREE* ("develop a *T*opic sentence, note *R*easons to provide support, *E*xamine the quality of each reason, and note an *E*nding for the writing").
2. *STOP* ("*S*uspend judgment, *T*ake a side, *O*rganize ideas, and *P*lan more as you write").
3. *DARE* ("*D*evelop your topic sentence, *A*dd supporting ideas, *R*eject possible arguments for the other side, and *E*nd with a conclusion").

Several meta-analyses of SRSD studies support the use of self-regulated strategy development to improve the writing skills of students (Graham & Harris, 2003; Graham & Perin, 2007). Studies show that SRSD is effective for students at a variety of ages, with average and low achievement, and with or without learning disabilities. In addition, SRSD promotes a positive attitude toward writing, motivation, content knowledge, and self-regulation skills.

Build Writing Vocabulary

As with reading comprehension, written expression requires the understanding and use of appropriate, interesting, and precise vocabulary. One component of SRSD focuses on vocabulary enrichment (Harris et al., 2008). Students are taught how to increase their use of action words (verbs), action helpers (adverbs), and describing words (adjectives). The five-step vocabulary strategy involves looking at a picture and writing down words of a certain type (e.g., action words), thinking of a good story idea to use the words, writing the story and incorporating the words, reading the story and reviewing the words, and editing the story and adding more words. After using the strategy, students count the number of words, graph this number, and set a goal to write more words on the next attempt. Having students brainstorm words to use in assignments can promote vocabulary development.

Teach Text Structures

Knowledge of genres, or text structures, enables students to be more successful writers. Explicit modeling and teaching of the text structure combined with strategy instruction leads to the best results. Common genres include narrative writing and expository writing. Students benefit from practice in planning, translating, and revising both narrative and expository genre (Berninger, 2008).

Narrative writing

This genre is most often represented by story writing, which is introduced early in a student's school career. Teachers can use a variety of strategies to help students plan and write stories. Story grammar graphics can be particularly helpful in organizing the structure of a story by reminding the writer of important story elements such as main character, location, time, initiating event or problem, attempts to solve, and resolution. SPACE LAUNCH is an example of a mnemonic strategy for planning a story. The first part of the mnemonic, SPACE, reminds the writer of the elements of a good narrative and the second part, LAUNCH, provides the steps to follow when writing the story. Rapid Reference 7.7 summarizes this strategy for narrative writing (Harris & Graham, 1996).

≡ *Rapid Reference 7.7*

Narrative Writing Strategy: SPACE LAUNCH

Elements of a Good Narrative

S = Setting
P = Problems
A = Actions
C = Consequences
E = Emotional reactions

Steps to Writing a Good Narrative

L = List idea words for my story
A = Ask if my ideas will meet my writing goals
U = Use encouraging self-talk
N = Now write a story with million-dollar words, sharp sentences, and lots of details
C = Challenge myself to develop more good ideas
H = Have fun

Another example of an evidence-based mnemonic strategy for story grammar is W-W-W, What = 2, and How = 2 (Graham & Harris, 1989; Harris et al., 2008), which may be used as a prewriting strategy. Prior to writing, the student answers the following questions:

1. *Who* is the main character? *Who* else is in the story?
2. *When* does the story take place?
3. *Where* does the story take place?
4. *What* does the main character do?
5. *What* happens when he or she tries to do it?
6. *How* does the story end?
7. *How* does the main character feel?

Expository writing

This type of writing means to explain, describe, define, instruct, persuade, or inform. Expository writing is used in writing reports and other types of nonfiction. Types of expository paragraphs or essays include: (a) sequential, (b) descriptive, (c) chronological, (d) compare/contrast, (e) cause and effect, and (f) problem-solution. The mnemonic DEFENDS, which is summarized in Rapid Reference 7.8, is an example of a strategy to assist with expository writing (Ellis & Colvert, 1996). The mnemonic DARE to DEFEND is a strategy for planning another type of expository writing—persuasive or opinion writing. The DARE portion of the mnemonic reminds the writer of the elements of good persuasive writing and the DEFEND mnemonic provides the steps for writing a good opinion paper. Rapid Reference 7.9 summarizes the steps in this persuasive writing strategy.

Teach Revising and Editing Strategies

Revising and editing are important elements of writing. Revising provides an opportunity for students to think about the content of writing in order to clarify and improve it. In reality, revising happens frequently during the process of writing, when ideas are reorganized, added, deleted, or clarified. Editing focuses on basic writing skills, such as correcting errors in spelling, punctuation, capitalization, and grammar. Rapid Refer-

≡ *Rapid Reference 7.8*

Expository Writing Strategy: DEFENDS

D = Decide on goals and themes

E = Estimate main ideas and details

F = Figure best order for main ideas and details

E = Express the theme in the first sentence

N = Note each main idea and supporting details

D = Drive home the message in the last statement

S = Search for errors and correct

≡ *Rapid Reference 7.9*

Expository Writing Strategy: DARE to DEFEND

Elements of Good Persuasive Writing

D = Develop a position statement

A = Add supporting arguments

R = Report and refute counterarguments

E = End with a strong conclusion

Steps to Good Persuasive Writing

D = Develop a list of idea words

E = Evaluate their importance

F = Find more ways to convince my reader

E = Encourage myself through self-talk

N = Now write an essay with clear ideas, sharp sentences, and great impact

D = Decide if I met my writing goals

CAUTION

Remember that the use of voice-activated writing programs or word processing does not replace the need for instruction in the editing/revising process.

ence 7.10 lists key principles for teaching revising or editing skills effectively (MacArthur, 2007).

Editing checklists

During the initial editing, students may use a checklist like COPS (Mulcahy, Marfo, Peat, & Andrews, 1986; Schumaker et al., 1981). This mnemonic strategy works with any genre and reminds students to check Capitalization, Overall Appearance, Punctuation, and Spelling. It is a short checklist, making it appropriate for primary grade students. Rapid Reference 7.11 illustrates the steps in this error-monitoring strategy.

≡ Rapid Reference 7.10

Effective Teaching of Editing and Revising Skills

- Teach specific evaluation criteria (by genre) so students know what to look for.
- Use critical reading (for comprehension) to identify problem areas in the writing.
- Use peer-revising and teacher-student dialogues.
- Use explicit strategy instruction to teach the revising process.
- Use word processing as a tool to simplify the physical aspects of revising.

≡ Rapid Reference 7.11

Steps in the COPS Checklist

Cue	Error	Correction
C	CAPITALS	Write over the error
O	OVERALL APPEARANCE	
	Fragments & Run-ons	Line out and write new sentence above
	Paragraph indent	→
	Margins	Write lines down the side of page
		Note marks, rips
P	PUNCTUATION	Circle each incorrect/omitted mark
S	SPELLING	Write SP above word

The COLA strategy (Singer & Bashir, 1999) has a more comprehensive checklist that is more suitable for older or more advanced writers. This strategy, however, is only applicable to expository and persuasive writing. The mnemonic strategy COLA reminds students to check the *C*ontent, *O*rganization, *L*anguage, and *A*ppearance. Another mnemonic checklist, SEARCH (Ellis & Friend, 1991), has two unique aspects: setting goals and peer-editing. The student is expected to set writing goals before beginning to write and then determine if the goals were met after writing and revising are completed. In addition, the student works with a peer to double-check editing. The mnemonic SEARCH reminds students to *S*et goals, *E*xamine writing to see if it makes sense, *A*sk if they said what they meant, *R*eveal picky errors, *C*opy over neatly, and *H*ave a last look for errors.

CDO strategy

The CDO strategy for individual revising (De La Paz, Swanson, & Graham, 1998) reminds students to *C*ompare, *D*iagnose, and *O*perate. This strategy requires more self-regulation on the part of the writer, making it a more powerful tool than the checklists. A prompt sheet is used that lists the three steps. The first step, Compare, asks the student to identify discrepancies between what was written and what was intended. The second step, Diagnose, asks the student to select a specific reason for the discrepancy found in the first step (if any). The third step, Operate, asks the student to fix the problem and evaluate whether or not the change is effective. The student goes through these steps a minimum of two times so that specific as well as more global

CAUTION

Using mnemonic strategies can complicate learning for some students. Will they remember what the mnemonic means or how to use it? Explicit teaching of how, when, and where the student should use the strategy is essential. Cue cards are needed while learning the strategy.

problems can be identified and revised. During the first pass, the student attends to each sentence. In the second review, the student attends to each paragraph.

Technology

Technology changed the world of writing. The use of word processors eliminates the need to erase or recopy and provides spelling and grammar checks. Some individuals may benefit from voice recognition software programs that translate their spoken words to text. Others may benefit from programs that "speak" the text as it is typed or predict the word the student is trying to write. Rapid Reference 7.12 provides examples of technology that can assist students in the writing process.

Writing Workshop

The writing workshop is an instructional model that focuses on the process of writing more than the end product. An emphasis is placed on student values and interests and self-determination. Many teachers use some variation of the writing workshop as the main vehicle for writing instruction. To ensure effective instruction, certain characteristics should be present. For example, high-quality writing

≡ *Rapid Reference 7.12*

Technology for Assisting Writers

(www.donjohnston.com)
- Draft: Builder (helps plan, organize, draft writing)
- Co-Writer (word prediction software)
- Write: OutLoud (talking word processor and writing software program)
- Read: OutLoud (reads text aloud)

Franklin Spelling Tools (www.franklin.com)

6 Trait Power Write (online writing program) (www.perfectionlearning.com)

workshops should include: explicit modeling, frequent conferencing, high expectations, flexibility, cooperative learning, and self-regulation.

Other Writing Tools

Teachers can use a number of tools to facilitate writing instruction. For example, the teacher may ask students to maintain writing notebooks to record ideas, plan writing, and make initial drafts. Writing folders can be used to organize the different phases of the writing process. Students may keep a personal journal, which may or may not be shared with others, as a way to foster writing outside of the classroom.

Writing portfolio

A writing portfolio is a valuable tool for providing students feedback about how well they are incorporating the writing skills being taught. Also, a portfolio provides an opportunity for the student to comment and reflect on their writings and to monitor progress.

Writing frames

Writing frames can help struggling writers use appropriate text organization for summarizing content-area information. The frames facilitate organization by providing partially completed sentences or transition words, commonly referred to as *cohesive ties*. For example, a student can learn to write a sequential paragraph using the words *first, then, next,* and *finally.* As students become familiar with each type of frame (e.g., compare-contrast), the prompts can be reduced or eliminated.

Graphic organizers

Graphic organizers can also help students plan what they want to say before beginning writing. Some provide the basic structure for the type of text to be written, such as a narrative story map. Others, like a semantic web, may help the student organize ideas and see how they relate to one another. *Inspiration* is a software program that helps students move back and forth between traditional outlines and graphic organiz-

ers for planning, organizing, and elaborating their thoughts (www
.inspiration.com).

Writing prompts

Use of a writing prompt, or story starter, can help stimulate the writer's
thinking. Prompts provide the topic or idea to begin the writing process.

Provide models

Examples of good writing can also provide guidance for writers. When
teachers provide models of effective passages, student performance is
enhanced (Graham & Perin, 2007).

Accommodations and Modifications

Students having difficulty with written expression may benefit from
certain accommodations or modifications to the learning environment, the instructional materials, or the task demands. For example,
some students may require preferential seating, or a quiet work space,
or a different desk or chair. Rapid Reference 7.13 lists examples of ac-

---

≡ Rapid Reference 7.13

Example Accommodations of Instructional Materials

- Highlight key words or phrases
- Simplify language used in writing prompts
- Use graphic organizers and procedural checklists
- Display mnemonic strategies in the classroom so students can ac-
  cess these cues
- Develop individual spelling lists and have students keep personal
  dictionaries of troublesome words
- Provide (as needed) pencil grips, raised- or color-line paper, per-
  sonal alphabet strips, and paper positioning marks on a student's
  desk

≡ Rapid Reference 7.14

Example Modifications of Task Demands

- Increase time to complete writing tasks
- Decrease length or complexity of writing assignment
- Use text frames (i.e., partially completed text)
- Reduce or eliminate copying tasks
- Permit use of dictation or a scribe
- Permit use of word processors (requires keyboarding skills)
- Use technology to support writing (e.g., spell checker, voice recognition, semantic mapping, outlining software)
- Allow other means of demonstrating assignment (e.g., oral versus written)

commodations to the instructional materials and Rapid Reference 7.14 lists modifications to tasks that may be appropriate. Students requiring accommodations or modifications must learn to advocate for themselves. This is especially important as students enter middle and high school, or college.

CONCLUSION

Writing is a highly complex task that is susceptible to difficulties in a multitude of areas. It has been called "an immense juggling act" (Berninger & Richards, 2002, p. 173). A good writer must integrate both low-level and high-level skills while monitoring his or her own performance. Students must be proficient and automatic with the low-level foundational skills of handwriting (or keyboarding) and spelling in order to build writing fluency and free cognitive resources for the higher-level tasks of planning, composing, and revising. While some educators may not think that handwriting instruction is important, research indicates that students benefit from this instruction.

The most effective writing instruction, whether designed to teach students handwriting or composing skills, is explicit instruction. When combined with explicit strategy instruction, students experience more success in developing the writing skills needed to clearly convey their ideas, their feelings, and their knowledge. The ability to express oneself in writing is an essential tool for school and work. If, as Abraham Lincoln said, writing is "the great invention of the world," we must ensure that appropriate instruction is provided.

🐟 TEST YOURSELF 🐟

1. **Writing is likely the most complex task students are asked to learn in school.** True or False?

2. **Writing is called the "Neglected R" because**

    (a) computers have eliminated the need for writing.

    (b) most teachers do not spend much time teaching it.

    (c) researchers and legislators have not focused on writing.

    (d) both b and c

3. **Automatic, fluent handwriting can improve the quality of composition because**

    (a) the student can work more quickly.

    (b) the student is thinking about letter formation and production.

    (c) the student's cognitive resources are free to think about *what* to write.

    (d) the student has good fine-motor skills.

4. **A reciprocal relationship exists between writing and reading.** True or False?

5. **Keyboarding skills should not be taught until the child has mastered handwriting.** True or False?

6. **List the five basic steps in the writing process approach.**

7. Effective writing instruction must

(a) be explicit.

(b) teach strategies.

(c) teach each step in the writing process explicitly.

(d) All of the above.

(e) None of the above.

8. Teaching text structures (genres) improves writing because

(a) the student does not need to think of a topic.

(b) the student knows what to include.

(c) the student knows how to organize the information.

(d) a and b

(e) b and c

9. Mnemonic strategies work for all students. True or False?

10. Why is writing such a complex task?

Answers: 1. True; 2. d; 3. c; 4. True; 5. False; 6. Prewriting, writing, revising, editing, publishing; 7. d; 8. e; 9. False; 10. It requires cognitive, linguistic, and motor skills and integrating low-level transcription skills with high-level composing skills. It places a heavy demand on working memory and executive functions.

Eight

BASIC MATH SKILLS

Preschoolers see the world as an arena for counting. Children want to count everything.
—*Gardner, 1991*

Although math problems are widespread, difficulties with mathematics have received less attention from researchers and educators than have difficulties with reading. Difficulties in mathematics must also be addressed. It is estimated that between 5 and 8% of school-age children have significant problems with math (Garnett, 1998; Geary, 2004); and more than 60% of students identified as having a learning disability in reading are also achieving below grade level in mathematics (McLeskey & Waldron, 1990). Difficulties with math may result from numerous sources, including impairments in: working memory, processing speed, language, attention, sequencing, spatial skills, or reasoning. In addition, a student's success in math reflects the efficacy of the instruction and can be negatively impacted by poor teaching, the design and materials of the curriculum, or both. Due to the hierarchical and cumulative nature of math with one skill building on another, poor instruction at any level may impede future success. Special education training programs and professional development opportunities also focus disproportionately on the delivery of reading rather than math interventions (Fuchs, Fuchs, Powell et al., 2008). Findings from research suggest that both special and general

CAUTION
....

Students struggling in math require careful instruction and close monitoring. No single approach or curriculum will work with all students.

educators take few courses in methods for teaching math and are often inadequately prepared to teach math skills, particularly at the secondary level (Maccini & Gagnon, 2006).

Some curriculum designs can be especially troublesome for students that struggle with math, including spiraling curriculums, teaching to mastery, and focusing on procedures versus understanding. A spiraling curriculum introduces a number of important concepts and then returns to those concepts in successive years. In any one year, the time devoted to a concept may be too limited for students that do not learn readily. Teaching to mastery without ample opportunities to practice "mastered" skills may lead to a false conclusion about the student's true skill level. Frequently, a struggling student's performance is uneven—the student demonstrates proficiency one day but not the next. When instruction focuses on procedural knowledge, learning the algorithms, students often fail to develop conceptual understanding. Teachers must be aware of these issues and realize that, as with reading, no single approach or curriculum will meet the needs of all students.

Characteristics of Individuals Struggling with Basic Math Skills

The major prevalent characteristic of a math disability in basic skills is difficulty storing and retrieving basic math facts (Geary, 1993, 2007; Rourke & Conway, 1997). In order for an accurate representation of the fact to be stored, the individual must hold all elements of the fact in working memory simultaneously (Geary, 2007). For example, in the addition fact $3 + 7 = 10$, all numbers must be held in working memory in order for an accurate representation of the fact to be learned and stored. If the individual uses inefficient strategies to solve the problem, such as counting all, or the *min strategy,* instead of automatic retrieval, the amount of time that all elements must be held in working memory increases. Thus the person's memory span, choice of strategy, and speed of processing come into play. As the solution time increases, there is more opportunity for one or more of the elements of the fact to fade from working memory, which in turn interferes with storing an accurate representation of the fact. Not surprisingly, students who struggle with basic math computations also have difficulty completing arithmetic problems that involve multisteps (Bryant, Bryant, & Hammill, 2000).

A history of academic failure can inhibit the student's desire to perform in mathematics as well as negatively impact his or her self-confidence regarding math (Montague, 1996, p. 85). These early failures in math can lead to anxiety about math performance that continues into adulthood.

An understanding of the cognitive and neuropsychological factors that contribute to math disabilities is of great importance for the assessment and identification of math disabilities, as well as the validation of effective interventions (Bryant et al., 2000). Researchers identified several cognitive correlates that can affect basic math performance, including: long-term memory (or store of acquired knowledge), memory span, working memory, attention, and processing speed (Fuchs, Fuchs, Stuebing et al., 2008; Geary, 2007). Fuchs, Fuchs, Stuebing et al. (2008) found that specific computational difficulty is associated with a strength in language, and weaknesses in attention and processing speed. Results from several additional studies support the finding that measures of processing speed are good predictors of computational competence (Bull & Johnston, 1997; Hecht, Torgesen, Wagner, & Rashotte, 2001).

Difficulties with the use of memory and strategies can create problems with conceptualizing mathematical operations and algorithms, representing and recalling math facts, and solving word problems. Frequently, students with mathematics disabilities do not learn to use strategies naturally (Montague, 1998). They do not know how to apply strategies effectively and end up switching from strategy to strategy.

Students may experience difficulty with the reading and writing demands of math because of weaknesses in oral language abilities. They may have difficulty understanding and discussing ideas about mathematics. Their language problems may result in confusion about terminology, difficulty following verbal explanations, and/or weak verbal skills for monitoring the steps of complex calculations.

Some researchers suggest that there may also be a phonological correlate because math disabilities often co-occur with reading disabilities (Geary, 1993), but the support for this hypothesis is inconsistent (Fuchs et al., 2006). For individuals with coexisting math and reading disabilities, a common problem appears to affect the encoding and maintenance of accurate phonological representations in working memory (Logie, Gilhooly, & Wynn, 1994).

Individuals who have math disabilities without reading problems typically do not have phonological deficits, but they frequently display visual-spatial difficulties (Geary, 2007). Problems with visual-spatial abilities can interfere with the student's conceptual understanding of problems, as well as how to address problems mathematically. For example, visual-spatial difficultes may result in failure to understand concepts, poor number sense, difficulty with pictorial representations, and/ or poorly controlled handwriting, confused arrangements, and trouble aligning numerals and signs on the page. Students with profoundly impaired conceptual understanding often have substantial perceptual-motor problems.

Geary (1993) identifies three math disability subtypes (see Rapid Reference 8.1), one of which is a visuospatial deficit. The visuospatial systems in the parietal cortex of the brain appear to be needed to estimate and form representations of magnitude (Dehaene, Spelke, Pinel, Stanescu, & Tsivkin, 1999). Further evidence of the connection between visual-spatial processing and math is provided by cases in which damage to the right parietal cortex resulted in deficits in spatial orientation and number line estimation (Zorzi, Priftis, & Umiltá, 2002).

NUMBER SENSE

Number sense refers to the child's fluidity and flexibility with numbers, as well as understanding of what numbers mean and their relationships to other numbers. This construct is difficult to define but easy to recognize (Case, 1998). Teachers and parents show recognition of the construct when they say things like "she is good with numbers" or "he just doesn't get numbers." Much as phonemic awareness is a key component underlying

≡ *Rapid Reference 8.1*

Three Math Disability Subtypes

• Procedural disorder: uses developmentally immature procedures, has a developmental delay in understanding concepts, makes frequent errors in execution of procedures

• Semantic disorder: has difficulty learning and retrieving math facts; facts that are retrieved are frequently incorrect

• Visuospatial disorder: has difficulty with the spatial representation of numbers (alignment or reversals), makes place value errors, has difficulty with spatial math (e.g., geometry)

early reading development, the concept of number sense may play a similar role in the field of mathematics (Gersten & Chard, 2001). Both are foundational skills that serve as prerequisites for academic success. In many cases, the beginning elements of both are acquired through informal interactions between parents and siblings before the child enters kindergarten. As with phonological awareness, this early conceptual knowledge of numbers usually develops during the preschool years and most children have an initial understanding in place by the ages of 4 to 5 years (Griffin & Case, 1997). If these elements are not acquired, formal instruction is required. Without an understanding of the basic concepts of number sense, students will have difficulty benefiting from future math instruction (Griffin, 2007).

Children with good number sense tend to display an understanding of the magnitude and relationship of numbers. They may invent ways to solve problems using concrete objects and use number words, such as "one, two, three." They demonstrate use of a mental number line—one of the big ideas in math. Without a mental number line, students may experience persistent problems in many areas of mathematics, especially those related to conceptual understanding and application of procedural knowledge to new problem-solving situations (Woodward & Baxter, 1997).

Number sense underlies automaticity in math—the ability to solve basic math computations. While number sense is necessary, it is not sufficient for developing problem-solving skills. There is no one best way to teach number sense, but some evidence suggests that instruction in number sense can reduce failure in early mathematics (Griffin, Case, & Siegler, 1994). Use of a problem-centered curriculum that emphasized student interaction and self-generated solutions was found to improve the number sense of second graders (Cobb, 1991). These students developed a variety of strategies to solve a wide range of problems and demonstrated increased persistence on more difficult problems. Even older children can benefit from instruction in number magnitude, mental computation, and estimation (Markovits & Sowder, 1994).

MATH FACTS AND FLUENCY

Some children have inordinate difficulty learning and retrieving basic math facts—a characteristic that is often associated with math difficulties (Geary, 1993; Miller & Mercer, 1997). Poor arithmetic fact retrieval is often described as a cardinal characteristic of children with specific math disabilities (Andersson, 2008; Gersten, Jordan, & Flojo, 2005). Despite conceptual understanding and good effort, they have trouble remembering that 6 + 7 = 13 or 3 x 4 = 12. To solve these problems, they continue to use developmentally immature approaches such as counting on their fingers or drawing marks on their papers. They fail to come up with and apply more efficient strategies on their own.

Drill and practice approaches are frequently recommended for helping students master math facts (Pellegrino & Goldman, 1987). This recommendation is based on the belief that automaticity with math facts increases overall math competence. Again, researchers draw a parallel between reading and math. Just as automatic word recognition would increase reading comprehension, automatic math fact recall would enhance problem solving. The hypothesis is that those who lack automaticity at the basic skill level exhaust their cognitive resources trying to recall math facts and, therefore, have few resources left for solving problems.

Computer-assisted instruction was introduced as a means to provide the necessary drill and practice (Hasselbring, Goin, & Bransford, 1988). A positive aspect of the software is the inclusion of immediate corrective feedback and controlled response times, in addition to the provision of extensive practice. Researchers conclude that computer-aided instruction leads to increased automaticity with math facts for most students.

As children work on building automaticity of facts, they should continue to receive instruction in more complex computation and problem solving. During problem-solving activities, supports such as pocket-size fact charts should be allowed for reference. As students master facts, they can block them out in the chart. This will decrease their reliance on the chart and increase their motivation by allowing them to see their progress.

> **CAUTION**
>
> Some children have advanced conceptual knowledge in math but struggle with basic math fact calculation. Be careful not to ignore their more advanced problem-solving abilities.

EFFECTIVE INSTRUCTION

Research suggests that important concepts in mathematics must be developed through a carefully sequenced set of learning opportunities that incorporates scaffolding of instruction (National Research Council, 2001). Teacher modeling and student verbal rehearsal of that modeling are important for developing conceptual understanding. Using visuals and multiple representations also shows promise in the process of developing conceptual understanding.

Two evidence-based approaches that have broad application to teaching math, as well as other academic areas, are direct instruction and

≡ Rapid Reference 8.2

Effective Instruction for Basic Math Skills

- Direct, explicit instruction with cumulative review (Fuchs, Fuchs, Powell et al., 2008; Kroesbergen & Van Luit, 2003; Miller, Butler & Lee, 1998; Swanson, 1999)
- Strategy instruction (Miller et al., 1998; Owen & Fuchs, 2002; Swanson, 1999)
- Concrete level (manipulatives) instruction (Miller et al., 1998)
- Concrete, representational/semiconcrete, abstract teaching sequence (Miller et al., 1998; Miller & Mercer, 1993, 1997; Miller, Mercer, & Dillon, 1992)
- Drill and practice (Fuchs, Fuchs, Powell et al., 2008)
- Ongoing monitoring of student performance, communicating progress, and reinforcing success continuously (Fuchs, Fuchs, Powell et al., 2008; Miller & Mercer, 1997)
- Teaching self-regulating behaviors (Fuchs, Fuchs, Powell et al., 2008; Miller et al., 1998; Miller & Mercer, 1997)
- Peer-mediated instruction (i.e., peer tutoring, cooperative learning groups) (Miller, Barbetta, Drevno, Martz, & Heron, 1996; Rivera, 1996)

strategy instruction. A combination of direct instruction and strategy instruction has a greater positive effect than either method in isolation (Ellis, 1993; Karp & Voltz, 2000; Swanson, 2001). For students to gain the maximum benefit from a lesson, teachers should include both direct instruction and strategy instruction. Rapid Reference 8.2 provides a summary of effective instructional approaches for math.

Direct Instruction

Direct instruction appears to be the most effective instructional approach for teaching basic or isolated skills (Harniss, Stein, & Carnine, 2002; Kroesbergen & Van Luit, 2003), including basic math facts. Direct instruction is a teacher-centered approach that includes demonstration or modeling by the teacher, followed by guided practice with immediate feedback, and then independent practice as the students begin to master the skills (Maccini & Gagnon, 2000). Direct instruction may or may not be scripted, but in any event, it is systematic with a step-by-step format requiring student mastery at each step. Rapid Reference 8.3 lists the 12 criteria associated with direct instruction (Swanson,

Rapid Reference 8.3

Is It Direct Instruction?

- Breaking down a task into small steps
- Administering probes
- Administering feedback repeatedly
- Providing a pictorial or diagram presentation
- Allowing independent practice and individually paced instruction
- Breaking the instruction down into simpler phases
- Instructing in a small group
- Teacher modeling a skill
- Providing set materials at a rapid pace
- Providing individual child instruction
- Teacher asking questions
- Teacher presenting the new (novel) materials

2001). When four or more of the criteria are present, direct instruction is occurring.

Strategy Instruction

Researchers found that strategy instruction in mathematics is also effective (Carnine, 1980; Case, Harris, & Graham, 1992; Hutchinson, 1993; Montague, 1992; Montague & Bos, 1986). To be understood and used, strategies need to be taught and practiced in a clear, explicit manner (Carnine, 1998).

One strategy that most children learn informally is called the *min strategy*. Children that use the min strategy recognize that it is more efficient to start with the larger number when solving a problem (e.g., 7 + 2 or 2 + 7). This strategy forms the basis for *counting on*. Siegler (1988)

≡ Rapid Reference 8.4

Progression of Strategies Used When Solving Simple Addition Problems

- Finger counting: counting all (the child lifts and counts all fingers representing the problem)
- Finger counting: counting on (the child says the larger number and then lifts fingers and counts the smaller number)
- Verbal counting: counting all (the child counts out the value of each number)
- Verbal counting: counting on (the child says the larger number, then counts the smaller number)
- Retrieval: the fact is retrieved directly from memory without signs of counting
- Decomposition: the child retrieves a related fact and then counts on (e.g., 8 + 7, the child retrieves 7 + 7 = 14 and then counts up 1 to 15)

≡ Rapid Reference 8.5

Representing Multiplication Facts (Two-Family) with Visual Images

2 × 2   skateboard with 2 sets of wheels

3 × 2   six pack of soda

4 × 2   spider with two sets of four legs

5 × 2   two hands with all fingers held up

6 × 2   dozen eggs in a carton

7 × 2   calendar with 2 weeks circled

8 × 2   two octopi, each with eight tentacles

9 × 2   18-wheel truck

determined that knowledge of this strategy is a key predictor of success in early mathematics. Geary (1994) describes the progressive strategies children use to solve simple addition problems. Rapid Reference 8.4 provides an overview of these strategies.

Other strategies incorporate mnemonics, such as visual images to represent math facts (Wood & Frank, 2000). Rapid Reference 8.5 provides an example of visual images that can be used when learning the two-family multiplication facts. Commercial flash cards are also available that use pictures and rhymes to teach addition and multiplication facts (e.g., www.CityCreek.com).

Practice

How do you get to Carnegie Hall? Practice, practice, practice. The importance of practice in developing skill and fluency with math facts cannot be downplayed. Practice with facts is required to build automaticity, which is at the core of fluency. Two major goals of early math in-

DON'T FORGET

Effective instruction of basic skills provides: modeling, guided practice, independent practice, feedback, error correction, goal setting, and progress monitoring.

tervention are to increase fluency and proficiency with basic math facts, as well as the accuracy and efficiency of counting strategies (Gersten et al., 2005). Without proficiency and fluency in basic math skills, the student's cognitive resources are less available for higher level math demands, such as problem solving. Fluency is a prerequisite skill that aids in generalizing and transferring knowledge to new situations. So ample practice not only makes it more likely the student will master the skill (Brophy & Good, 1986), but practice also can improve student behavior (Sutherland & Wehby, 2001). This phenomenon is observed when "drill and kill" changes to "drill and skill" and ultimately to "drill and thrill" (A. Archer, personal communication, August 12, 2004).

For effective student practice, the teacher should provide clear directions and model how to perform the task prior to beginning the practice activity. This is true for simple computations, as well as more advanced algorithms. In addition, the teacher should monitor the student's progress during practice and provide corrective feedback and reinforcement frequently. The activities need to be matched to the student's level of understanding and build upon prior conceptual knowledge.

Board games

Instructional games when used appropriately can provide a creative and motivational way for students to practice math skills (Mercer & Mercer, 2005). Before using a game, it is important to ensure that the student has an adequate level of accuracy on the target skill so that a reasonable chance of success is possible (Lavoie, 1993). Researchers found that playing numerical board games helps develop numerical understanding in young children. In addition to improving number line estimation, Ramani and Siegler (2005) found that playing numerical board games also improved preschoolers' ability to count, identify numbers, and make quantity comparisons. Children with greater exposure to numerical board games entered kindergarten with greater intuitive knowledge of numbers, or number sense (Case & Griffin, 1989; Phillips & Crowell, 1994).

Computer-assisted instruction

The use of computer-assisted instruction (CAI) is beneficial when students need to practice certain kinds of problems (Hasselbring et al., 1988; Howell, Sidorenko, & Jurica, 1987). Computer- or web-based activities can help students develop automaticity in skills (Cummings & Elkins, 1999), as well as strategies for recalling basic facts and solving problems (Atkinson, Derry, Renkl, & Wortham, 2000; Kalyuga, Chandler, Tuovinen, & Sweller, 2001; Ward & Sweller, 1990). In addition, computer-based activities can provide a motivating way to practice. Numerous commercial software programs are available to help students improve their basic skills (see Rapid Reference 8.8).

Self-correcting materials

A student can practice independently using self-correcting materials. For example, a student can study flash cards with the problem written on one side and the answer written on the back. This type of practice activity should focus on math processes that the student can perform independently and with a reasonable success rate. Self-correcting materials provide immediate, corrective feedback—an effective teaching technique.

Cover-copy-compare

Another way to provide practice that is also self-correcting is the use of a cover-copy-compare intervention. This procedure can be used to improve a student's ability to recall math calculations (Hayden & McLaughlin, 2004; Lee & Tingstrom, 1994; Skinner, Turco, Beatty, &

Rasavage, 1989). In this intervention, students are provided with training sheets (specially formatted pages of math problems) and prompted to read a math problem on the left side of the page where the correct answer is provided. The student covers the problem and solution (on the left-hand side) and is asked to write the math problem and answer from memory on the right-hand side of the training sheet. When finished, the student uncovers the problem on the left side and compares the answers. The student completes the problem when he or she arrives at the correct answer. (If incorrect, the student may require additional guidance before repeating the item.) When correct, the student moves on to the next problem on the left side of the training sheet. New training sheets are provided after the student reaches mastery of a page of problems. This intervention may be implemented individually or within a small-group setting. Of note, the benefits of cover-copy-compare may be bolstered by providing additional flash-card drills with a peer.

Error Analysis

One of the most effective ways to help resolve a student's errors on basic math computation is to analyze any mistakes he or she makes on standardized tests, classroom exams, school papers, and homework assignments. The evaluator or teacher should try to determine the reasons why a student missed certain problems. Students will continue to make the same types of errors unless intervention occurs. A teacher must task analyze the skills carefully and then provide student practice with the steps involved (Bryant et al., 2000). If it is impossible to determine why a student missed a problem, the

DON'T FORGET

An analysis of a student's errors can help pinpoint misunderstandings and increase the specificity and effectiveness of instruction.

evaluator or teacher should ask the student to explain step-by-step what he or she was doing when solving the problem. When listening to the student's explanation, the teacher should ask questions as needed to help discover why the student is making errors.

Monitor Student Progress

An important element of effective learning is increasing students' self-awareness and ability to monitor their own learning. Frequent feedback and charting progress are ways to help students become more aware of their growth. Additionally, continuous monitoring of student progress provides teachers with valuable information about the effectiveness of their instruction and whether or not adjustments are needed. Research suggests that continuous progress monitoring promotes positive learning outcomes (Allinder, Bolling, Oats, & Gagnon, 2000; Calhoon & Fuchs, 2003; Fuchs, Fuchs, Powell et al., 2008). Charting progress provides a tangible means for students to set goals for their own learning—an important aspect of self-regulation. Students who struggle with math will benefit greatly from seeing concrete proof that they are learning. Having students chart their own progress not only motivates the students, but it also frees the

DON'T FORGET

Ongoing opportunities to review and practice seemingly mastered skills are important, especially for students who struggle with recalling and using previously learned math skills and concepts. Brief maintenance activities (5 to 10 minutes) can be scheduled into class time several days a week. Old problems can be mixed in with new problems.

DON'T FORGET

The most essential principle of effective math instruction is ongoing progress monitoring to create individually tailored programs.

teacher from this task. Fuchs, Fuchs, Powell et al. (2008) state that ongoing progress monitoring to create individually tailored programs is the most essential principle of effective math instruction.

Concrete Representations

A critical element in developing a student's understanding is to illustrate math concepts with concrete objects, or manipulatives (Butler, Miller, Crehan, Babbitt, & Pierce, 2003; Cass, Cates, Smith, & Jackson, 2003; Siegler, 1988). Children can develop mental images of mathematical concepts by using concrete objects that serve as the basis from which abstract thinking may develop (Dunlap & Brennan, 1979). The use of manipulatives is not just for young children. Research shows that the use of concrete representations can be helpful at any age, especially when introducing a new mathematical concept (Driscoll, 1986; Williams, 1986). For example, when introducing the concepts of fractions, a teacher may demonstrate by cutting a large pizza into different size slices, beginning with 1/2 and gradually progressing to 1/16. When discussing the use of manipulatives in intermediate grades, Driscoll states, "If there is any risk related to the use of manipulatives in these grades, it derives from their being ignored or abandoned too quickly" (1986, p. 7). Instruction and guidance are provided to students as they learn to manipulate objects.

DON'T FORGET

Understanding comes before memorization. Children should not memorize facts and numbers until they fully understand the underlying concepts.

Number line

A number line provides a geometric representation of numbers. Each number has a unique point on the line and a specific distance from the origin. The number line helps students see the magnitude (size) and the direction (relationship) of each number. As students learn about different types of numbers (whole numbers, decimals, fractions, negative numbers, etc.), the number line helps develop numerical understanding and connects each number type.

Number names

Because English number names do not make clear the connection to the underlying base-10 system, many children require additional instruction to understand this connection. For example, the number name *eleven* does not communicate that $11 = 10 + 1$. Manipulatives or diagrams may be necessary to illustrate the quantities organized into ones, tens, hundreds, and so on. These types of conceptual supports that connect written numerals to actual quantities have been found to help students acquire insight into the base-10 number system (NRC, 2001).

Concrete-Representational-Abstract (CRA)

An evidence-based approach for teaching math is the concrete-representational-abstract (CRA) instructional sequence. Research indicates that students are more successful in learning mathematics when a CRA sequence of instruction is used (Allsopp, 1999; Maccini & Gagnon, 2000; Mercer & Mercer, 2005). Instruction begins at a concrete level, transitions to a semiconcrete or representational level (e.g., pictorial), and then evolves to the abstract level (e.g., numerals, symbols) (Dunlap & Brennan, 1979; Miller & Mercer, 1993; Morin & Miller, 1998). Students may require up to seven lessons at the concrete and semi-

CAUTION

Some students demonstrating correct procedural knowledge at the abstract level cannot represent the problem at the concrete or representational levels. This is an indication they lack conceptual understanding.

DON'T FORGET

Effective teachers provide students with ample opportunities to demonstrate mathematical understanding using two different response modes—recognition and demonstration.

concrete levels before being able to handle abstract-level problems (Miller & Mercer, 1993). Use of the CRA approach incorporates scaffolding of instruction—an effective teaching technique.

Explicit Timings

One proven means of increasing the rate of problems worked correctly and accurately is the use of explicit timings (Rathovan, 1999). Using math worksheets of 100 basic math facts, the teacher explains that the session will be timed as a means to help students improve their performance, and that 1-minute timings will be conducted throughout the session. The teacher begins each 1-minute timing by saying, "Pencils up, ready, begin." At the end of the 1-minute interval, the teacher says "Stop." The students are directed to draw a line after the last problem answered. This procedure is repeated throughout the math period. The total time available for the math session will vary, but should allow for multiple timings (10 or more). A typical session may be 20 to 30 min-

Rapid Reference 8.6

1-Minute Timings

1. Provide students with a worksheet of problems that cannot be completed within 1 minute.
2. Have students complete as many problems as they can within the minute.
3. Ask students to stop after 1 minute.
4. Score the sheet by counting the number of correct and incorrect digits written.
5. Plot the total number of correct digits on a graph.

utes in length. The students' accuracy and fluency are evaluated using the number of correct problems per 1-minute interval. This information can be graphed or charted so students can see their growth.

The use of a similar procedure, *1-Minute Timings,* is another evidence-based practice for increasing fluency with math computations (Miller & Hudson, 2007). Rapid Reference 8.6 describes the steps in this procedure. After the timing and graphing, students may then review errors with the teacher or a peer or correct any errors with a calculator.

Additional strategies for building math fact competence are provided within most math curricu-

Rapid Reference 8.7

Strategies for Building Math Fact Competence

- Use motivational materials (e.g., games) for intensive practice.
- Work on small groups of facts at one time (then practice with mixed groups).
- Emphasize reverses or turn-arounds (e.g., 2 + 4 and 4 + 2, 6 × 4 and 4 × 6).
- Practice in small doses (i.e., distributed practice).
- Provide instruction (teach strategies such as doubles, or doubles + 1).
- Encourage students to monitor their own progress.

lums. Rapid Reference 8.7 lists some of the most common strategies that are recommended (Garnett, Frank & Fleischner, 1983).

Reciprocal Peer Tutoring

Reciprocal peer tutoring not only improves math performance, but it also improves students' perceptions of their own academic competence and self-control (Fantuzzo, King, & Heller, 1992). This approach incorporates several effective practices including active engagement and student monitoring of progress. Working in pairs, the students act as instructional partners. Together, they set a team goal, identify individual goals or contributions, and select a reward activity. This information is recorded on a card. Each pair receives a set of flash cards with one problem on each card. The problem is shown on one side of the card and the problem with computational steps and the answer are shown on the other side. The pairs also receive sheets of paper divided into four sections labeled Try 1, Try 2, Help, and Try 3. The student acting as the tutor holds up a card for the other student to solve in the Try 1 section of the worksheet. If correct, the tutor praises the student and moves to a new problem. If incorrect, the tutor gives instructional prompts read from a prompt card and tells the student to try again. If Try 2 is incorrect, the tutor demonstrates the correct computation in the Help section while explaining each step and answering any student questions. Then the tutor tells the student to try again in the Try 3 section. After 10 minutes, the students switch roles.

During the tutoring sessions, the classroom teacher supervises the activities, identifies strategies that the tutors can use to help their students, and answers any questions that the tutor cannot answer. In addition, the teacher meets with each pair weekly to assure that an appropriate team goal has been selected.

After the tutoring sessions are completed (about 20 minutes), the teacher distributes a practice worksheet to each student. The students work independently for an additional 7 to 10 minutes. Then the student pairs switch papers to correct each other's work. The teacher can provide the answers orally or provide answer sheets to the students. Then the pairs determine the team's total number correct and compare it to the goal they set at the beginning of the class. If the pair meets or exceeds the team goal, they receive a sticker on their card. Once the pair has earned 5 stickers, a time is scheduled for the pair to engage in the reward activity that they selected previously.

Peer-Assisted Learning Strategies and Cross-Age Tutoring

Peer-assisted learning strategies (PALS) and cross-age tutoring are other examples of peer-tutoring interventions. Many students can benefit from using a peer-tutoring format, especially if the students are taught explicitly how to work together and provided with guided practice. In a study of first-graders, peer-mediated drill and practice of math facts had strong and lasting effects (Greenwood, Delquadri, & Hall, 1989). In a meta-analysis of peer-mediated interventions, Kunsch, Jitendra, and Sood (2007) found that peer-mediated interventions were highly effective for helping elementary-age students at risk for math failure improve their computation skill in general education classrooms. These types of interventions were not, however, as effective for improving higher order mathematical skills.

Commercial Products

Number Worlds
Number Worlds is an intensive intervention program designed to assist students in Grades 1 through 8 who are one or more grade levels behind in elementary math. A prevention program for PreK through Grade 1 and an algebra readiness program for Grades 8 and 9 are also available. In efficacy studies, the treatment group's performance using Number Worlds surpassed the control group's performance. In addition, the treatment group, by the end of kindergarten, approached the conceptual and procedural knowledge level of a normative comparison group (Griffin & Case, 1996; Griffin et al., 1994). More information about Number Worlds can be found at www.sranumberworlds.com or at www.clarku.edu/numberworlds.

PALS Math
Peer-Assisted Learning Strategies Math offers a combination of teacher-led and dyadic practice. PALS Math has been found to be

effective for first graders (Fuchs, Fuchs, Yazdian, & Powell, 2002) and has been approved by the U.S. Department of Education's Program Effectiveness Panel for inclusion in the National Diffusion Network on effective educational practices. In addition, this program is listed as having strong evidence of effectiveness on the Johns Hopkins University web site, Best Evidence Encyclopedia (www.bestevidence.org/math). More information about PALS can be found at http://kc.vanderbilt.edu/pals/.

TouchMath

TouchMath is a sequential, multisensory learning system designed to help students develop math skills. The curriculum covers counting, addition, subtraction, multiplication, division, story problems, time, money, and fractions. This program is typically used with preschool through Grade 6 in both general and special education, and it is also used as a supplement for older students struggling with math. The key to TouchMath is that each number, one through nine, has "touchpoints" that correspond to the digit's quantity. Students touch these points as they count aloud, integrating multiple senses in the process. More information about TouchMath can be found at www.touchmath.com.

Structural Arithmetic

Structural Arithmetic is a complete curriculum for building number concepts in Grades K through 3. It makes use of manipulatives (colored cubes, boxes, and grooves) to help children develop reasoning and insight into the relationships between numbers. Self-discovery and self-correction are elements of the program. Although sequential in nature, it can be used as a supplement to any math program. More information about Structural Arithmetic can be found at www.sternmath.com.

Software and Web-based resources

Kidspiration is a software program for Grades K through 5 that combines proven visual learning methodologies and technology to help children develop number sense, spatial reasoning, and understanding of the four basic operations. More information about Kidspiration can be found at www.inspiration.com. Rapid Reference 8.8 lists basic math skills software programs that received the Readers' Choice Awards (eSchool News, April, 2005). Rapid Reference 8.9 lists helpful math-related web sites for teachers and students. For example, one web site, www.unicog.org, offers a free,

Rapid Reference 8.8

Software for Teaching Basic Math Skills (in alphabetical order)

- Accelerated Math (Renaissance Learning)
- Destination Math Series (Riverdeep Interactive Learning)
- Larson's Elementary Math (Larson Learning)
- Math Amigo (Valiant Technology)
- Math Blasters Series (Knowledge Adventure)
- Math + Music (Mind Institute)
- Skills Tutor (Achievement Technology)
- Success Maker (Pearson Digital Learning)

research-based software program—The Numbers Race. The program is designed to remediate, or prevent, dyscalculia in children aged 4 to 8 and helps teach number sense. Currently, this software is available in five languages: English, Spanish, French, German, and Dutch.

CONCLUSION

Individuals must be proficient with basic math skills to function productively in the modern world. In testimony given in February of 2006 before the U.S. Senate Committee on Health, Education, Labor, and

≡ *Rapid Reference 8.9*

Math Websites (in alphabetical order)

- www.aaamath.com
- www.aplusmath.com
- www.coolmath.com
- www.edinformatics.com
- www.edu4kids.com
- www.figurethis.org (National Council of Teachers of Mathematics)
- www.funbrain.com (Pearson Education)
- www.iknowthat.com
- http://illuminations.nctm.org
- www.k8accesscenter.org
- www.math.com
- www.mathforum.com (Drexel University)
- www.multiplication.com
- www.nctm.org (National Council of Teachers of Mathematics)
- http://nlvm.usu.edu (National Library of Virtual Manipulatives/Utah State University)
- www.planemath.com (InfoUse and NASA)
- www.unicog.org/main/pages.php?page=NumberRace

Pensions, U.S. Secretary of Education Margaret Spellings, stated that "... almost half of our 17-year olds do not have the basic understanding of math needed to qualify for a production associate's job at a modern auto plant."

Because of the number of students with low levels of math achievement, there is a sense of urgency that teachers must provide intensive instruction to students with weaknesses and disabilities in math (Bryant, 2005). Although educators have long been aware that many students lack basic math skills, education has not addressed this problem successfully. Educators must have an understanding of the developmental nature of math and be able to employ effective instructional principles to reduce math difficulties.

🔖 TEST YOURSELF 🔖

1. **What percentage of school-age children has significant math difficulties?**
   (a) 10–15%
   (b) 5–8%
   (c) less than 5%
   (d) more than 15%

2. **Phonemic awareness is to reading as** _____ **is to math.**
   (a) calculation
   (b) reasoning
   (c) number sense
   (d) fluency

3. **All children who struggle with basic math facts have poor conceptual math knowledge.** True or False?

4. **When instruction includes teacher demonstration, followed by guided practice with immediate corrective feedback, it is best described as**
   (a) peer-mediated instruction.
   (b) strategy instruction.
   (c) cooperative learning.
   (d) direct instruction.

5. **What is the *min strategy*?**
   (a) start with the larger number when adding
   (b) use of explicit 1-minute timings
   (c) *minus* means take away
   (d) *less than* means smaller

6. **Manipulatives can be appropriate for teaching math to students of all ages.** True or False?

7. **Concrete-Representational-Abstract (CRA) is best described as**

   (a) a math curriculum.

   (b) a teaching sequence.

   (c) an art form.

   (d) a math principle.

8. **Which is an example of peer-mediated instruction?**

   (a) reciprocal peer tutoring

   (b) paired instructional partners

   (c) cooperative learning groups

   (d) All of the above.

   (e) None of the above.

9. **Why is practice important in building basic math skills and fluency?**

10. **List the three subtypes of math learning disability identified by Geary (1993, 2004).**

Answers: 1. b; 2. c; 3. False; 4. d; 5. a; 6. True; 7. b; 8. d; 9. Practice develops automaticity, which is required for fluency. Fluency is necessary to transfer and generalize knowledge to new situations. Automaticity and fluency allow the individual to focus more attention to higher-level demands; 10. Semantic, procedural, and visuospatial

Nine

MATH PROBLEM SOLVING

Solving problems is not only a goal of learning mathematics, but also a major means of doing so.
—*National Council of Teachers of Mathematics, 2000*

Problem solving is natural to young children because the world is new to them, and they exhibit curiosity, intelligence, and flexibility as they face new situations.
—*NCTM, 2000*

MATHEMATICS

Mathematics is one of the most challenging academic areas because it is comprised of numerous domains that continue to increase in complexity. Knowledge develops in a cumulative manner toward increasingly complex topics (Woodward, 2004). Previously mastered math skills are necessary but insufficient for success in the higher level math domains. Although parallels have been drawn between the acquisition of basic math and basic reading skills, it is difficult to continue this analogy with higher level math and reading comprehension. Once you are an accomplished reader, although the material and vocabulary may become more difficult, the process of reading does not increase in complexity. The same is not true for mathematics. Math continues to increase in complexity, placing more and more demands on the knowledge and reasoning abilities of the individual learner. This is why most children identify math rather than reading as being the "hard" subject. This might also explain why almost one fifth of the U. S. population experiences high levels of math anxiety (Ashcraft, Krause, & Hopko, 2007).

Historically, different terms have been applied to learning difficulties with math, including: dyscalculia, arithmetic disorder, math learning disability, and even the generic term math difficulties. However, the term *math difficulty* encompasses a broad array of individuals that may not have a math learning disability but rather struggle with math due to low ability or poor instruction (Mazzocco, 2007). Distinguishing between individuals who have a math learning disability and those who have math difficulties continues to be a struggle for researchers, partly due to lack of stringent criteria or a clearly articulated definition. Although math disabilities are thought to be biologically based, they represent a behaviorally defined condition. For example, Geary (2003) found that individuals struggling with math often use immature behaviors, such as counting on their fingers.

Characteristics of Individuals Struggling with Math Problem Solving

Currently, researchers are not in complete agreement about the core cognitive deficits for math learning disabilities. Whereas reading research has clearly identified core deficits for reading disability, such as phonemic awareness or rapid naming, the research regarding math is not as definitive. One possibility for the lack of consensus may be that the cognitive correlates vary based on which math domain is being considered. In addition, the majority of research has focused on math facts and simple computations with not as many studies focusing on the cognitive dimensions of math problem solving. Results from one comprehensive study with first through third graders indicate that nonverbal reasoning, algorithmic recognition for problem solution, processing speed, short-term memory, and working memory each accounted for variance in arithmetic word-problem performance (Swanson & Beebe-Frankenberger, 2004). Findings from another study with a large sample of third graders (n = 924) indicate that difficulties in problem solving are primarily associated with deficient oral language abilities, as well as race and poverty (Fuchs, Fuchs, Stuebing et al., 2008).

Working memory and executive functions are also frequently mentioned as cognitive correlates of mathematics problem solving (LeBlanc & Weber-Russell, 1996; Passolunghi & Siegel, 2001; Swanson & Beebe-Frankenberger, 2004; Swanson & Sachse-Lee, 2001). Geary and Hoard (2005) found that executive functions including planning, inhibiting responses, shifting attention, and monitoring strategy use were related to math difficulties. Some individuals with difficulty in math problem solving have trouble organizing the necessary steps or inhibiting irrelevant information, which suggests a problem with executive functions (Passolunghi, Cornoldi, & De Liberto, 1999).

These problems with working memory and executive functions may also explain why over 30% of individuals diagnosed with Attention-Deficit/Hyperactivity Disorder (ADHD) are also diagnosed with math learning disabilities (McInnes, Humphries, Hogg-Johnson, & Tannock, 2003). Students with ADHD have difficulty sustaining attention and manipulating verbal information in working memory (Hecht et al., 2001), both necessary for math problem solving. Thus, successful math problem solving requires both cognitive and linguistic processes, as well as self-regulation strategies. Individuals must be able to read and understand the problem, identify what information is missing, come up with a plan to solve the problem, per-

DON'T FORGET

Over 30% of individuals diagnosed with Attention-Deficit/ Hyperactivity Disorder (ADHD) are also diagnosed with math learning disabilities.

form the necessary computations, and evaluate the answer for correctness. This complex activity requires processing linguistic information, employing various cognitive processes, and applying basic math knowledge (see Chapter 8 of this text).

Math Problem Solving in the Classroom

Although problem solving is recognized as a critical element of mathematics by researchers and national organizations alike, the emphasis in classrooms, especially special education classrooms, continues to be largely on memorization of facts and computational procedures. Little time is spent on developing the conceptual and procedural knowledge and strategies necessary for problem solving.

CAUTION

Many teachers lack necessary mathematical knowledge (Ball & Bass, 2000; Fuchs, Fuchs, Powell et al., 2008) and tend to focus instruction on procedures rather than concepts (Stigler & Perry, 1990).

Instructional time

Over 90% of the time, in a typical eighth-grade math class in the United States, is spent practicing routine procedures, whereas in an eighth-grade math class in Japan only 40% of the time is spent on these routine procedures. Forty-five percent of the class time in Japan is spent inventing new procedures and analyzing new situations, whereas virtually no time is spent on this in U. S. classrooms (TIMSS Video Study, 1999). This reality helps explain why students with math difficulties often fail to develop higher level math skills.

Textbooks

In addition to not enough time being devoted to instruction in mathematics, the mathematic textbooks used in a classroom may not employ the most effective instructional practices. In some school districts, the math textbooks are the primary means for instruction and the only forms of curriculum that exist (Jitendra et al., 2005). In a review of basal mathematics textbooks used in the primary grades, Bryant et al. (2008) found that the critical features of effective instruction were not being fully incorporated. Rapid Reference 9.1 provides a summary of the evidence-based features, based partially on the work of Jitendra et al.

≡ Rapid Reference 9.1

Evidence-Based Features of Effective Math Instruction

1. Clarity of objectives: Objectives state specific and measurable student behaviors.

2. One skill or concept: The focus is on only one new skill or concept so that adequate resources of working memory are available for learning.

3. Use of manipulatives or representations: Manipulatives and representation techniques are used to increase conceptual understanding, understanding, and organization.

4. Instructional approach: Explicit instructional procedures are used that employ modeling and an explanation of steps.

5. Teacher examples: Examples are presented for teachers to teach the target skill or concept.

6. Provision of adequate practice: Sufficient opportunities to practice are provided.

7. Review of prerequisite math skills: Review is provided of important prior skills.

8. Error correction and feedback: Corrective instructive feedback is provided that allows students to analyze their performances.

9. Vocabulary: Key vocabulary is introduced and reviewed.

10. Strategies: Cognitive strategies are taught and practiced.

11. Progress monitoring: Procedures are described for ensuring student progress and mastery.

(2005), that were used to evaluate the instructional principles incorporated into the textbooks. Results from these reviews suggest that if teachers are expected to teach to the NCTM Standards then the textbooks need to adhere to and align with these instructional design principles.

Elements of Problem Solving

When teachers of students with learning disabilities rated the frequency of mathematical problems across the ages, word problems were ranked as being the most problematic (Bryant et al., 2000). Often times, students with problem-solving difficulties have trouble following the multiple steps of problems as well as understanding exactly what the problem is asking them to do. Effective problem solving requires that an individual can: (a) represent the problem accurately, (b) visualize the elements of the problem, (c) understand the relationships among numbers, (d) use self-regulation, and (e) understand the meaning of the language and vocabulary.

Problem representation

The basis of understanding a problem relies on the individual being able to represent the problem accurately. In contrast to computation, problem solving involves the addition of linguistic information that requires students to construct a problem model (Fuchs, Fuchs, Stuebing et al., 2008). Difficulty with problem representation often results in difficulty with problem solution. Young children typically can only represent a problem that they understand and that uses numbers within their counting ranges. Children will represent problems using real objects and acting out the relationships described in problems.

Visualization

As children's skills develop, visualization is often used as a strategy for representing problems. Students are often instructed to act out, draw a

≡ Rapid Reference 9.2

Characteristics of Good Problem Solvers

- Use a variety of strategies, including self-monitoring strategies
- Read the problem for understanding (reread as necessary)
- Paraphrase the problem
- Identify key information (may underline it)
- Ask themselves "what is the question, what am I looking for?"
- Visualize—create a schematic representation
- Formulate a plan to solve problem using both verbal and visual information
- Estimate the answer
- Compute and check the answer
- Understand the language of mathematics

picture, or make a diagram of problems. However, pictorial representations, characteristic of poor problem solvers, may not always represent the relationships between the components of the problem and, therefore, may not lead to understanding or solving the problem.

Visualizing the relationships among the parts of a problem is called a *schematic representation* (van Garderen & Montague, 2003), which is a characteristic of good problem solvers. Good problem solvers use cognitive processes efficiently and apply metacognitive strategies. They can visualize and estimate problems, tell themselves what to do, monitor their performance, and evaluate the results. Poor problem solvers must be taught to do these things. Rapid Reference 9.2 identifies characteristics of good problem solvers and Rapid Reference 9.3 identifies the characteristics of poor problem solvers.

≡ Rapid Reference 9.3

Characteristics of Poor Problem Solvers

- Poor number sense
- Little or no use of various strategies
- Little or no use of self-monitoring strategies
- Little or no use of visualization (may create limited pictorial representations)
- Little or no planning
- Little or no use of estimation
- Limited mathematical vocabulary
- May compute prior to understanding problem
- Little or no checking of procedures or answers for accuracy

Understanding relationships among numbers

Converging evidence suggests that conceptual knowledge regarding numbers and their relationships is an important correlate of math achievement involving rational numbers (Hecht, Close, & Santisi, 2003). Some children have difficulty developing number sense (see Chapter 8 for a more thorough discussion of this topic). *Number sense* refers broadly to a student's ability to fluidly and flexibly perform mental mathematics and make quantitative comparisons with ease (Chard et al., 2008). Without this conceptual knowledge, or number sense, progress can be limited. For example, solving problems involving fractions is often difficult for students and creates a barrier to more advanced math topics

DON'T FORGET

Problem solving requires both representing and solving problems. In other words, math problem solving requires both conceptual understanding and procedural fluency.

(Loveless, 2003; Smith, 1995). On the 2003 National Assessment of Educational Progress (NAEP) only 55% of eighth graders could solve a word problem involving the division of one fraction by another (National Center for Education Statistics [NCES], 2006). These limits in conceptual knowledge of fractions may stem from inadequate number sense, which then affects fraction problem solving.

Self-regulation

Problem solving requires metacognition, or executive functions. Self-regulation includes strategies that help learners use the cognitive processes that facilitate learning, such as self-instruction, self-questioning, self-monitoring, self-evaluation, and self-reinforcement (Montague, 2008). To be an effective problem solver, students must think about the problem, be aware of what they do and do not know, plan how to solve the problem, inhibit irrelevant information, compute, and check the answer for reasonableness, all the while monitoring their own performance. These are characteristics of good problem solvers (see Rapid Reference 9.2). In addition, use of self-regulating strategies improves a student's problem solving and facilitates transfer to, or the ability to solve, novel problems (Fuchs et al., 2003a).

Language and vocabulary

Limited knowledge of mathematical vocabulary can also affect problem-solving skill (Bryant et al., 2008). In addition, language ability is an important factor affecting problem-solving ability (Fuchs, Fuchs, Stuebing et al., 2008). Mathematics is conceptually dense and difficult and unlike reading, contextual clues are limited or nonexistent (Bryant et al., 2000; Wiig & Semel, 1984).

EFFECTIVE INSTRUCTION

Research identified strategies and methods that are effective in improving a teacher's ability to teach mathematics, thus leading to enhanced

DON'T FORGET

The combination of direct/explicit instruction and cognitive strategy instruction is the most effective intervention for students struggling with math problem solving.

student achievement. Because a teacher's influence on the learner is powerful, and because math is so susceptible to inadequate instruction, it is essential that teachers incorporate research-based strategies in their teaching. These interventions must not only be effective, but also efficient (Montague, 2008). Rapid Reference 9.4 describes ten instructional practices that were found to be effective

≡ Rapid Reference 9.4

Ten Effective Instructional Practices that Improve Math Achievement

1. Opportunity to learn: provide ample exposure and practice
2. Focus on meaning: teach important mathematical ideas
3. Problem solving: build conceptual understanding to improve procedural knowledge
4. Opportunities to invent and practice: provide time for students to invent ways of solving problems and to apply skills being learned
5. Openness to student solutions and student interactions: use understanding of how students construct knowledge
6. Small-group learning: provide cooperative learning activities
7. Whole-class discussions: encourage sharing of various student solutions
8. Focus on number sense: help students determine reasonableness of solutions
9. Use of concrete materials: provide manipulatives to increase student achievement
10. Use of calculators: encourage the use of technology to increase student achievement and improve attitude

≡ Rapid Reference 9.5

Four Effective Instructional Practices for Teaching Math and Their Benefits

1. Teach within authentic contexts (demonstrates significance of math for real-life problem solving, promotes interest).
2. Build meaningful student connections (links new learning to previous knowledge).
3. Provide explicit Concrete-Representational-Abstract (CRA) instruction with modeling/scaffolding (matches instruction to student's current level of understanding).
4. Teach problem-solving strategies (develops metacognitive skills and fosters independence).

in teaching math and improving student achievement (Grouws & Cebulla, 2002). Allsopp, Kyger, and Lovin (2007) identified four effective instructional practices for teaching math. Rapid Reference 9.5 lists these four practices and identifies associated student benefits. In a meta-analysis of intervention studies in learning disabilities, Swanson (1999) found direct instruction and cognitive strategy instruction to be the most powerful interventions for students with learning disabilities. These findings have been replicated by Kroesbergen and Van Luit (2003) in their meta-analysis of math interventions for elementary students with special needs.

From a survey regarding the instructional practices of secondary general and special education teachers, Maccini and Gagnon (2006) found that the most common techniques and practices employed by general education teachers during multistep problem solving were use of a calculator, individualized instruction by the teacher, extended time on assignments, and peer or cross-age tutoring. Across special education teachers, the four most common instructional practices were prob-

> ### CAUTION
>
> Educators must understand how children learn mathematics and use developmentally appropriate instruction or the instruction will be ineffective (Kamii, 2000).

lems read to the student, individualized instruction by the teacher, extended time, and calculators. In discussing their findings, Maccini and Gagnon conclude that special education teachers need more instruction in the content of secondary mathematics, whereas general education teachers need additional preparation in the use of accommodations and instructional practices with students who have special needs.

Direct/Explicit Instruction

The terms *direct instruction* and *explicit instruction* essentially mean the same thing, although direct instruction is frequently associated with scripted lessons found in programs such as *Distar® Arithmetic* (Engelmann & Carnine, 1975) or *Corrective Reading* (Engelmann, 1975). Both direct instruction and explicit instruction are teacher-directed instructional approaches that use research-based practices and instructional procedures such as cueing, modeling, verbal rehearsal, and feedback. Both use lessons that are highly organized and structured, fast-paced, provide for ongoing interaction between teacher and student, and leave nothing to chance. Students are actively engaged in learning and practicing the objective of the lesson. Immediate, corrective, and positive feedback on performance is provided to each student. The goal is for the student to achieve mastery and automaticity of the skill being taught. While direct/explicit instruction has been found to be most effective for teaching basic skills (Kroesbergen & Van Luit, 2003; Swanson, 1999), this instructional approach underlies cognitive strategy instruction, which is a primary means of developing math problem-solving skills.

In addition, the use of explicit instruction, examples, and guided practice is important for teaching math vocabulary and the meanings of different abstract symbols (Bryant et al., 2000; Rivera & Smith, 1997). When preparing a lesson, a teacher can identify the important vocabulary and teach it explicitly, reinforcing the meanings throughout the lesson (Bryant, 2005). As with reading comprehension, instruction that actively engages students, such as the use of graphic organizers, as well as small group instruction on a small number of words, is most beneficial (Bryant, 2005).

DON'T FORGET

Not all students require explicit instruction to learn, but it is essential for those students who are struggling to learn.

Modeling

Initially, the teacher demonstrates what good problem solvers do when solving problems. The teacher says aloud everything he or she is thinking or doing while solving the problem. Students are given opportunities to see and hear good problem-solving behaviors before practicing. The teacher will also model incorrect problem-solving behaviors so that students can see how to use self-regulation strategies to monitor their performance. One aspect of problem solving that must be explicitly taught for many students is problem representation. Typically, visualization is the means used for constructing a schematic representation of the important information in the problem. The teacher models how to portray both linguistic and numerical information in a manner that shows the relationships among the problem parts. Students use paper and pencil to create pictures, diagrams, tables, charts, or other graphic displays. As they progress, students may move from concrete images to mental images.

Verbal rehearsal

Verbal rehearsal is a memory strategy for recalling the math problem-solving processes and strategies. Acronyms are frequently used to assist students in remembering the steps they are rehearsing verbally so they can internalize the processes. Eventually, after guided practice, the students move from saying the steps aloud to private speech. This increases problem-solving efficiency.

Strategy Instruction

In addition to using effective teaching principles and extensive practice, strategy instruction has been found to be most effective for teaching problem solving in mathematics (Kroesbergen & Van Luit, 2003). Swanson (1999) found that cognitive strategy instruction was one of the most powerful interventions for students with learning disabilities. All students appear to benefit from learning self-regulation strategies, such as self-instruction, self-questioning, and self-checking (Montague, 2006). Consistent use of strategies appears to have a reciprocal relationship with conceptual understanding—gains in one create gains in the other. Some evidence indicates that conceptual understanding is facilitated by developing procedural knowledge first (Rittle-Johnson, Siegler, & Alibali, 2001). Rapid Reference 9.6 provides additional ideas for developing problem-solving skills. The problem-solving strategies shown in Rapid Reference 9.7 are from the Northwest Regional Education Laboratory (NWREL).

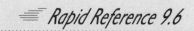

Rapid Reference 9.6

Tips for Teaching Problem Solving

- Teach specific strategies.
- Use think-aloud techniques when modeling steps to solve problems.
- Provide guided practice before independent practice to ensure student success.
- Allow time to practice the strategies regularly.
- Have students verbalize their understanding and rationale of the strategies they employ.
- Use diagrams and hands-on materials to aid problem solving.

Problem-solving strategies

Cognitive strategies can help students work through and remember the multiple steps inherent in mathematical problems (Bryant et al., 2000). Two examples of effective learning strategies for problem solving are Pólya's four-step problem-solving process (Van de Walle, 2007) and Montague's seven-step process (Montague, 2003). The four steps in Polya's process include: (1) understand the problem, (2) develop a plan to solve the problem, (3) carry out the plan, and (4) look back to be sure the answer solves the problem.

Montague identified the following seven problem-solving processes along with self-regulating strategies to facilitate each process: Read, Paraphrase, Visualize, Hypothesize, Estimate, Compute, and Check. Each process is accompanied by self-regulating strategies organized into three steps: Say, Ask, and Check. As an example, the self-regulating strategies for the first process, Read, are:

Say: Read the problem. If I do not understand, read it again.

Ask: Have I read and understood the problem?

Check: Be sure I understand as I solve the problem.

A validated math problem-solving curriculum, *Solve It!*, resulted from Montague's research with upper-elementary, middle-school, and secondary students with learning disabilities. The curriculum explicitly

≡ *Rapid Reference 9.7*

Math Problem-Solving Strategies

- Draw a picture, make a model, or act it out.
- Work backward from the answer.
- Make a table or a systematic list.
- Guess, check, and revise.
- Look for a pattern.
- Solve a simpler, related problem.
- Break it down into subordinate problems.
- Eliminate possibilities.
- Use algebra.

CAUTION

Strategies are important to math, but they do not work unless the student knows how and when to use them. Explicit modeling and scaffolding must be used when teaching strategies. In addition, strategies should not focus on teaching students to search for key words, such as *how many* means to add. Students need to grasp the entire meaning of the problem, rather than rely on the possible meanings of specific words.

teaches students to apply the cognitive processes and self-regulating strategies in the context of math problem solving.

Schema-Based Strategy Instruction

Schema-based strategy instruction is a well-researched, effective approach for teaching procedural and conceptual understanding related to mathematical word problem solving to students with disabilities (Fuchs & Fuchs, 2007; Hegarty & Kozhevnikov, 1999; Xin, Jitendra, & Deatline-Buchman, 2005). The semantic properties of a problem are important to schema-based problem solving (Silver & Marshall, 1990). As the individual maps relationships between pieces of acquired knowledge in a domain, a schema is formed. Recalling one piece of information will activate the connected pieces, facilitating the problem-solving process. When students use schemas to solve novel problems, they employ a framework that facilitates transferring their acquired knowledge, skills, and strategies to a new situation.

One schema-based problem-solving model (Xin & Jitendra, 2006) involves applying four procedural steps—identification, representation, planning, and solution—to already known problem types, or schemas. The student first reads the problem and *identifies* the problem schema. Next, the student *represents* the problem by diagramming the key information. Then the student *plans* how to solve the problem by selecting the appropriate operation(s) and writing out the math equation. Finally, the student *solves* the problem.

Explicit instruction in problem-solving rules combined with

schema-based instruction and peer practice improves problem-solving skills (Fuchs et al., 2003b). Further improvement is noted when instruction incorporates self-regulating strategies, especially for those students who have math learning disabilities (Fuchs et al., 2003a). The Peer-Assisted Learning Strategies (PALS) math program resulted from research conducted over a number of years by Drs. Lynn and Douglas Fuchs in effective ways to teach math problem solving.

Concrete-Representational-Abstract (CRA)

The concrete-representational-abstract (CRA) instructional sequence moves from a concrete level, to a semiconcrete or representational level, and then to the abstract level (e.g., Morin & Miller, 1998). Using concrete materials or manipulatives helps develop understanding of the underlying mathematical concept and prepares the student to deal with the abstract representations. Not only do students develop better mental representations and understanding of mathematical ideas, but motivation and time on task improves (Harrison & Harrison, 1986; Suydam & Higgins, 1977). Concrete materials are helpful when developing a variety of mathematical concepts, ranging from early concepts such as place value to more complex concepts such as probability and statistics. For example, when the CRA teaching sequence was applied to algebra, the problem-solving skills of the students improved dramatically (Maccini & Hughes, 2000). Clements (1996) found that virtual manipulatives were also effective in supporting the development of math concepts.

When the CRA instructional sequence includes explicit teacher modeling and scaffolding, mathematics becomes more meaningful and accessible to struggling learners (Allsopp et al., 2007).

> **DON'T FORGET**
> ....
> The use of hands-on activities and manipulatives promotes mathematical learning for young children, as well as older learners (Kamii, Lewis, & Kirkland, 2001).

Demonstration Plus Permanent Model

This instructional routine was developed to teach long division (Rivera & Smith, 1988). The teacher first demonstrates the steps in the algorithm. The correct teacher-solution becomes the permanent model. Then students try to solve similar problems while the teacher provides corrective feedback as needed. Once the student solves a problem correctly, additional problems are worked independently.

Mnemonic Strategies

A number of mnemonic strategies exist for assisting students with mathematical problem solving. The strategies can be presented as acronyms, pictures, acrostics (a phrase in which the first letter in each word represents a step), graphics, or cue sheets. Following are four examples of strategies that use acronyms and one that uses an acrostic.

STAR

This first-letter mnemonic helps students, especially older students, recall the steps used to solve word problems or equations involving integers (Maccini & Hughes, 2000; Maccini & Ruhl, 2000).

> S = Search the word problem
> T = Translate the words into an equation in picture form
> A = Answer the problem
> R = Review the solution

DRAW

This mnemonic incorporates the CRA strategy and is helpful for solving problems involving addition, subtraction, multiplication, and division (Mercer & Mercer, 1998).

> D = Discover the sign (find, circle, and say name of computation sign)
> R = Read the problem

A = Answer or draw tallies and/or circles and check your answer

W = Write the answer

ORDER

This mnemonic helps students remember which operation should be solved first when learning to solve multioperation problems (Allsopp, 1999).

O = Observe the problem

R = Read the signs

D = Decide which operation to do first

E = Execute the rule of order (*Many Dogs Are Smelly* = ×, /, +, −)

R = Relax, you're done!

EQUAL

This acronym provides a learning strategy for determining greater than, less than, and equal to.

E = Examine what is on each side

Q = Question: Is it addition or multiplication?

U = Use circles and lines for addition; use groups and tallies for multiplication

A = Answer by drawing the totals for each side

L = Label equal (=) or not equal (≠)

Please Excuse My Dear Aunt Sally

This is an example of an acrostic mnemonic that is useful in teaching the order in which to execute operations.

*P*lease (parentheses)

*E*xcuse (exponents)

*M*y (multiplication)

*D*ear (division)

*A*unt (addition)

*S*ally (subtraction)

DON'T FORGET

Effective math problem-solving instruction is explicit, teaches problem-solving rules and schemas, includes self-regulating strategies, and provides peer-mediated practice.

Algebra

Empirically validated instructional approaches for teaching algebra are summarized in Rapid Reference 9.8. Many of these instructional approaches have already been discussed in this chapter. One additional teacher-directed sequence, LIP, directs the teacher to link new information to prior knowledge, identify objectives of the lesson, and provide the rationale for learning when teaching. Allsopp (1997) demonstrates that classwide peer tutoring for general education low-achieving students and peers with learning disabilities could be effective. This intervention used trained peer tutors to provide additional support and instruction for low-achieving students.

Rapid Reference 9.8

Effective Instruction for Teaching Algebra

• Teacher-based activities
• Concrete-Representational-Abstract teaching sequence
• Direct/Explicit instruction—modeling
• LIP (Link, Identify, Provide)—Teach prerequisites
• Computer-assisted instruction
• Strategy instruction
• Metacognitive strategies (e.g., self-questioning)
• Structured worksheets
• Mnemonics (e.g., STAR, PEMDAS)
• Graphic organizers

Technology

The use of technology, such as calculators, allows an individual to focus on the higher level thinking required for math problem solving. The individual's cognitive resources, working memory in particular, are freed from the burden of computation. Important ideas in the problem receive the individual's full attention when computing technology is used. In addition, technology, such as video and gaming applications, allows learning to occur in meaningful contexts. This has a positive effect on a student's mathematical learning, especially those students with learning difficulties (Bottge, Heinrichs, Chan, Mehta, & Watson, 2003).

Computers

Computer- and Web-based activities may be useful supplements to a math curriculum. Many of these activities and tools provide a visual representation of the math problem, which is a critical component of problem solving. In addition, these representations are typically dynamic and interactive, assisting students in seeing patterns and recognizing critical elements (Ahmed, Clark-Jeavons, & Oldknow, 2004; Arcavi, 2003; Sloutsky & Yarlas, 2000). Students may develop a better understanding of abstract, symbolic concepts through analysis of these representations (Butler et al., 2003; Stylianou, 2002). An important factor in problem solving is the ability to translate from one form of representation to another (Gagatsis & Shiakalli, 2004), so combining Web- or computer-based activities with more traditional approaches may foster the students' problem-solving skills. In fact, computer-assisted instruction was found to be an effective intervention for improving student performance on math word problems (NRC, 2001; Shiah, Mastropieri, Scruggs, & Mushinski-Fulk, 1995).

Unlike textbooks with a fixed number of problems, Web- or computer-based activities provide opportunities for students to solve as many problems as needed to develop the skill. In addition, the technology options typically provide immediate feedback—a critical element for effective learning.

DON'T FORGET

Computer-assisted instruction was found to be effective for improving student performance on math word problems.

Calculators

Studies have shown that calculator use helps improve the student's conceptual understanding, use of strategies, and attitude toward math. Unfortunately, only about one third of secondary educators and approximately half of special educators allow students with mild disabilities to use calculators during multiple-step problems (Maccini & Gagnon, 2006). The use of calculators is encouraged especially when problems require the computation of large numbers. A review of the research indicated that incorrect student responses resulted primarily from the increased opportunity for errors when using large numbers (Cawley, Parmar, Yan, & Miller, 1996, 1998; Cawley, Shepard, Smith, & Parmar, 1997). For example, calculators may be recommended to solve division problems for items exceeding two-digit into four-digit combinations. Research also indicates that the understanding and learning of algebraic representation are both enhanced if instruction makes productive use of computer and calculator technology (NRC, 2001).

CAUTION

Students need a variety of experiences to ensure they learn how to use a calculator (Glover, 1992).

Commercial Products

The What Works Clearinghouse (http://ies.ed.gov/ncee/wwc/) identifies several commercial programs that demonstrate evidence of effectiveness at the elementary- or middle-school levels. The only one listed as having potentially positive effects on math achievement at the elementary level (Grades 3–5) was *Everyday Mathematics,* a program developed by University of Chicago School Mathematics Project and currently published by Wright Group/McGraw-Hill (www.wrightgroup.com).

At the middle-school level, several programs demonstrated evidence of positive or potentially positive effects on math achievement. The studies typically were done with students in eighth or ninth grade. Two programs demonstrated positive effects on math achievement: *I CAN Learn® Pre-Algebra* and *Algebra* (www.icanlearn.com) and *Saxon Middle School Math* (www.saxonpublishers.com). Programs that had potentially positive effects on math achievement included *The Expert Mathematician* (www.expertmath.org), *Cognitive Tutor®* (www.carnegielearning.com), and the *University of Chicago School Mathematics Project (UCSMP) Algebra* (3rd edition available at www.wrightgroup.com).

The Johns Hopkins University Center for Data-Driven Reform in Education (www.bestevidence.org) is another resource for determining what programs or methods have evidence of effectiveness. Their review includes math curricula, computer-assisted instruction, and instructional process strategies. In general, evidence of effectiveness ranged from limited for math curricula, moderate for computer-assisted instruction, and strong for instructional process strategies. Similar to the findings regarding reading instruction, these findings suggest that how math is taught is more important than which text or program is used. Instructional processes showing strong evidence of effectiveness include: classwide peer tutoring, Missouri Mathematics Program, Peer-Assisted Learning Strategies (PALS), Student Teams-Achievement Divisions (STAD), and TAI math. Rapid Reference 9.9 provides a brief description of each of these instructional processes and contact information for obtaining further information. *Classworks* (www.curriculumadvantage.com) was the only computer-assisted program reviewed that had evidence of effectiveness (moderate). Additional resources for reviewing the effectiveness of materials and methods include the Promising Practices Network (www.promisingpractices.net) and the National Dissemination Center for

> **DON'T FORGET**
>
> The instructional methods used to teach math are more important and more effective in improving math achievement than either a text or computer-assisted instruction.

≡ Rapid Reference 9.9

Instructional Processes with Strong Evidence of Effectiveness

Classwide Peer Tutoring (CPT)	Paired learning approach Students take turns as teacher and learner (greenwood@ku.edu)
Missouri Mathematics Program	Focuses on active teaching, classroom management, and motivation (good@u.arizona.edu)
Peer-Assisted Learning Strategies (PALS)	Structured pair learning strategy Students take turns as teacher and learner (www.kc.vanderbilt.edu/pals)
Student Teams-Achievement Divisions (STAD)	Structured cooperative learning program Students work in teams of four (nmadden@jhu.edu)
Team Accelerated Instruction Math (TAI Math)	Structured cooperative learning program Explicit instruction by teacher Students work in four-member teams (www.charlesbridge.com)

Children with Disabilities (http://research.nichcy.org). Rapid Reference 9.10 lists web sites that provide resources for teaching math problem solving. (See Chapter 8 in this text for additional math-related web sites.)

CAUTION

Limited independent research exists on many published materials.

CONCLUSION

Existing research in mathematics suggests that instructional practices are more important and effective in teaching problem solving than any curricula.

≋ Rapid Reference 9.10

Web sites Related to Math Problem Solving

http://coe.jmu.edu/mathvidsr
  MathVIDS (Mathematics Video Instructional Development Source)
  (Developers: Allsopp, Kyger, & Ingram)

www.goENC.com
  Offers a fee-based subscription service for math and science resources for grades K through 12 (formerly Eisenhower National Clearinghouse for Math and Science)

www.Big6.com
  Widely used approach for teaching information
  (Developers: Eisenberg & Berkowitz)

www.mathplayground.com
  Provides activities for elementary- and middle-school students to
practice their math skills and logic

www.mathcounts.org
  A national enrichment, coaching, and competition program that
promotes middle-school mathematics achievement through grassroots
involvement in every U.S. state and territory

www.intmath.com
  Interactive math designed for secondary and undergraduate students or teachers of math

A direct/explicit instructional approach is most effective for teaching basic math skills, but this type of approach also underlies effective strategy instruction. Strategy instruction, in procedures and self-regulation, is most effective for improving students' math problem-solving skills. Students who are struggling with problem solving must be shown the how, when, where, and why of strategies—in other words, they must be taught explicitly the procedures, steps, and applications of strategies. Problem solving is both the process and the content of mathematics and is an important instructional priority.

🐟 TEST YOURSELF 🐟

1. **Children often consider math a harder subject than reading.** True or False?

2. **Most U.S. classrooms spend the majority of instructional time in math on developing problem-solving skills.** True or False?

3. **List two ways to represent a problem without using numerals.**

4. **List three characteristics of good problem solvers.**

5. **Strategy instruction is one of the most effective ways to develop problem-solving skills.** True or False?

6. **What is an effective way to ensure the student knows how and when to use strategies?**

7. **What is CRA?**

8. **What is the purpose of the acrostic Please Excuse My Dear Aunt Sally?**

9. **Which of the following was most effective in developing problem-solving skill?**

   (a) Explicit instruction in problem-solving rules combined with schema-based instruction incorporating self-regulating strategies and peer practice.

   (b) Explicit instruction in problem-solving rules and computer-assisted instruction.

   (c) Explicit instruction in problem-solving rules combined with schema-based instruction.

   (d) Explicit instruction in problem-solving rules combined with schema-based instruction and peer practice.

10. Which of the following are cognitive correlates of math problem solving?

(a) working memory and executive functions

(b) visual-spatial processing and reasoning

(c) processing speed

(d) All of the above.

(e) None of the above.

Answers: 1. True; 2. False; 3. Any two: Using concrete objects, visualizing, drawing a picture, diagramming; 4. Any three: Use self-regulation strategies (self-monitor, metacognition), visualize the relationship between the parts of a problem (schematic representation), create a plan, identify key information, read problem carefully and reread as necessary, estimate answer, compute, check for correctness; 5. True; 6. Explicit instruction (modeling) and scaffolding; 7. Concrete-Representational-Abstract (teaching or instructional sequence); 8. To teach the order in which to execute operations; 9. a; 10. d

Ten

THE RELEVANCE OF COGNITIVE ABILITIES TO ACADEMIC INTERVENTIONS

The hypotheses explaining the scores, rather than the scores themselves, form the basis for making recommendations.
—*Kaufman, 1979*

In a book about evidence-based instruction, it may be surprising to see a chapter related to cognitive abilities. On the other hand, it may be equally surprising to find a book about evidence-based instruction in the Essentials series of assessment books. This conundrum is similar to the state of education today. The line is blurring between general and special education. Both are focused on student outcomes as determined by the student's response-to-instruction or response-to-intervention (RTI) using evidence-based instruction. Educators and evaluators alike are concerned about RTI and the implementation of effective instruction. There is change brewing, and at times confusion, regarding the need for and benefit of comprehensive assessments. Whether or not assessment has a role in planning interventions is not the issue. RTI models require ongoing assessment, typically curriculum based, as well as frequent progress monitoring. The question is whether or not comprehensive, diagnostic assessments that include cognitive abilities are necessary. Are cognitive assessments needed to identify a specific learning disability? Are they needed for determining eligibility for special education services? Are the results helpful for selecting accommodations and choosing the most effective instructional programs for students?

Professionals rejecting the importance of cognitive assessments for instructional planning may be basing that decision on their knowledge of older tests and older models of intelligence. Modern models of intelligence and the tests that operationalize those theories can help identify important cognitive and linguistic abilities that impact achievement. Currently, the Cattell-Horn-Carroll (CHC) theory provides the most comprehensive framework for understanding cognitive abilities. For an in-depth description of CHC theory, see McGrew (2005) or McGrew and Woodcock (2001). Seven broad abilities included in CHC theory are: verbal ability (Gc), fluid reasoning (Gf), long-term retrieval (Glr), auditory processing (Ga), visual processing (Gv), processing speed (Gs), and short-term memory (Gsm). Rapid Reference 10.1 provides a brief description of these seven broad abilities and lists a sampling of the narrow abilities for each.

As was stated in Chapter 1, a comprehensive assessment is often needed to determine an individual's strengths and weaknesses in all areas related to achievement, which includes cognitive and linguistic abilities. In addition, the determination of a pattern of strengths and weaknesses is relevant to the identification of a specific learning disability and is one criterion for determining eligibility for special education services (IDEA, 2004). Researchers are learning more each day about how the brain learns as well as how various cognitive abilities relate to academic performance. Understanding the relationships among cognitive abilities and achievement areas can help an evaluator identify a person's unique strengths and weaknesses, formulate diagnostic impressions, and inform instructional planning.

DON'T FORGET

Exploring the relationship between cognitive, linguistic, and academic skills and abilities is essential for determining an individual's pattern of strengths and weaknesses. Understanding these patterns is an important part of determining eligibility for special services and informing instruction.

≣ *Rapid Reference 10.1*

Summary of Seven Broad CHC Abilities

1. Verbal Ability (Gc)

Also referred to as *comprehension-knowledge* or *crystallized intelligence*, Gc is a store of acquired knowledge that includes both declarative and procedural knowledge. Includes lexical knowledge, general information, language development, and listening ability.

2. Fluid Reasoning (Gf)

Refers to problem-solving skills and mental flexibility, especially in novel situations. Includes inductive, deductive (general sequential reasoning), and quantitative reasoning.

3. Short-Term Memory (Gsm)

The ability to hold information in immediate awareness for a brief time. Includes memory span and working memory.

4. Long-Term Retrieval (Glr)

The ability to encode, store, and retrieve information. Includes associative memory, naming facility, ideational fluency, meaningful memory, figural fluency, and free recall memory.

5. Auditory Processing (Ga)

The ability to analyze and synthesize auditory information. Includes phonemic awareness, auditory discrimination, phonetic coding, speech/sound discrimination, sound localization, and resistance to auditory stimulus distortion.

6. Visual Processing (Gv)

The ability to analyze and synthesize visual information. Includes spatial relations, visual memory, closure speed, visualization, spatial scanning, and flexibility of closure.

7. Processing Speed (Gs)

The ability to process simple information quickly. Includes perceptual speed, number facility, rate of test taking, and speed of reasoning.

CONNECTION TO ACHIEVEMENT

A growing body of research helps delineate how cognitive abilities differentially relate to the achievement domains of reading, writing, and mathematics (e.g., Berninger, Abbott, Vermeulen, et al., 2006; Floyd, Evans, & McGrew, 2003; Fuchs et al., 2006; Geary, 2003; Hale, Fiorello, Kavanagh, Hoeppner, & Gaitherer, 2001; Rourke & Conway, 1997; Swanson et al., 2003). The following section provides a brief review of the cognitive correlates for the academic areas of reading, writing, and mathematics. It is important to keep in mind that cognitive abilities do not work in isolation, but rather are interrelated, one influencing the other. The skilled clinician must consider this interplay when determining an individual's pattern of strengths and weaknesses.

Reading Achievement

A variety of cognitive and linguistic abilities are related to reading achievement (e.g., Evans et al., 2002). Lower level cognitive processes are more related to the acquisition of word recognition skill and fluency, whereas higher level linguistic and reasoning abilities are related to reading comprehension.

Phonemic awareness in kindergarten is the best predictor of word reading ability in the elementary grades (e.g., Adams, 1990). Both sound blending and segmentation influence the ease of learning to apply phonics when reading. Processing speed, especially the rapid processing of visual symbols, resembles the perceptual demands of reading. Research confirms a relationship between slow perceptual speed and poor word reading ability (Berninger, 1990; McGrew, 1993; McGrew, Flanagan, Keith, & Vanderwood, 1997; Urso, 2008). Reading fluency and the ability to read exception words are related to rapid automatized naming, or how quickly one can identify colors, objects, letters, and digits, as well as orthographic processing, the ease and speed at which word parts and words are recognized (e.g., Fletcher et al., 2007; Scarborough, 1998; Torgesen, 1997).

A significant relationship exists between reading comprehension and verbal abilities such as level of oral vocabulary (e.g., Baumann & Kame'enui, 1991; Berninger & Abbott, 1994) and background knowledge (Anderson & Pearson, 1984). In fact, reading comprehension can be no stronger than the oral comprehension of language (Fletcher et al., 2007). Vocabulary, in particular, is a good predictor of reading comprehension and, even though a child may decode a word if the meaning is unknown, comprehension will be impaired (Tannenbaum, Torgesen, & Wagner, 2006). Regarding reasoning abilities, although most children can draw inferences from text by second grade, many cannot (Hall, 1989). Students with poor comprehension have trouble making inferences that require interpretation and integration of text (Fletcher et al., 2007). In some cases, understanding a text is influenced by poor word recognition skill or a slow reading rate. Clearly, the reasoning required for comprehension is influenced not only by oral language and background knowledge, but also by how fluently the reader reads (Snow, 2002).

Working memory is another significant predictor of both listening and reading comprehension ability (Cain, Oakhill, Barnes, & Bryant, 2001; Fletcher et al., 2007). Once again the automaticity of decoding influences the effectiveness of working memory. If a reader must try to figure out a new word, working memory is engaged in the decoding process, making it less likely that the reader will comprehend what he or she reads (Pressley, 2000). Research also indicates that skilled reading by third grade depends on skill in the use of a variety of comprehension strategies and thinking skills (NRP, 2000). Rapid Reference 10.2 provides a brief summary of the cognitive abilities most related to reading achievement.

≡ Rapid Reference 10.2

Cognitive Abilities and Reading Achievement

- Auditory Processing (phonemic awareness)
- Short-Term Memory (working memory, memory span)
- Long-Term Retrieval (associative memory, rapid automatized naming)
- Processing Speed (speed of lexical access, perceptual speed—e.g., orthographic processing)
- Fluid Reasoning (inductive, deductive, quantitative)
- Verbal Ability (lexical knowledge, background knowledge, listening ability)

Written Language Achievement

Floyd, McGrew, and Evans (2008) found that a number of cognitive abilities were related to writing, including verbal ability, reasoning, long-term retrieval, working memory, and processing speed (see Rapid Reference 10.3). As with reading, the factors that affect spelling development differ from the ones related to written expression.

Spelling ability is primarily related to the ability to segment sounds in words—an aspect of phonological awareness—as well as the ability to recall letter strings or the orthographic patterns that exist. In addition, knowledge of morphology, or the meaning units of language, is necessary for adding word parts and word endings.

As with reading comprehension, oral language ability serves as the foundation for, and is positively related to, subsequent success in written expression (Glazer, 1989; Stanovich, 1986; Strickland & Feeley, 1991; Wiig & Semel, 1984). Executive processing, or functioning, is often mentioned as another important aspect of written language. Both

≡ Rapid Reference 10.3

Cognitive Abilities and Written Language Achievement

- Processing Speed (perceptual speed)
- Auditory Processing (phonemic awareness)
- Long-Term Retrieval (associative memory)
- Working Memory
- Fluid Reasoning (inductive, deductive)
- Verbal Ability (lexical knowledge, background knowledge, listening ability)

fluid reasoning and working memory are executive functions, as are attention and self-regulation. The importance of these abilities combined with the complexity of writing may help explain why writing disorders are so prevalent in individuals with attention deficits.

Mathematics Achievement

A number of cognitive abilities are related to achievement in mathematics (Floyd et al., 2003; Geary, 2007; Rourke & Conway, 1993) and are summarized in Rapid Reference 10.4. The abilities that affect mastery of basic skills differ from those that affect math problem solving.

Geary (1993) discusses the speed of reasoning, which may underlie the development of accurate representations of math facts that is necessary for automatic fact recall. Individuals with math disabilities frequently have difficulty with representation and retrieval of math facts (Geary 1993, 2007), implicating weaknesses in the storage and retrieval process. Successful achievement in arithmetic depends on automatic retrieval from stored information (Siegler & Shrager, 1984). Working memory and memory span both involve immediate awareness and are

≡ Rapid Reference 10.4

Cognitive Abilities and Mathematics Achievement

- Auditory Processing
- Processing Speed (scanning)
- Short-Term Memory (working memory, memory span)
- Long-Term Retrieval (associative memory)
- Visual Processing (pattern recognition, spatial skills)
- Fluid Reasoning (inductive, deductive, quantitative)
- Verbal Ability (lexical knowledge, background knowledge, listening ability)

limited-capacity abilities. Therefore, different factors, such as speed of processing, choice of strategy, or automaticity of fact recall, may impact memory span and working memory and, thus, affect development and performance in mathematics. Furthermore, limited basic math skills stress working memory and inhibit performance on more complex problems (Fuchs et al., 2006). Individuals with math disabilities have more limited working memory than do their normal age mates (Bull & Johnston, 1997).

Findings from studies also indicate a relationship between processing speed and the development of basic math skills. Fuchs et al. (2006) found that processing speed, phonological processing, and attention were all related to basic math skills. In another study, processing speed was found to be the best predictor of arithmetic competence in 7-year-olds (Bull & Johnston, 1997).

Oral language abilities and reasoning abilities are highly related to success in math problem solving. Within the research on mathematics, reasoning is sometimes referred to as *concept formation* or *adaptive problem solving* (Rourke & Conway, 1993). Students with math difficulties often have weaknesses in multiple domains of mathematical thinking, as well as language impairments (Fletcher et al., 2007). Fuchs et al. (2006) found that attention, language, nonverbal problem solving, and concept formation were all related to the ability to solve word problems.

A few research studies also indicated a relationship between visual processing and higher level math achievement, such as geometry or calculus (Hegarty & Kozhevnikov, 1999). Visuospatial skills appear to be required for estimating, forming representations of magnitude, and visualizing a mental number line (Dehaene et al., 1999; Phillips & Crowell, 1994). Geary (1993) identified a visuospatial disorder math disability subtype characterized by difficulty with spatial representations (e.g., alignments, geometry) and place value errors.

CAUTION

Trying to examine cognitive abilities in isolation is like "slicing smoke" (Horn, 1991, p. 198). Practitioners must keep in mind the interplay of abilities and how they affect one another.

EFFECTIVE INSTRUCTION

The guiding principles of effective instruction are presented in Chapter 1 of this text. Those principles are effective in large part because they coincide with how the brain learns. For example, the human brain seeks patterns. New information is examined to determine if it is familiar and if it fits with some existing knowledge. It is easier to learn something new when the learner can connect the information to something that is already known. To facilitate new learning, instruction must help students make associations between new and known information.

The brain also seeks meaning. It attends to information that makes sense and diverts attention from things that make no sense. To keep a student's attention, instruction must be clear and meaningful. The brain has a large visual cortex and can remember nonlinguistic information readily. For students to successfully learn and remember, instruction must capitalize on the brain's visual capabilities. It is no wonder that effective teaching principles such as activating prior knowledge, actively engaging the learner, using advance organizers, and teaching in a clear and explicit manner work. These methods capitalize on how the brain works. The brain is the learning organ (e.g., Hart, 1983). Effective instruction incorporates methods that use the brain's natural tendencies.

> **DON'T FORGET**
> ....
> The brain seeks patterns and meaning. Relating new information to prior knowledge is an effective teaching and learning principle.

Although the plasticity of the brain is well documented, it is best to intervene early before the brain matures. Numerous studies demonstrate that the brain's ability to learn spoken language is best during the first 10 years of life (Sousa, 2005).

If interventions are not provided to students in a timely fashion, they get further and further behind and learning requires more effort. This is why there has been such increased focus on the need for early intervention with reading. The longer a student's difficulties continue, the harder it becomes to resolve them.

Interventions for Limitations in Cognitive Abilities

The purpose of exploring interventions for cognitive processing weaknesses is not necessarily to "fix" the ability, but rather to plan instruction that addresses these weaknesses. Cognitive interventions can be applied within the context of the academic area(s) of concern. In other words, knowledge of how the brain works is used to facilitate learning. For example, if a student with reading difficulties has a significant deficit in phonemic awareness, instruction can focus on the development of these abilities within the context of reading instruction. Phonemic awareness not only has a causal relationship with learning to read, but it has a reciprocal one as well. Developing skills in reading helps increase phonological awareness.

The effective teaching principles discussed in Chapter 1 are appropriate for teaching individuals with limits in one or more cognitive ability. As a brief review, Rapid Reference 10.5 summarizes the effective teaching principles (see Chapter 1 for more information). It is important to employ these effective principles when teaching any student, but it is critically important when teaching students who are struggling to learn.

Cognitive strategy instruction

Cognitive strategy instruction (CSI) is an instructional approach that focuses on developing thinking skills in order to improve learning outcomes. Research found CSI to be effective in improving achievement

---

≡ Rapid Reference 10.5

Summary of Effective Teaching Principles

- Activate prior knowledge
- Actively engage learner
- Teach explicitly
- Scaffold instruction
- Differentiate instruction
- Teach strategies
- Use advance organizers
- Engage higher order thinking skills (similarities/differences, summarizing)
- Provide feedback (relevant, immediate, frequent)
- Establish a climate of success and appropriate expectations
- Use peer-mediated instruction
- Make use of nonlinguistic representations (models or images)

for a variety of students, especially for individuals with learning difficulties (Swanson, 2001). Many students with learning disabilities are passive learners. CSI engages those students and makes them active participants who are responsible for their learning. Additionally, CSI supports the development of improved executive functioning, which is often cited as a problem area for struggling learners (Lee & Riccio, 2005). One likely reason for the effectiveness of cognitive strategy instruction is that it provides strategies for students whose problems go beyond the achievement areas.

Throughout this book, strategy instruction is included as an effective instructional approach across all academic areas. It is equally, if not more, important for individuals with limitations in one or more cognitive ability. Cognitive strategy instruction is designed to help students learn the strategies employed by successful learners so that they can also succeed. This includes developing metacognitive skills as well as how to select and use strategies as an aid to learning. Many times struggling learners do not monitor their own thinking or performance. They do not think about what they know and do not know when approaching a task. These self-regulating skills are the essence of metacognition. CSI provides the optimal learning strategies to accomplish the learning goal. Typically, both metacognitive (self-regulating) skills and specific learning strategies are taught simultaneously. Self-regulation strategies empower the learner to be aware of and responsible for his or her own learning. Learning strategies provide a framework, or game plan, for the learner to follow.

Strategies must be taught explicitly with teacher demonstration using a think-aloud procedure followed by guided practice with feedback. Not only must the students learn what the strategy is, but they must learn how and when to use the strategy, as well as why the strategy is important to use. Strategy instruction actively engages the learner in thinking about the task and monitoring performance. Instruction and practice must be ongoing so that the strategies can become automatic,

DON'T FORGET

Metacognition is thinking about one's thinking: knowing what is known and what is not known. Self-awareness is an important characteristic of successful learners.

DON'T FORGET

Cognitive strategy instruction is a proven means to improve achievement, especially for students with learning problems.

CAUTION

Simply showing or telling students about how to use a cognitive strategy will be insufficient for students with learning challenges; these students require extensive coaching and practice in the use and application of the strategy (Gildroy & Deshler, 2008).

allowing the learner to focus on the information to be learned.

Most cognitive strategy instruction designed to enhance metacognitive skills has three main components: self-instruction, goal setting, and self-reinforcement. Self-instruction is basically self-talk. Overt verbalization makes the steps of a strategy explicit and can guide problem solving (Dehn, 2008). Most people have used some type of private speech, or self-talk, to help perform a task at some point in their lives. This strategy, self-talk, is a normally occurring strategy. Young children use self-talk, spoken aloud, when engaged in a task. As the children increase in age, the self-talk becomes covert, or silent. CSI teaches students to talk to themselves for specific purposes such as organizing or structuring behavior, or completing a task. Self-talk may include self-statements to guide behavior, such as "I must finish my work before recess"; "I need to raise my hand if I have a question"; "I failed that test, but I'm not stupid. I have to figure out a better way to study"; or "I don't understand what to do. I'd better ask for help." Self-instruction can also be used to guide the learner through a series of steps to accomplish a task. Many times mnemonics are used to help the learner remember the steps in a task.

For example, when teaching middle or upper grade students a comprehension strategy for reading content-area books, the mnemonic SCROL has been used (Grant, 1993). SCROL includes five steps: (1) Survey the headings, (2) Connect, (3) Read the text, (4) Outline, and (5) Look back. As another example, Schumaker, Denton, and Deshler (1984) developed the RAP strategy for teaching students how to paraphrase. RAP reminds the student to: (a) Read the paragraph; (b) Ask yourself, "What were the main ideas and details in the paragraph?"; and (c) Put the main idea and details into your own words. The first letter of each step forms a mnemonic that helps with memory (Gildroy & Deshler, 2008).

Goal setting is the second component in CSI. Successful learners set goals. Goals allow progress to be monitored, attention to be focused, and even increase motivation. Performance improves when the goals are clearly articulated, are of appropriate difficulty (not too easy or too hard), and can be reached in the near future.

The third component is self-reinforcement. Once the learner accomplishes the goal, then he or she may select a reward. When employing all of these components, the learner becomes self-regulating.

Self-regulating strategy development (Harris & Graham, 1996) is one model for implementing cognitive strategy instruction. This model is presented in Chapter 7 as a writing strategy. However, one benefit of self-regulating strategy development (SRSD) is that it is flexible and can be applied to numerous tasks. Rapid Reference 10.6 summarizes the basic steps to follow when implementing SRSD.

Mnemonics

Mnemonics are memory aids that are frequently used in cognitive strategy instruction. Some mnemonics use acronyms—first letter cues—

☰ *Rapid Reference 10.6*

Steps to Implementing the Self-Regulating Strategy Development

1. Develop and activate background knowledge.

   a. Determine prerequisite skills through task analysis.

   b. Teach students necessary pre-skills or knowledge for task.

2. Discuss the strategy.

   a. Explain the importance and how it will help the student.

   b. Describe the steps of the strategy.

   c. Explain where and when to use the strategy.

3. Model the strategy.

   a. Demonstrate the how and the why of the strategy.

   b. Use a think-aloud procedure to show students the metacognitive aspects of the task.

4. Memorize the strategy.

   a. Memorize the steps of the strategy so the focus can be on accomplishing the task.

   b. Provide ample practice and variation.

5. Support the strategy.

   a. Use scaffolding to ensure success (gradually shift responsibility to learner).

   b. Use cooperative groups and collaboration.

   c. Provide practice in a variety of settings .

6. Independent performance.

   a. Allow individual adaptations of the strategy as long as the end result is improved performance.

   b. Monitor performance and strategy use (ongoing).

whereas others use acrostics— cue words that form a sentence. Still others use visual clues, rhymes, or songs. Mnemonics can help the individual recall numerous things including the steps in a task, a list of items, vocabulary words, or metacognitive skills. Throughout this text,

> ## CAUTION
>
> It is better to teach a few strategies thoroughly than to try to teach too many strategies. Effectively teaching strategies so that students will actually use them requires an investment of time.

mnemonics have been presented, when appropriate, as part of effective instruction. For example, in Chapter 5, the keyword method that uses mnemonics for learning new vocabulary words is described (Mastropieri & Scruggs, 1998). This intervention is particularly effective for mastering new words in content areas, such as science and history. As with all strategies, students must be taught how to implement the mnemonic strategies and practice using them.

Rehearsal, overlearning, and elaboration

Individuals with weaknesses in the cognitive abilities of long-term retrieval and/or short-term memory will benefit from repetition when learning new information. Rehearsing and reviewing the new information immediately as well as across time are most effective for learning. Distributed practice, with intervening activities and varying time intervals, is an important component of rehearsal. Additional benefits can be obtained by what is commonly called *overlearning*. Overlearning occurs when a skill is practiced after it has been mastered and it becomes easier and easier to use. Even one additional rehearsal after mastery has been reached can have a positive impact on learning and retention. Elaboration during practice goes beyond simple repetition, requiring the learner to think deeply about the information. Connections are made between the new information and prior knowledge. Advance organizers are one way to help engage students in forming connections between the new information and their existing knowledge.

Visual representations

Individuals with low verbal ability, long-term retrieval, auditory processing, fluid reasoning, processing speed, or short-term memory may benefit from the use of visual representations. Connecting verbal information with a visual cue or image can enhance learning. One memory strategy that uses visual imagery is the method of loci. When trying to remember a list, a person can visualize each item and place it in a common scene or location. The individual mentally strolls through the scene, recalling each item. The peg word mnemonic is another memory strategy that uses visual representations to aid students in remembering lists of information or steps in a procedure. Students begin by learning the set of rhyming pegwords, such as one and bun, two and shoe, three and tree. Each item to be remembered is then visually linked to the pegword image.

Chunking strategies

Individuals with limits in short-term memory or difficulty with encoding, storing, and retrieving information will benefit from using chunking, or grouping strategies. *Chunking* refers to pairing or associating individual elements into groups, making them easier to remember (Dehn, 2008). It is difficult to recall the individual numbers of a 10-digit phone number. When the numbers are grouped into area code, prefix, and line number, they are much easier to store and recall.

Interventions Organized by Cognitive Ability

Evidence-based interventions also exist for each of the CHC cognitive abilities. Some of the interventions, depending on the cognitive ability, are similar to those identified for achievement areas. Verbal ability, for example, has many of the same types of interventions as those de-

≣ *Rapid Reference 10.7*

Effective Interventions for Verbal Ability (*Gc*)

- Create a language- and experience-rich environment (e.g., Hart & Risley, 1995).
- Provide frequent exposure and practice with words (e.g., Hart & Risley, 1995).
- Read aloud to the child (e.g., Adams, 1990).
- Use text talks (e.g., Beck & McKeown, 2001).
- Increase time spent reading (e.g., Cunningham & Stanovich, 1991).
- Read for different purposes (e.g., NRP, 2000).
- Provide direct instruction in morphology (e.g., Carlisle, 2004).
- Provide intentional, explicit word instruction (e.g., NRP, 2000).
- Develop word consciousness (e.g., Graves & Watts-Taffe, 2002).
- Use relevant computer programs (e.g., Davidson, Elcock, & Noyes, 1996).

scribed in Chapter 5 for vocabulary and reading comprehension. A summary of effective interventions for verbal ability (*Gc*) is presented in Rapid Reference 10.7. Auditory processing, which includes phonemic awareness, shares the same types of interventions that were described for phonological awareness and beginning phonics in Chapter 2. Rapid Reference 10.8 summarizes evidence-based interventions for auditory processing (*Ga*). Short-term memory and long-term retrieval share a number of interventions (see Rapid Reference 10.9). Interventions for fluid reasoning (*Gf*) are listed in Rapid Reference 10.10, and Rapid Reference 10.11 presents interventions for visual processing (*Gv*). Individuals with limitations in processing speed (*Gs*) may benefit from repeated practice, speed drills, and computer games that require him or her to make decisions quickly (Merzenich & Sameshina, 1993; Tallal et al., 1996).

≡ Rapid Reference 10.8

Effective Interventions for Auditory Processing (*Ga*)

- Expose young children to sounds, music, rhythms, and language (e.g., Strickland, 1991).
- Read aloud to the child (e.g., Adams, 1990).
- Provide opportunities to explore and manipulate sounds, words, and language (e.g., Adams, 1990).
- Provide daily practice with language (e.g., Bridge, Winograd, & Haley, 1983).
- Use explicit, systematic, synthetic phonics instruction (e.g., NRP, 2000).
- Use decodable texts for daily practice (e.g., Meyer & Felton, 1999).
- Listen to books on tape (e.g., Carbo, 1989).

≡ Rapid Reference 10.9

Effective Interventions for Short-Term Memory (*Gsm*) or Long-Term Retrieval (*Glr*)

- Rehearse information to be learned (e.g., Parente & Herrmann, 1996).
- Present activities that require elaboration (deep thinking) (e.g., Squire & Schacter, 2003).
- Provide overlearning (practice beyond mastery) (e.g., Squire & Schacter, 2003).
- Use mnemonics (e.g., Wolfe, 2001).
- Employ visual representations (e.g., Greenleaf & Wells-Papanek, 2005).
- Teach chunking strategies (e.g., Hardiman, 2003).

≡ Rapid Reference 10.10

Effective Interventions for Fluid Reasoning (*Gf*)

- Provide opportunities to sort, classify, and categorize (e.g., Quinn, 2004).
- Use teacher demonstrations with a think-aloud procedure followed by guided practice with feedback (e.g., Klauer, Willmes, & Phye, 2002).
- Make use of graphic organizers (e.g., Marzano et al., 2001).
- Teach metacognitive and problem-solving strategies (e.g., Manning & Payne, 1996).
- Use cooperative groups and reciprocal teaching.

≡ Rapid Reference 10.11

Effective Interventions for Visual Processing (*Gv*)

- Employ multisensory teaching methods (e.g., Williams, Richman, & Yarbrough, 1992).
- Provide activities designed to develop discrimination of visual features, matching, and recalling visual information (e.g., Greenleaf & Wells-Papanek, 2005).
- Use language to describe visual information.
- Teach cognitive-behavioral intervention of private speech (e.g., Meichenbaum, 1977).

Accommodations

At times, specific accommodations are necessary to provide a student with access to learning. Accommodations should not alter the nature of the underlying task, but rather make it possible for the student to participate in the task. They adjust the manner in which testing and instruc-

CAUTION

For accommodations to be most effective the teacher must support them and the student must be willing to use them.

tion are presented and/or evaluated so that students can access information or demonstrate knowledge in a fair, equitable manner (Gregg & Lindstrom, 2008). Rapid Reference 10.12 summarizes some common classroom accommodations. Accommodations may be offered by teachers in general education when students struggle, or, if students are identified with a disability, they may be mandated. Students with Individual Educational Programs (IEPs) or 504 Plans have a legal right to the accommodations specified in their plans. In addition, if a student with an identified disability is planning to attend college, the College Board is

≣ *Rapid Reference 10.12*

Examples of Common Classroom Accommodations

- Provide extended time on assignments and tests
- Provide preferential seating
- Stand near the student when giving directions
- Display classroom rules and/or daily routine in writing
- Allow tape recording of class discussions or lectures
- Accept word-processed assignments (instead of handwritten)
- Allow oral or audio-taped assignments (instead of written)
- Combine visual media with oral instruction (e.g., overhead, document camera)
- Incorporate technology (e.g., computers, calculators, PDAs)
- Provide an outline of content to be covered in the lesson
- Use peer tutoring
- Individualize assignments (e.g., adjust length or due dates)

⚊ *Rapid Reference 10.13*

Accommodations that May Be Allowed by the College Board (individual basis)

Presentation

- Large print, fewer items on a page
- Read, sign, or orally present instructions
- Colored paper, highlighter, color overlays, plastic covered pages
- Visual or auditory magnification, audio cassette
- Braille, Braille graphs, Braille device for written responses

Responding

- Verbal (dictated to a scribe)
- Tape recorder, computer without spell or grammar check or cut/paste features
- Record answers in test booklet, large block answer sheet

Timing/Scheduling

- Frequent breaks, extended time
- Multiple days, specified time of day

Setting

- Small group, private room, screens to block out distractions
- Special lighting, special acoustics, adaptive/special furniture or tools
- Alternative test site (proctor present)
- Preferential seating

responsible for ensuring that the student receives appropriate accommodations on the college entrance exam. The College Board divides accommodations into four categories: presentation, responding, timing/scheduling, and setting (see Rapid Reference 10.13). More information can be found at www.collegeboard.com/ssd/student/accom.html.

CAUTION

Accommodations do not replace instruction, but rather are adaptations to facilitate access to learning or demonstration of one's learning and knowledge (Gregg & Lindstrom, 2008).

Accommodations for limits in short-term memory or long-term retrieval

Individuals with limits in short-term memory or in the storage and retrieval processes may benefit from accommodations in the presentation of information. For example, oral directions should be kept short and simple. Asking the individual to paraphrase the directions can help ensure the directions are understood. Visual cues serve as a more permanent reminder and may be helpful. These students will also need to spend more time studying and rehearsing information.

Accommodations for limits in auditory processing

Students with weaknesses in auditory processing may perform better in a quiet learning environment so that it is easier to attend to the relevant auditory stimuli (Bellis, 2003). Another accommodation could involve seating the individual close to the primary channels of auditory information (Zentall, 1983). These students often have difficulty perceiving speech sounds, which affects spelling, so they may need to obtain a copy of class notes or use a tape recorder to reduce the need to take notes. Depending upon the level of writing skill, students may need extended time or shorter assignments. Additionally, students with auditory processing deficits may benefit from seeing visual representations of the information that is presented orally.

Accommodations for limits in visual processing

Of all of the cognitive abilities, visual processing is least related to academic performance (Floyd et al., 2003). Thus, students with weaknesses in visual processing may not require any accommodations. If a student has trouble interpreting visual information, possible accommodations include enlarging print materials, reducing the amount of visual information the individual sees at one time, making use of color-coding, or providing repeated exposures to printed visuals.

Accommodations for limits in processing speed

Accommodations that compensate for limitations in processing speed include providing extended time and/or reducing the quantity of work required (breaking large assignments into two or more component assignments). In addition, activities requiring copying information from a book or the board should be limited or eliminated.

Modifications for limits in oral language or reasoning

Students with poor oral language or reasoning abilities will usually require changes in the type of instruction, rather than just accommodations, such as a differing format to the materials or the provision of more time. The major modification often necessary for students with more limited language and reasoning abilities is an adjustment in the difficulty level of the materials: The amount of material needs to be reduced, the level of vocabulary simplified, and the concepts thoroughly explained with numerous examples. The materials are still challenging, but at an appropriate level of difficulty for the student so that learning and mastery are possible and supported. As we note throughout this book, oral language is the basis for development of reading comprehension, written expression, and math problem solving so adjustments will need to be made in much of the academic content. Students must also be allotted sufficient time for review and practice, as well as time to share and discuss their ideas. In addition, students who are slow processors of language will benefit from increased "wait" times after questions are asked as well as after responses are given. As Thomas Jefferson said, "There is nothing as unequal as the equal treatment of unequals." Children with low language and/or reasoning will need access to a modified curriculum that is tailored to their ability levels.

CONCLUSION

Is knowledge of an individual's cognitive abilities relevant to planning appropriate academic interventions and accommodations? It seems clear that the answer is *yes*. Knowledge of the individual's unique pattern of strengths and weaknesses informs the instructional planning process, helps determine the need for and types of accommodations, and helps verify the presence of a specific learning disability. If two individuals have reading difficulties, an appropriate instructional program cannot be determined without understanding the underlying reasons for their poor reading achievement. This is particularly true if these children have failed to respond adequately to instruction. One has to ask: Why are they not responding? If one has a weakness in verbal ability and the other has adequate verbal ability, but poor phonemic awareness, the selection of instructional plans will be quite different. Each learner is unique and instruction must be differentiated to meet these unique needs.

In the past, intelligence testing was often focused on global scores and discrepancies between that global score and achievement. That information was not valuable to instruction. Modern cognitive tests are based on well-researched theories and measure an array of important cognitive and linguistic abilities. Scores on these specific measures provide far more meaningful information than a single global score. The challenge for assessment professionals is to understand the relationship between cognitive abilities and achievement and then use that information when diagnosing certain disabilities, identifying the necessary supports and accommodations, and planning differentiated instructional interventions.

Both educators and evaluators alike must try to incorporate research findings into their daily practices, recognize and plan for individual differences in learning abilities, and match instructional methods and materials to the unique needs of each learner. This is not an easy task. For children with learning problems, learning is hard work, and for their teachers, instruction is hard work and requires an enormous amount of training and support (Semrud-Clikeman, 2005). Despite these challenges, our job is to embrace the task of helping to ensure that all students are provided with appropriate and effective instruction throughout their school years. As noted by Cruickshank, "Diagnosis must take second place to instruction, and must be made a tool of instruction, not an end in itself" (1977, p. 193). Comprehensive evaluations are necessary for understanding a student's unique pattern of strengths and weaknesses, and then using that information to design an efficacious, individually tailored instructional program.

🐊 TEST YOURSELF 🐊

1. **Cognitive abilities have different correlations with different areas of achievement.** True or False?

2. **It is easy to examine cognitive abilities in isolation.** True or False?

3. **Effective teaching principles are effective because**

    (a) they have been around a long time.

    (b) they use the brain's natural tendencies.

    (c) they require active engagement of the learner.

    (d) b and c

4. **Cognitive strategy instruction is effective for improving achievement, especially for students with learning disabilities.** True or False?

5. **Metacognition is** _____.

6. **Self-instruction is**

    (a) doing work independently.

    (b) self-talk.

    (c) instruction about the individual.

    (d) All of the above.

    (e) None of the above.

(continued)

7. A mnemonic may be

(a) a rhyme.

(b) an acronym.

(c) an acrostic.

(d) All of the above.

(e) None of the above.

8. Interventions for low verbal ability are similar to interventions for _____.

9. An appropriate intervention for an individual with weak short-term memory is _____.

10. Cognitive abilities are relevant to academic interventions. True or False?

Answers: 1. True; 2. False; 3. d; 4. True; 5. thinking about your thinking (being self-aware and self-regulating); 6. b; 7. d; 8. reading (vocabulary); 9. teaching chunking strategies (rehearsal, overlearning, elaboration, mnemonics, visual representations); 10. True

References

Abbott, M. (2001). Identifying reliable generalizations for spelling words: The importance of multilevel analysis. *Elementary School Journal, 101,* 233–245.

Ackerman, P. T., Weir, N. L., Metzler, D. P., & Dykman, R. A. (1996). A study of adolescent poor readers. *Learning Disabilities Research & Practice, 11,* 68–77.

Adams, M. J. (1990). *Beginning to read: Thinking and learning about print.* Cambridge, MA: MIT Press.

Adams, G., & Brown, S. (2003). *Six-minute solution.* Longmont, CO: Sopris West Educational Services.

Ahmed, A., Clark-Jeavons, A., & Oldknow, A. (2004). How can teaching aids improve the quality of mathematics education. *Educational Studies in Mathematics, 56,* 313–328.

Allinder, R. M., Bolling, R. M., Oats, R. G., & Gagnon, W. A. (2000). Effects of teacher self-monitoring on implementation of curriculum-based measurement and mathematics computation achievement of students with disabilities. *Remedial and Special Education, 21,* 219–226.

Allington, R. (1983). Fluency: The neglected reading goal. *Reading Teacher, 36,* 556–561.

Allsopp, D. H. (1997). Using classwide peer tutoring to teach beginning algebra problem-solving skills in heterogeneous classrooms. *Remedial and Special Education, 18,* 367–379.

Allsopp, D. H. (1999). Using modeling, manipulatives, and mnemonics with eighth-grade math students. *Teaching Exceptional Children, 32,* 78–81.

Allsopp, D. H., Kyger, M. M., & Lovin, L. H. (2007). *Teaching mathematics meaningfully: Solutions for reaching struggling learners.* Baltimore: Paul H. Brookes Publishing Co.

Anders, P., & Bos, C. (1986). Semantic feature analysis: An interactive strategy for vocabulary development and text comprehension. *Journal of Reading, 9,* 610–616.

Anderson, R. C. (1996). Research foundations to support wide reading. In V. Greaney (Ed.), *Promoting reading in developing countries* (pp. 55–77). Newark, DE: International Reading Association.

Anderson, R. C., & Nagy, W. E. (1992). The vocabulary conundrum. *American Educator, 16,* 14–18, 44–47.

Anderson, R. C., & Pearson, P. D. (1984). A schema-theoretic view of basic processes in reading comprehension. In P. D. Pearson, R. Barr, M. L. Kamil, & P. B. Mosenthal (Eds.), *Handbook of reading research* (Vol. 1, pp. 255–291). New York: Longman.

Andersson, U. (2008). Mathematical competencies in children with different types of learning difficulties. *Journal of Educational Psychology, 100,* 48–66.

Anthony, J. L., & Francis, D. J. (2005). Development of phonological awareness. *Current Directions in Psychological Science, 14,* 255–259.

Arcavi, A. (2003). The role of visual representations in the learning of mathematics. *Educational Studies in Mathematics, 52,* 215–241.

Archer, A., & Isaacson, S. (1989). *Design and delivery of academic instruction.* Reston, VA: Council for Exceptional Children.

Armbruster, B. B., Lehr, F., & Osborn, J. (2001). *Put reading first: The research building blocks for teaching children to read.* Jessup, MD: National Institute for Literacy.

Ashcraft, M. H., Krause, J. A., & Hopko, D. R. (2007). Is math anxiety a mathematical learning disability? In D. B. Berch & M. M. M. Mazzocco (Eds). *Why is math so hard for some children? The nature and origins of mathematical learning difficulties and disabilities* (pp. 329–348). Baltimore: Paul H. Brookes Publishing Co.

Atkinson, R. K., Derry, S. J., Renkl, A., & Wortham, D. W. (2000). Learning from examples: Instructional principles from the worked examples research. *Review of Educational Research, 70,* 181–214.

August, D., Carlo, M., Dressler, C., & Snow, C. (2005). The critical role of vocabulary development for English language learners. *Learning Disabilities: Research & Practice 20,* 50–57.

Baker, S. K., Simmons, D. C., & Kameenui, E. J. (1995). *Vocabulary acquisition: Synthesis of the research.* Eugene: University of Oregon. Technical Report 13.

Ball, D. L., & Bass, H. (2000). Interweaving content and pedagogy in teaching and learning to teach: Knowing and using mathematics. In J. Boaler (Ed.), *Multiple perspectives on the teaching and learning of mathematics* (pp. 83–104). Stamford, CT: Ablex.

Baumann, J. F., Font, G., Edwards, E. C., & Boland, E. (2005). Strategies for teaching middle-grade students to use word-part and context clues to expand reading vocabulary. In E. H. Hiebert & M. L. Kamil (Eds.), *Teaching and learning vocabulary: Bringing research to practice* (pp. 179–205). Mahwah, NJ: Erlbaum.

Baumann, J. F., & Kame'enui, E. J. (1991). Research on vocabulary instruction: Ode to Voltaire. In J. Flood, D. Lapp, & J. R. Squire (Eds.), *Handbook of research on teaching the English language arts* (pp. 604–632). New York: Macmillan.

Baumann, J. F., Kame'enui, E. J., & Ash, G. E. (2003). Research on vocabulary instruction: Voltaire redux. In J. Flood, D. Lapp, J. R. Squire, & J. M.

Jensen (Eds.), *Handbook on research on teaching the English language arts* (2nd ed., pp. 752–785). Mahwah, NJ: Erlbaum.

Bear, D. R., Invernizzi, M., Templeton, S., & Johnston, F. (2008). *Words their way: Word study for phonics, vocabulary, and spelling instruction* (4th ed.). Upper Saddle River, NJ: Prentice-Hall.

Beck, I. L., Hamilton, R., Kucan, L., & McKeown, M. (1997). *Questioning the author: An approach for enhancing student engagement with text.* Newark, DE:International Reading Association.

Beck, I. L., & McKeown, M. G. (2001). Text talk: Capturing the benefits of read-aloud experiences for young children. *The Reading Teacher,* 55, 10–20.

Beck, I. L, & McKeown, M. G. (2005). *Text talk: Robust vocabulary instruction for grades K–3.* New York: Scholastic.

Beck, I. L., McKeown, M. G., & Kucan, L. (2002). *Bringing words to life: Robust vocabulary instruction.* New York: Guilford.

Bellis, T. J. (2003). *Assessment and management of central auditory processing disorders in the educational setting from science to practice.* Clifton Park, NY: Thomson.

Benson, V., & Cummins, C. (2000). *The power of retelling: Developmental steps for building comprehension.* Bothell, WA: Wright Group/McGraw-Hill.

Bereiter, C., & Bird, M. (1985). Use of thinking aloud in identification and teaching of reading comprehension strategies. *Cognition and Instruction, 2,* 131–156.

Berninger, V. (1990). Multiple orthographic codes: Key to alternative instructional methodologies for developing the orthographic phonological connections underlying word identification. *School Psychology Review, 19,* 518–533.

Berninger, V. (2008). Written language during early and middle childhood. In R. Morris & N. Mather (Eds.), *Evidence-based interventions for students with learning and behavioral challenges* (pp. 215–235). New York: Routledge.

Berninger, V., & Abbott, R. (1994). Redefining learning disabilities. Moving beyond aptitude-treatment discrepancies to failure to respond to validated treatment protocols. In G. R. Lyon (Ed.), *Frames of reference for the assessment of learning disabilities: New views on measurement issues* (pp. 163–202). Baltimore: Paul H. Brookes Publishing Co.

Berninger, V., & Abbott, S. (2003). *PAL research-supported reading and writing lessons.* San Antonio, TX: The Psychological Corporation.

Berninger, V., Abbott, R., Thomson, J., Wagner, R., Swanson, H. L., Wijsman, E., et al. (2006). Modeling developmental phonological core deficits within a working-memory architecture in children and adults with developmental dyslexia. *Scientific Study of Reading, 10,* 165–198.

Berninger, V., Abbott, R., Vermeulen, K., & Fulton, C. M. (2006). Paths to reading comprehension in at-risk second-grade readers. *Journal of Learning Disabilities, 39,* 334–351.

Berninger, V., & Amtmann, D. (2003). Preventing written expression disabilities through early and continuing assessment and intervention for handwriting and/or spelling problems: Research into practice. In H. L. Swanson, K. R. Harris, & S. Graham (Eds.), *Handbook of learning disabilities* (pp. 345–363). New York: Guilford.

Berninger, V., & Graham, S. (1998). Language by hand: A synthesis of a decade of research on handwriting. *Handwriting Review 12,* 11–25.

Berninger, V., & Richards, T. (2002). *Brain literacy for educators and psychologists.* San Diego, CA: Academic Press.

Berninger, V., Vaughn, K., Abbott, R., Abbott, S., Rogan, L., Brooks, A. et al. (1997). Treatment of handwriting problems in beginning writers: Transfer from handwriting to composition. *Journal of Educational Psychology, 89,* 652–666.

Berninger, V., & Winn, W. (2006). Implications of advancements in brain research and technology for writing development, writing instruction, and educational evolution. In C. MacArthur, S. Graham, & J. Fitzgerald (Eds.), *Handbook of writing research* (pp. 96–114). New York: Guilford.

Biancarosa, C., & Snow, C. E. (2004). *Reading next: A vision for action and research in middle and high school literacy.* Report from Carnegie Corporation of New York. Washington, DC: Alliance for Excellent Education.

Biemiller, A. (2004). Teaching vocabulary in the primary grades. In J. F. Baumann & E. J. Kame'enui (Eds.), *Vocabulary instruction: Research to practice* (pp. 28–40). New York: Guilford.

Blachman, B. A., Ball, E. W., Black, R., & Tangel, D. M. (2000). *Road to the code: A phonological awareness program for young children.* Baltimore: Paul H. Brookes Publishing Co.

Blachowicz, C. (2005). *Vocabulary essentials: From research to practice for improved instruction.* Glenview, IL: Scott Foresman.

Blachowicz, C., & Fisher, P. (2000). Vocabulary instruction. In M. Kamil, P. Mosenthal, P. D. Pearson, & R. Barr (Eds.), *Handbook of reading research* (Vol. 3, pp. 503–523). Mahwah, NJ: Erlbaum.

Blachowicz, C., & Fisher, P. (2004). Keeping the "fun" in fundamental: Encouraging word awareness and incidental word learning in the classroom through word play. In In J. F. Baumann & E. J. Kame'enui (Eds.), *Vocabulary instruction: Research to practice* (pp. 218–237). New York: Guilford.

Blachowicz, C., Fisher, P. J., & Watts-Taffe, S. (2005). *Integrated vocabulary instruction: Meeting the needs of diverse learners in grades K–5.* Naperville, IL: Learning Point Associates.

Block, C. C., & Pressley, M. (2002). Introduction. In C. C. Block & M. Pressley (Eds.), *Comprehension instruction: Research-based best practices* (pp. 1–7). New York: Guilford.

Bond, G. L., & Dykstra, R. ([1967]; 1997). The cooperative research program in first-grade reading instruction. *Reading Research Quarterly, 32,* 348–427.

Bottge, B. A., Heinrichs, M., Chan, S., Mehta, Z. D., & Watson, E. (2003). Effects of video-based and applied problems on the procedural math skills of average- and low-achieving adolescents. *Journal of Special Education Technology, 18,* 5–22.

Bridge, C. A., Winograd, P. N., & Haley, D. (1983). Using predictable materials vs. preprimers to teach beginning sight words. *The Reading Teacher, 36,* 884–891.

Brophy, J., & Good, T. (1986). Teacher behavior and student achievement. In M. Wittock (Ed.), *Third handbook of research on teaching* (pp. 328–375). Chicago: Rand McNally.

Brown, A. L., Palincsar, A. S., & Purcell, L. (1986). Poor readers: Teach, don't label. In U. Neisser (Ed.), *The academic performance of minority children: New perspectives* (pp. 105–143). Hillsdale, NJ: Erlbaum.

Bruck, M. (1988). The word recognition and spelling of dyslexic children. *Reading Research Quarterly, 23,* 51–69.

Bryant, B. R., Bryant, D. P., Kethley, C., Kim, S. A., Pool, C., & Seo, Y. (2008). Preventing mathematics difficulties in the primary grades: The critical features of instruction in textbooks as part of the equation. *Learning Disabilities Quarterly, 31,* 21–35.

Bryant, D. P. (2005). Commentary on early identification and intervention for students with mathematical difficulties. *Journal of Learning Disabilities, 38,* 340–345.

Bryant, D. P., Bryant, B. R., & Hammill, D. D. (2000). Characteristic behaviors of students with LD who have teacher-identified math weaknesses. *Journal of Learning Disabilities, 33,* 168–177.

Bull, R., & Johnston, R. S. (1997). Children's arithmetical difficulties: Contributions from processing speed, item identification, and short-term memory. *Journal of Experimental Child Psychology, 65,* 1–24.

Burchers, S. (1997). *Vocabulary cartoons.* Punta Gorda, FL: New Monic Books.

Burchers, S. (2000). *Vocabulary cartoons II.* Punta Gorda, FL: New Monic Books.

Butler, F. M., Miller, S. P., Crehan, K., Babbitt, B., & Pierce, T. (2003). Fraction instruction for students with mathematics disabilities: Comparing two teaching sequences. *Learning Disabilities Research & Practice, 18,* 99–111.

Cain, K., Oakhill, J. V., Barnes, M. A., & Bryant, P. E. (2001). Comprehension skill, inference-making ability, and their relation to knowledge. *Memory and Cognition, 29,* 850–859.

Calderón, M., August, D., Slavin, R., Duran, D., Madden, N., & Cheung, A. (2005). Bring words to life in classrooms with English-language learners. In

E. H. Hiebert & M. L. Kamil (Eds.), *Teaching and learning vocabulary: Bringing research to practice* (pp. 115–136). Mahwah, NJ: Erlbaum.

Calhoon, M. B., & Fuchs, L. S. (2003). The effects of peer-assisted learning strategies and curriculum-based measurement on the mathematics performance of secondary students with disabilities. *Remedial and Special Education, 24,* 235–245.

Campbell, K. U. (1998). *Great leaps reading program* (4th ed.). Gainesville, FL: Diarmuid.

Campbell, K. U. (2005). *Great leaps reading program grades 3–5.* Gainesville, FL: Diarmuid.

Carbo, M. (1989). *How to record books for maximum reading gains.* New York: National Reading Styles Institute.

Carlisle, J. F. (1987). The use of morphological knowledge in spelling derived forms by learning-disabled and normal students. *Annals of Dyslexia, 37,* 90–108.

Carlisle, J.F. (2004). Morphological processes influencing literacy learning. In K. Apel, B. Ehren, E. Silliman, & C.A. Stone (Eds.), *Handbook of language and literacy* (pp. 318-339). New York: Guilford.

Carlisle, J. F., & Rice, M. S. (2002). *Improving reading comprehension: Research-based principles and practices.* Baltimore: York Press.

Carnine, D. (1980). Relationships between stimulus variation and the formation of misconceptions. *Journal of Educational Research, 74,* 106–110.

Carnine, D. (1998). Instructional design in mathematics for students with learning disabilities. In D. Rivera (Ed.), *Mathematics education for students with learning disabilities* (pp. 119–138). Austin, TX: Pro-Ed.

Carnine, D.W., Silbert, J., Kame'enui, E.J., & Tarver, S.G. (2004). *Direct instruction reading* (4th ed.). Upper Saddle River, NJ: Pearson Education.

Carreker, S. (2005a). Teaching reading: Accurate decoding and fluency. In J. R. Birsh (Ed.), *Multisensory teaching of basic language skills* (2nd ed., pp. 141–182). Baltimore: Paul H. Brookes Publishing Co.

Carreker, S. (2005b). Teaching spelling. In J. R. Birsh (Ed.), *Multisensory teaching of basic language skills* (2nd ed., pp. 257–295). Baltimore: Paul H. Brookes Publishing Co.

Carver, R. P. (1990). *Reading rate: A review of research and theory.* San Diego, CA: Academic Press.

Case, R. (1998, April). *A psychological model of number sense and its development.* Paper presented at the annual meeting of the American Educational Research Association, San Diego.

Case, R., & Griffin, S. (1989). Child cognitive development: The role of central conceptual structures in the development of scientific and social thought. In C. A. Hauert (Ed.), *Advances in psychology: Developmental psychology* (pp. 193–230). Amsterdam: Elsevier.

Case, L. P., Harris, K. R., & Graham, S. (1992). Improving the mathematical problem-solving skills of students with learning disabilities: Self-regulated strategy development. *Journal of Special Education, 26,* 1–19.

Cass, M., Cates, D., Smith, M., & Jackson, C. (2003). Effects of manipulative instruction on solving area and perimeter problems by students with learning disabilities. *Learning Disabilities Research & Practice, 18,* 112–120.

Cawley, J. F., Parmar, R. S., Yan, W. E., & Miller, J. H. (1996). Arithmetic computation abilities of students with learning disabilities: Implications for instruction. *Learning Disabilities Research & Practice, 11,* 230–237.

Cawley, J. F., Parmar, R. S., Yan, W. E., & Miller, J. H. (1998). Arithmetic computation performance of students with learning disabilities: Implications for curriculum. *Learning Disabilities Research & Practice, 13,* 68–74.

Cawley, J. F., Shepard, T., Smith, M., & Parmar, R. (1997). Item mass and complexity and the arithmetic computation of students with learning disabilities. *Learning Disabilities: A Multidisciplinary Journal, 8,* 97–107.

Chall, J. S. (1996). *Stages of reading development.* New York: McGraw-Hill.

Chall, J. S., Jacobs, V. A., & Baldwin, L. E. (1990). *The reading crisis: Why poor children fall behind.* Cambridge, MA: Harvard University Press.

Chard, D. J., Baker, S. K., Clarke, B., Jungjohann, K., Davis, K., & Smolkowski, K. (2008). Preventing early mathematics difficulties: The feasibility of a rigorous kindergarten mathematics curriculum. *Learning Disability Quarterly, 31,* 11–20.

Chard, D. J., & Osborn, J. (1999). Phonics and word recognition instruction in early reading programs: Guidelines for accessibility. *Learning Disabilities Research & Practice, 14,* 107–117.

Chard, D. J., Vaughn, S., & Tyler, B. J. (2002). A synthesis of research on effective interventions for building reading fluency with elementary students with learning disabilities. *Journal of Learning Disabilities, 35,* 386–406.

Clay, M. M. (1982). *Observing the young reader.* Auckland, New Zealand: Heinemann.

Clements, D. (1996). Rethinking "concrete" manipulatives. *Teaching Exceptional Children, 2,* 270–279.

Cobb, P. (1991). Reconstructing elementary school mathematics. *Focus on Learning Problems in Mathematics, 13,* 3–32.

Connelly, V., Campbell, S., MacLean, M., & Barnes, J. (2006). Contribution of lower-order skills to the written composition of college students with and without dyslexia. *Developmental Neuropsychology, 29,* 175–196.

Coyne, M. D., Simmons, D. C., & Kame'enui, E. J. (2004). Vocabulary instruction for young children at risk of experiencing reading difficulties: Teaching word meanings during shared storybook readings. In J. F. Baumann & E. J.

Kame'enui (Eds.), *Vocabulary instruction: Research to practice* (pp. 41–58). New York: Guilford.

Cruickshank, W. M. (1977). Least-restrictive placement: Administrative wishful thinking. *Journal of Learning Disabilities, 10,* 193–194.

Cummings, J. J., & Elkins, J. (1999). Lack of automaticity in the basic addition facts as a characteristic of arithmetic learning problems and instructional needs. *Mathematical Cognition, 5,* 149–180.

Cunningham, A. E., & Stanovich, K. E. (1991). Tracking the unique effects of print. *Journal of Educational Psychology, 83,* 264–274.

Cunningham, A. E., & Stanovich, K. E. (1997). Early reading acquisition and its relation to reading experience and ability 10 years later. *Developmental Psychology, 33,* 934–945.

Cunningham, A. E., & Stanovich, K. E. (1998). What reading does for the mind. *American Educator, 22* (1 & 2), 8–15.

Cunningham, J. W. (1982). Generating interactions between schemata and text. In J. A. Niles & L. A. Harris (Eds.), *New inquiries in reading research and instruction* (pp. 42–47). Rochester, NY: National Reading Conference.

Cunningham, P. M., & Cunningham, J. W. (1992). Making WORDS: Enhancing the invented spelling-decoding connection. *Reading Teacher, 46,* 106–115.

Davidson, J., Elcock, J., & Noyes, P. (1996). A preliminary study of the effect of computer-assisted practice on reading attainment. *Journal of Research in Reading, 19*(2), 102–110.

Dehaene, S., Spelke, E., Pinel, P., Stanescu, R., & Tsivkin, S. (1999). Sources of mathematical thinking: Behavioral and brain-imaging evidence. *Science, 284,* 970–974.

Dehn, M. J. (2008). Cognitive processing deficits. In R. Morris & N. Mather (Eds.), *Evidence-based interventions for students with learning and behavioral challenges* (pp. 258–287). New York: Routledge.

De La Paz, S., Swanson, P. N., & Graham, S. (1998). The contribution of executive control to the revising by students with writing and learning difficulties. *Journal of Educational Psychology, 90,* 448–460.

Denton, C. A., Fletcher, J. M., Anthony, J. L., & Francis, D. J. (2006). An evaluation of intensive interventions for students with persistent reading difficulties. *Journal of Learning Disabilities, 39,* 447–466.

Diamond, L., & Gutlohn, L. (2006). *Vocabulary handbook.* Baltimore: Paul H. Brookes Publishing Co.

Dickson, S., Simmons, D. C., & Kame'enui, E. J. (1998). Text organization: Research bases. In D. C. Simmons & E. J. Kame'enui (Eds.), *What reading research tells us about children with diverse learning needs* (pp. 239–277). Mahwah, NJ: Erlbaum.

Driscoll, M. (1986). *Stories of excellence: Ten case studies from a study of exemplary mathematics programs.* Reston, VA: NCTM.

Duke, N. K., & Pearson, P. D. (2002). Effective practices for developing reading comprehension. In A. E. Farstrup & S. J. Samuels (Eds.), *What research has to say about reading instruction* (3rd ed., pp. 205–242). Newark, DE: International Reading Association.

Dunlap, W. P., & Brennan, A. H. (1979). Developing mental images of mathematical processes. *Learning Disability Quarterly, 2,* 89–96.

Durkin, D. (1993). *Teaching them to read* (6th ed.). Boston: Allyn & Bacon.

Echevarria, J., Vogt, M. E., & Short, D. (2004). *Making content comprehensible for English language learners: The SIOP model* (2nd ed.). Boston: Pearson/Allyn & Bacon.

Edwards, C. E., Font, G., Baumann, J. F., & Boland, E. (2004). Unlocking word meanings: Strategies and guidelines for teaching morphemic and contextual analysis. In J. F. Baumann & E. J. Kame'enui (Eds.), *Vocabulary instruction: Research to practice* (pp. 159–176). New York: Guilford.

Ehri, L. C. (1995). Teachers need to know how word reading processes develop to teach reading effectively to beginners. In C. Hedley, T. Antonacci, & M. Rabinowitz (Eds.), *Literacy and thinking: The mind at work in the classroom* (pp. 167–188). Hillsdale, NJ: Erlbaum.

Ehri, L. C. (1998). Grapheme-phoneme knowledge is essential for learning to read words in English. In J. L. Metsala & L. C. Ehri (Eds.), *Word recognition in beginning literacy* (pp. 3–40). Mahwah, NJ: Lawrence Erlbaum.

Ehri, L. C. (2000). Learning to read and learning to spell: Two sides of a coin. *Topics in Language Disorders, 20*(3), 19–36.

Ehri, L. C. (2004). Teaching phonemic awareness and phonics. In P. M. McCardle & V. Chhabra (Eds.), *The voice of evidence in reading research* (pp. 153–186). Baltimore: Paul H. Brookes Publishing Co.

Ehri, L. C. (2006). Alphabetics instruction helps students learn to read. In R. M. Joshi & P. G. Aaron (Eds.), *Handbook of orthography and literacy* (pp. 649–677). Mahwah, NJ: Erlbaum.

Eldredge, J. L. (2005). Foundations of fluency: An exploration. *Reading Psychology, 26,* 161–181.

Elkonin, D. B. (1973). U.S.S.R. In J. Downing (Ed.), *Comparative reading: Cross national studies of behavior and processes in reading and writing* (pp. 551–579). New York: Macmillan.

Ellis, E. S. (1993). Integrative strategy instruction: A potential model for teaching content area subjects to adolescents with learning disabilities. *Journal of Learning Disabilities, 26,* 358–383.

Ellis, E. S., & Colvert, G. (1996). Writing strategy instruction. In D. D. Deshler,

E. S. Ellis, & B. K. Lenz (Eds.), *Teaching adolescents with learning disabilities* (2nd ed. pp. 127–207). Denver, CO: Love Publishing Company.

Ellis, E. S., & Friend, P. (1991). Adolescents with learning disabilities. In B. Y. L. Wong (Ed.), *Learning about learning disabilities* (pp. 505–561). San Diego, CA: Academic Press.

Ellis, E. S., Worthington, L. A., & Larkin, M. J. (1994). *Effective teaching principles and the design of quality tools for educators.* A commissioned paper for the National Center to Improve the Tools of Education (NCITE). Eugene, OR: The University of Oregon.

Engelmann, S. (1975). *Your child can succeed.* New York: Simon & Schuster.

Engelmann, S., & Carnine, D. (1975). *Distar Arithmetic.* Columbus, OH: SRA.

Engelmann, S., & Carnine, D. (1982). *Theory of instruction: Principles and applications.* New York: Irvington.

eSchool News (2005, April). *Readers' choice awards* (pp. 31–33). Bethesda, MD: Author.

Evans, J. J., Floyd, R. G., McGrew, K. S., & Leforgee, M. H. (2002). The relations between measures of Cattell-Horn-Carroll (CHC) cognitive abilities and reading achievement during childhood and adolescence. *School Psychology Review, 31,* 246–262.

Fantuzzo, J., & Ginsburg-Block, M. (1998). Reciprocal peer tutoring: Developing and testing effective peer collaborations for elementary school students. In K. Topping & S. Ehly (Eds.) *Peer-assisted learning* (pp. 121–144). Mahwah, NJ: Erlbaum.

Fantuzzo, J. W., King, J., & Heller, L. R. (1992). Effects of reciprocal peer tutoring on mathematics and school adjustment: A component analysis. *Journal of Educational Psychology, 84,* 331–339.

Feldman, K., & Kinsella, K. (2004). *Narrowing the language gap: The case for explicit vocabulary instruction.* Scholastic Professional Paper. New York: Scholastic.

Fernald, G. (1943). *Remedial techniques in basic school subjects.* New York: McGraw-Hill.

Figueredo, L., & Varnhagen, C. K. (2004). Detecting a problem is half the battle: The relation between error type and spelling performance. *Scientific Studies of Reading, 5,* 337–356.

Fletcher, J. M., Lyon, G. R., Fuchs, L. S., & Barnes, M. A. (2007). *Learning disabilities: From identification to intervention.* New York: Guilford.

Flood, J. & Lapp, D. (1991). Reading comprehension instruction. In J. Flood, J. M. Jensen, D. Lapp, & J. R. Squire (Eds.), *Handbook of research on teaching the English language arts* (pp. 732–742). New York: Macmillan.

Flood, J., Lapp, D., & Fisher, D. (2005). Neurological impress method plus. *Reading Psychology, 26,* 147–160.

Floyd, R. G., Evans, J. J., & McGrew, K. S. (2003). Relations between measures of Cattell-Horn-Carroll (CHC) cognitive abilities and mathematics achievement across the school-age years. *Psychology in the Schools, 40,* 155–171.

Floyd, R. G., McGrew, K. S., & Evans, J. J. (2008). The relative contribution of the Cattell-Horn-Carroll cognitive abilities in explaining writing achievement during childhood and adolescence. *Psychology in the Schools, 45,* 132–144.

Foorman, B., Seals, L., Anthony, J., & Pollard-Durodola, S. (2003). Vocabulary enrichment program for third and fourth grade African American students: Description, implementation, and impact. In B. Foorman (Ed.) *Preventing and remediating reading difficulties: Bringing science to scale* (pp. 419–441). Austin, TX: Pro-Ed.

Francis, D. J., Shaywitz, S. E., Stuebing, K. K., Shaywitz, B. A., & Fletcher, J. M. (1996). Developmental lag versus deficit models of reading disability: A longitudinal, individual growth curves analysis. *Journal of Educational Psychology, 88,* 3–17.

Frayer, D., Frederick, W. C., & Klausmeier, H. J. (1969). *A schema for testing the level of cognitive mastery.* Madison, WI: Wisconsin Center for Education Research.

Frederickson, N. (2002). Evidence based practice and educational psychology. *Educational and Child Psychology, 19,* 96–111.

Fry, E. B. (1977). *Elementary reading instruction.* New York: McGraw-Hill.

Fuchs, D., Fuchs, L. S., Mathes, P. G., & Martinez, E. A. (2002). Preliminary evidence on the social standing of students with learning disabilities in PALS and No-PALS classrooms. *Learning Disabilities Research & Practice, 17,* 205–215.

Fuchs, D., & Fuchs, L. S., & Maxwell, L. (1988). The validity of informal reading comprehension measures. *Remedial and Special Education, 9,* 20–28.

Fuchs, L. S., & Fuchs D. (1995). Acquisition and transfer effects of classwide peer-assisted learning strategies in mathematics. *School Psychology Review, 24,* 604–620.

Fuchs, L. S., & Fuchs, D. (2007). Mathematical problem solving: Instructional intervention. In D. B. Berch & M. M. M. Mazzocco (Eds). *Why is math so hard for some children? The nature and origins of mathematical learning difficulties and disabilities,* (pp. 397–414). Baltimore: Paul H. Brookes Publishing Co.

Fuchs, L. S., Fuchs, D., Compton, D. L., Powell, S. R., Seethaler, P. M., Capizzi, A. M., et al. (2006). The cognitive correlates of third-grade skill in arithmetic, algorithmic computation, and arithmetic word problems. *Journal of Educational Psychology, 98*(1), 29–43.

Fuchs, L. S., Fuchs, D., Hamlett, C. L., Phillips, N. B., Karns, K., & Dutka, S. (1997). Enhancing students' helping behavior during peer tutoring with conceptual mathematical explanations. *Elementary School Journal, 97,* 223–250.

Fuchs, L. S., Fuchs, D., Hosp, M. K., & Jenkins, J. (2001). Oral reading fluency as an indicator of reading competence: A theoretical, empirical, and historical analysis. *Scientific Studies of Reading, 5,* 239–256.

Fuchs, L. S., Fuchs, D., & Kazdan, S. (1999). Effects of peer-assisted learning strategies on high school students with serious reading problems. *Remedial and Special Education, 20,* 309–318.

Fuchs, L. S., Fuchs, D., Mathes, P. G., & Simmons, D. C. (1997). Peer-assisted learning strategies: Making classrooms more responsive to academic diversity. *American Education Research Journal, 34,* 174–206.

Fuchs, L. S., Fuchs, D., Powell, S. R., Seethaler, P. M., Cirino, P. T., & Fletcher, J. M. (2008). Intensive intervention for students with mathematics disabilities: Seven principles of effective practice. *Learning Disability Quarterly, 31,* 79–92.

Fuchs, L. S., Fuchs, D., Prentice, K., Burch, M., Hamlett, C. L., Owen, R., et al. (2003a). Explicitly teaching for transfer: Effects on third-grade students' mathematical problem solving. *Journal of Educational Psychology, 95,* 293–304.

Fuchs, L. S., Fuchs, D., Prentice, K., Burch, M., Hamlett, C. L., Owen, R., et al. (2003b). Enhancing third-grade students' mathematical problem solving with self-regulated learning strategies. *Journal of Educational Psychology, 95,* 306–315.

Fuchs, L. S., Fuchs, D., Stuebing, K., Fletcher, J. M., Hamlett, C. L., & Lambert, W. (2008). Problem solving and computational skill: Are they shared or distinct aspects of mathematical cognition? *Journal of Educational Psychology, 100,* 30–47.

Fuchs, L. S., Fuchs, D., Yazdian, L., & Powell, S. R. (2002). Enhancing first-grade children's mathematical development with peer-assisted learning strategies. *School Psychology Review, 31,* 569–583.

Gagatsis, A., & Shiakalli, M. (2004). Ability to translate from one representation of the concept of function to another and mathematical problem solving. *Educational Psychology, 24,* 645–657.

Gallagher, M., & Pearson, P. D. (1989). *Discussion, comprehension, and knowledge acquisition in content area classrooms* (Tech. Rep. No. 480). Urbana, IL: University of Illinois, Center for the Study of Reading.

Gardner, H. (1991). *The unschooled mind: How children think and how schools should teach.* New York: Basic Books.

Garnett, K. (1998). Math learning disabilities. *Learning Disabilities Journal.* LD Online. Retrieved February 11, 2008, from http://www.ldonline.org/ld_in-depth/math_skills/garnett.html.

Garnett, K., Frank, B., & Fleischner, J. E. (1983). *A strategies generalization approach to basic fact learning.* Research Institute for the Study of Learning Disabilities. New York: Teachers College, Columbia University.

Geary, D. C. (1993). Mathematical disabilities: Cognitive, neuropsychological, and genetic components. *Psychological Bulletin, 114,* 345–362.

Geary, D. C. (1994). *Children's mathematical development: Research and practical applications.* Washington, DC: American Psychological Association.

Geary, D. C. (2003). Learning disabilities in arithmetic: Problem-solving differences and cognitive deficits. In H. L. Swanson, K. R. Harris, & S. Graham (Eds.), *Handbook of learning disabilities* (pp. 199–212). New York: Guilford.

Geary, D. C. (2004). Mathematics and learning disabilities. *Journal of Learning Disabilities, 37,* 4–15.

Geary, D. C. (2007). An evolutionary perspective on learning disabilities in mathematics. *Developmental Neuropsychology, 32,* 471–519.

Geary, D. C., & Hoard, M. K. (2005). Learning disabilities in arithmetic and mathematics. In J. I. D. Campbell (Ed.), *Handbook of mathematical cognition* (pp. 253–267). New York: Psychology Press.

Gersten, R., & Baker, S. (1999). *Teaching expressive writing to students with learning disabilities: A meta-analysis.* Eugene, OR: University of Oregon.

Gersten, R., & Chard, D. (2001). Number sense: Rethinking arithmetic instruction for students with mathematical disabilities. *Journal of Special Education, 33,* 18–28.

Gersten, R., Fuchs, L. S., Williams, J. P., & Baker, S. (2001). Teaching reading comprehension strategies to students with learning disabilities: A review of the research. *Review of Educational Research, 71,* 279–320.

Gersten, R., Jordan, N. C., & Flojo, J. R. (2005). Early identification and interventions for students with mathematics difficulties. *Journal of Learning Disabilities, 38,* 293–304.

Gildroy, P., & Deshler, D. (2008). Effective learning strategy instruction. In R. Morris & N. Mather (Eds.), *Evidence-based interventions for students with learning and behavioral challenges* (pp. 288–301). New York: Routledge.

Glazer, S. M. (1989). Oral language and literacy. In D. S. Strickland & L. M. Morrow (Eds.), *Emerging literacy: Young children learn to read and write* (pp. 16–26). Newark, DE: International Reading Association.

Glover, M. A. (1992). The effect of the hand-held calculator on the computation and problem-solving achievement of students with learning disabilities. (State University of New York at Buffalo, 1991). Dissertation Abstracts International, 52, 3888A.

Goodlad, J. (1984). *A place called school.* New York: McGraw-Hill.

Grace, K. (2007). *Phonics and spelling through phoneme-grapheme mapping.* Longmont, CO: Sopris West.

Graham, S., Berninger, V., Abbott, R. D., Abbott, S. P., & Whitaker, D. (1997).

Role of mechanics in composing of elementary school students: A new methodological approach. *Journal of Educational Psychology, 89,* 170–182.

Graham, S., & Harris, K. R. (1989). Improving learning disabled students' skills at composing essays: Self-instructional strategy training. *Exceptional Children, 56,* 201–214.

Graham, S., & Harris, K. R. (1997). It can be taught, but it does not develop naturally: Myths and realities in writing instruction. *School Psychology Review, 26,* 414–424.

Graham, S., & Harris, K. R. (2002). Prevention and intervention for struggling writers. In M. Shinn, H. Walker, & G. Stoner (Eds.), *Interventions for academic and behavior problems II: Preventive and remedial techniques* (pp. 589–610). Washington, DC: The National Association of School Psychologists.

Graham, S., & Harris, K. R. (2003). Students with learning disabilities and the process of writing: A meta-analysis of SRSD studies. In H. L. Swanson, K. R. Harris, & S. Graham (Eds.), *Handbook of learning disabilities* (pp. 323–344). New York: Guilford.

Graham, S., & Harris, K. R. (2005). *Writing better: Effective strategies for teaching students with learning difficulties.* Baltimore: Paul H. Brookes Publishing Co.

Graham, S., Harris, K. R., & Fink, B. (2000). Is handwriting causally related to learning to write: Treatment of handwriting problems in beginning writers. *Journal of Educational Psychology, 92,* 620–630.

Graham, S., Harris, K., & Troia, G. (2000). Self-regulated strategy development revisited: Teaching writing strategies to struggling writers. *Topics in Language Disorders, 20*(4), 1–14.

Graham, S., & Madan, A. J. (1981). Teaching letter formation. *Academic Therapy, 16,* 389–396.

Graham, S., & Perin, D. (2007). A meta-analysis of writing instruction for adolescent students. *Journal of Educational Psychology, 99,* 445–476.

Grant, R. (1993). Strategic training for using text headings to improve students' processing of content. *Journal of Reading, 36,* 482–488.

Graves, M. F. (2000). A vocabulary program to complement and bolster a middle-grade comprehension program. In B. M. Taylor, M. F. Graves, & P. van den Broek (Eds.), *Reading for meaning: Fostering comprehension in the middle grades* (pp. 116–135). New York: Teachers College Press.

Graves, M. F. (2004). Teaching prefixes: As good as it gets? In J. F. Baumann & E. J. Kame'enui (Eds.), *Vocabulary instruction: Research to practice* (pp. 81–99). New York: Guilford.

Graves, M. F. (2006). *The vocabulary book: Learning & instruction.* New York: Teachers College Press.

Graves, M. F., Juel, C., & Graves, B. B. (2004). *Teaching reading in the 21st century* (3rd ed.). Boston: Allyn & Bacon.

Graves, M. F., & Watts-Taffe, S. (2002). The role of word consciousness in a research-based vocabulary program. In A. Farstrup & S. J. Samuels (Eds.), *What research has to say about reading instruction* (pp. 140–165). Newark, DE: International Reading Association.

Greenleaf, R. K. (2005). *Brain based teaching.* Newfield, ME: Greenleaf & Papanek Publications.

Greenleaf, R. K., & Wells-Papanek, D. (2005). *Memory, recall, the brain & learning.* Newfield, ME: Greenleaf & Papanek Publications.

Greenwood, C. R., Delquadri, J. C., & Hall, R. V. (1989). Longitudinal effects of classwide peer tutoring. *Journal of Educational Psychology, 81,* 371–383.

Greenwood, C. R., Horton, B. T., & Utley, C. A. (2002). Academic engagement: Current perspectives on research and practice. *School Psychology Review, 31,* 328–349.

Gregg, N., & Lindstrom, J. H. (2008). Accommodation of instructional and testing situations. In R. Morris & N. Mather (Eds.), *Evidence-based interventions for students with learning and behavioral challenges* (pp. 302–318). New York: Routledge.

Griffin, S. (2007). *Number Worlds: A mathematics intervention program for grades prek–6.* Columbus, OH: SRA/McGraw-Hill.

Griffin, S. A., & Case, R. (1996). Evaluating the breadth and depth of training effects when central conceptual structures are taught. *Society for Research in Child Development Monographs, 59,* 90–113.

Griffin, S. A., & Case, R. (1997). Re-thinking the primary school math curriculum: An approach based on cognitive science. *Issues in Education, 3,* 1–49.

Griffin, S. A., Case, R., & Siegler, R. S. (1994). Rightstart: Providing the central conceptual prerequisites for first formal learning of arithmetic to students at risk for school failure. In K. McGilly (Ed.) *Classroom lessons: Integrating cognitive theory and classroom practice* (pp. 24–49). Cambridge, MA: MIT Press.

Grognet, A., Jameson, J., Franco, L., & Derrick-Mescua, M. (2000). *Enhancing English language learning in elementary classrooms: Study guide.* Washington, DC: Center for Applied Linguistics.

Grouws, D. A., & Cebulla, K. J. (2002). Improving student achievement in mathematics, Part 1: Research findings. ERIC Digest. Retrieved January, 2008 from http://www.ericse.org/digests/dse00-09.html.

Hale, J. B., Fiorello, C. A., Kavanagh, J. A., Hoeppner, J. B., & Gaitherer, R. A. (2001). WISC-III predictors of academic achievement for children with learning disabilities: Are global and factor scores comparable? *School Psychology Quarterly, 16,* 31–35.

Hall, T. (2002). Differentiated instruction. Wakefield, MA: National Center on Accessing the General Curriculum. http://www.cast.org/publications/ncac/ncac_diffinstruc.html.

Hall, W. S. (1989). Reading comprehension. *American Psychologist, 44,* 157–161.

Hardiman, M. M. (2003). *Connecting brain research with effective teaching.* Lanham, MD: Rowman & Littlefield Education.

Harniss, M. K., Stein, M., & Carnine, D. (2002). Promoting mathematics achievement. In M. A. Shinn, H. M. Walker, & G. Stoner (Eds.), *Interventions for academic and behavior problems II: Preventive and remedial approaches* (pp. 571–587). Bethesda, MD: National Association of School Psychologists.

Harris, K. R., & Graham, S. (1996). *Making the writing process work: Strategies for composition and self-regulation.* Cambridge, MA: Brookline Books.

Harris, K. R., Graham. S., Mason, L. H., & Friedlander, B. (2008). *Powerful writing strategies for all students.* Baltimore: Paul H. Brookes Publishing Co.

Harrison, M., & Harrison, B. (1986). Developing numeration concepts and skills. *Arithmetic Teacher, 33,* 18–21.

Hart, B., & Risley, T. R. (1995). *Meaningful differences in the everyday experience of young American children.* Baltimore: Paul H. Brookes Publishing Co.

Hart, L. (1983). *Human brain and human learning.* Village of Oak Creek, AZ: Books for Educators.

Hasbrouck, J. E., Ihnot, C., & Rogers, G. (1999). Read Naturally: A strategy to increase oral reading fluency. *Reading Research and Instruction, 39,* 27–38.

Hasbrouck, J. E., & Tindal, G. (2005). *Oral reading fluency: 90 years of measurement* (Tech. Rep. No. 33). Eugene: University of Oregon, College of Education, Behavioral Research and Teaching.

Hasselbring, T. S., Goin, L., & Bransford, J. D. (1988). Developing math automaticity in learning handicapped children: The role of computerized drill and practice. *Focus on Exceptional Children, 20,* 1–7.

Hayden, J., & McLaughlin, T. F. (2004). The effects of cover, copy, and compare and flash card drill on correct rate of math facts for a middle school student with learning disabilities. *Journal of Precision Teaching & Celebration, 20,* 17–21.

Hebb, D. O. (1949). *The organization of behavior.* New York: Wiley.

Hecht, S., Close, L., & Santisi, M. (2003). Sources of individual differences in fraction skills. *Journal of Experimental Child Psychology, 86,* 277–302.

Hecht, S. A., Torgesen, J. K., Wagner, R. K., & Rashotte, C. A. (2001). The relations between phonological processing abilities and emerging individual differences in mathematical computational skills: A longitudinal study from second to fifth grades. *Journal of Experimental Child Psychology, 79,* 192–227.

Heckelman, R. G. (1969). A neurological-impress method of remedial-reading instruction. *Academic Therapy, 4,* 277–282.

Heckelman, R. G. (1986). N.I.M. revisited. *Academic Therapy, 21,* 411–420.

Hegarty, M., & Kozhevnikov, M. (1999). Types of visual-spatial representations and mathematical problem-solving. *Journal of Educational Psychology, 91,* 684–689.

Heimlich, J. E., & Pittelman, S. D. (1986). *Semantic mapping: Classroom applications.* Newark, DE: International Reading Association.

Henderson, E. H., & Templeton, S. (1986). A developmental perspective of formal spelling instruction through alphabet, pattern, and meaning. *Elementary School Journal, 86,* 292–316.

Henry, M. K. (2003). *Unlocking literacy: Effective decoding & spelling instruction.* Baltimore: Paul H. Brookes Publishing Co.

Henry, M. K. (2005). The history and the structure of written English. In J. R. Birsh (Ed.), *Multisensory teaching of basic language skill* (2nd ed., pp. 151–170). Baltimore: Paul H. Brookes Publishing Co.

Holmes, V. M., & Castles, A. E. (2001). Unexpectedly poor spelling in university students. *Scientific Studies of Reading, 5,* 319–350.

Horn, J. L. (1991). Measurement of intellectual capabilities: A review of theory. In K. S. McGrew, J. K. Werder, & R. W. Woodcock (Eds.), *WJ-R Technical Manual* (pp. 197–232). Rolling Meadows, IL: Riverside.

Howell, R., Sidorenko, E., & Jurica, J. (1987). The effects of computer on the acquisition of multiplication facts by a student with learning disabilities. *Journal of Learning Disabilities, 20,* 336–341.

Hudson, R. F., Lane, H. B., & Pullen, P. C. (2005). Reading fluency assessment and instruction: What, why, and how? *Reading Teacher, 58,* 702–714.

Huey, E. B. (1968). *The psychology and pedagogy of reading.* Cambridge, MA: MIT Press.

Hutchinson, N. L. (1993). Effects of cognitive strategy instruction on algebra problem solving of adolescents with learning disabilities. *Learning Disability Quarterly, 16,* 34–63.

Ihnot, C., Mastoff, J., Gavin, J., & Hendrickson, I. (2001). *Read naturally.* St. Paul, MN: Read Naturally.

Individuals with Disabilities Education Improvement Act (IDEA) of 2004, PL 108-446.

International Reading Association. (2002). *What is evidence-based reading instruction?* Newark, DE: Author.

International Reading Association & National Council of Teachers of English. (2003). *Insert comprehension strategy.* ReadWriteThink materials at www.readwritethink.org. IRA/NCTE.

Invernizzi, M., & Hayes, L. (2004). Developmental-spelling research: A systematic imperative. *Reading Research Quarterly, 39,* 216–228.

Jenkins, J. R., & Jewell, M. (1993). Examining the validity of two measures for formative teaching: Reading aloud and maze. *Exceptional Children, 59,* 421–432.

Jitendra, A. K., Edwards, L. L., Sacks, G., & Jacobsen, L. A. (2004). What research says about vocabulary instruction for students with learning disabilities. *Exceptional Children, 70,* 299–322.

Jitendra, A. K., Griffin, C., Deatline-Buchman, A., Dipipi-Hoy, C., Sczesniak, E., Sokol, N. G., et al. (2005). Adherence to mathematics professional standards and instructional criteria for problem-solving in mathematics. *Exceptional Children, 71,* 319–337.

Johnson, D. J., & Myklebust, H. R. (1967). *Learning disabilities: Educational principles and practices.* New York: Grune & Stratton.

Johnson, D. W., & Johnson, R. T. (1987). *Learning together and alone: Cooperation, competition, and individualization* (2nd ed.). Englewood Cliffs, NJ: Prentice-Hall.

Jones, D. (2004, December). *Automaticity of the transcription process in the production of written text.* Doctor of Philosophy Thesis, Graduate School of Education, University of Queensland, Australia.

Jones, D., & Christensen, C. A. (1999). The relationship between automaticity in handwriting and students' ability to generate written text. *Journal of Educational Psychology, 91,* 44–49.

Juel, C. (1988). Learning to read and write: A longitudinal study of 54 children from first through fourth grades. *Journal of Educational Psychology, 80,* 443–447.

Kalyuga, S., Chandler, P., Tuovinen, J., & Sweller, J. (2001). When problem solving is superior to studying worked examples. *Journal of Educational Psychology, 93,* 579–588.

Kame'enui, E. J., & Simmons, D. C. (1990). *Designing instructional strategies: The prevention of academic problems.* Columbus, OH: Merrill.

Kamii, C. (2000). *Young children reinvent arithmetic* (2nd ed.). New York: Teachers College Press.

Kamii, C., Lewis, B. A., & Kirkland, K. (2001). Manipulatives: When are they useful? *The Journal of Mathematical Behavior, 20*(1), 21–31.

Karp, K. S., & Voltz, D. L. (2000). Weaving mathematical instructional strategies into inclusive settings. *Intervention in School and Clinic, 35,* 206–215.

Kaufman, A. S. (1979). *Intelligent testing with the WISC-R.* New York: Wiley.

Keene, E. O., & Zimmerman, S. (1997). *Mosaic of thought: Teaching comprehension in a readers' workshop.* Portsmouth, NH: Heinemann.

Kelley, R. (2007). The writing on the wall. *Newsweek.* Retrieved February 28, 2008, from www.newsweek.com/id/67956.

Kim, A., Vaughn, S., Wanzek, J., & Wei, S. (2004). Graphic organizers and their effects on the reading comprehension of students with LD: A synthesis of research. *Journal of Learning Disabilities, 37,* 105–118.

Kintsch, W., & Rawson, K. A. (2007). Comprehension. In M. J. Snowling & C. Hulme (Eds.), *The science of reading: A handbook* (pp. 209–226). Victoria, Australia: Blackwell Publishing.

Kirk, S. A., Kirk, W. D., Minskoff, E. H., Mather, N., & Roberts, R. (2007). *Phonic reading lessons: Skills.* Novato, CA: Academic Therapy.

Klauer, K. J., Willmes, K., & Phye, G. D. (2002). Inducing inductive reasoning: Does it transfer to fluid intelligence? *Contemporary Educational Psychology, 27,* 1–25.

Klingner, J. K., & Vaughn, S. (1996). Reciprocal teaching of reading comprehension strategies for students with learning disabilities who use English as a second language. *Elementary School Journal, 96,* 275–293.

Klingner, J. K., & Vaughn, S. (1998). Using collaborative strategic reading. *Teaching Exceptional Children, 30*(6), 32–37.

Klingner, J. K., Vaughn, S., Dimino, J., Schumm, J. S., & Bryant, D. P. (2001). *Collaborative strategic reading: Strategies for improving comprehension.* Longmont, CO: Sopris West.

Klingner, J. K., Vaughn, S., & Schumm, J. S. (1998). Collaborative strategic reading during social studies in heterogeneous fourth-grade classrooms. *Elementary School Journal, 99,* 3–22.

Kroesbergen, E. H., & Van Luit, J. E. H. (2003). Mathematical interventions for children with special educational needs. *Remedial and Special Education, 24,* 97–114.

Kuhn, M. R., & Stahl, S. A. (2003). Fluency: A review of developmental and remedial practices. *Journal of Educational Psychology, 95,* 3–21.

Kunsch, C. A., Jitendra, A. K., & Sood, S. (2007). The effects of peer-mediated mathematics instruction for students with disabilities: A review of the literature. *Learning Disabilities Research & Practice, 22,* 1–12.

LaBerge, D., & Samuels, S. J. (1974). Toward a theory of automatic processing in reading. *Cognitive Psychology, 6,* 293–323.

Landerl, K., & Wimmer, H. (2008). Development of word reading fluency and spelling in a consistent orthography: An 8-year follow up. *Journal of Educational Psychology, 1,* 150–161.

Lavoie, R. H. (1993). *Discovering mathematics.* Boston: PWS Publishing Co.

LeBlanc, M. D., & Weber-Russell, S. (1996). Text integration and mathematics connections: A computer model of arithmetic work problem solving. *Cognitive Science, 20,* 357–407.

Lee, D., & Riccio, C. A. (2005). Understanding and implementing cognitive neuropsychological retraining. In R. C. D'Amato, E. Fletcher-Janzen, &

C. R. Reynolds (Eds.), *Handbook of school neuropsychology* (pp. 701–720). Hoboken, NJ: Wiley.

Lee, M. J., & Tingstrom, D. H. (1994). A group math intervention: The modification of cover, copy, and compare for group application. *Psychology in the Schools, 31,* 133–145.

Light, P. L., & Littleton, K. (1999). *Social processes in children's learning.* Cambridge, England: Cambridge University Press.

Logie, R. H., Gilhooly, K. J., & Wynn, V. (1994). Counting on working memory in arithmetic problem solving. *Memory & Cognition, 22,* 395–410.

Loveless, T. (2003). Trends in math: The importance of basic skills. *Brookings Review, 21,* 40–43.

Lovett, M. W., Lacerenza, I., & Borden, S. I. (2000). Putting struggling readers on the PHAST track: A program to integrate phonological and strategy-based remedial reading instruction and maximize outcomes. *Journal of Learning Disabilities, 33,* 458–476.

Lyon, G. R. (1995). Toward a definition of dyslexia. *Annals of Dyslexia, 45,* 3–27.

MacArthur, C. A. (2007). Best practices in teaching evaluation and revision. In S. Graham, C. A. MacArthur, & J. Fitzgerald (Eds.), *Best practices in writing instruction* (pp. 141–162). New York: Guilford.

Maccini, P., & Gagnon, J. C. (2000). Best practices for teaching mathematics to secondary students with special needs. *Focus on Exceptional Children, 32,* 1–22.

Maccini, P., & Gagnon, J. C. (2006). Mathematics instructional practices and assessment accommodations by secondary special and general educators. *Exceptional Children, 72,* 217–234.

Maccini, P., & Hughes, C. A. (2000). Effects of a problem-solving strategy on the introductory algebra performance of secondary students with learning disabilities. *Learning Disabilities Research & Practice, 15,* 10–21.

Maccini, P., & Ruhl, K. L. (2000). Effects of a graduated instructional sequence on the algebraic subtraction of integers by secondary students with learning disabilities. *Education and Treatment of Children, 23,* 465–489.

Madden, N. A., & Slavin, R. E. (1983). Effects of cooperative learning on the social acceptance of mainstreamed academically handicapped students. *Journal of Special Education 17,* 171–82.

Maheady, L., Sacca, K., & Harper, G. F. (1988). Classwide peer tutoring with mildly handicapped high school students. *Exceptional Children, 55,* 52–59.

Manning, B., & Payne, B. (1996). *Self-talk for teachers and students.* Needham, MA: Allyn & Bacon.

Markovits, Z., & Sowder J. T. (1994). Developing number sense: An intervention study in grade 7. *Journal for Research in Mathematics Education, 25*(1), 4–29.

Marzano, R. J., Pickering, D. J., & Pollock, J. E. (2001). *Classroom instruction that works.* Alexandria, VA: Association for Supervision and Curriculum Development.

Mastropieri, M. A. (1988). Using the keyboard (sic) method. *Teaching Exceptional Children, 20*(2), 4–8.

Mastropieri, M. A., Leinart, A., & Scruggs, T. E. (1999). Strategies to increase reading fluency. *Intervention in School and Clinic, 5,* 278–284.

Mastropieri, M. A., & Scruggs, T. E. (1998). Enhancing school success with mnemonic strategies. *Intervention in School and Clinic, 33,* 201–208.

Mather, N., & Urso, A. M. (2008). Younger readers with reading difficulties. In R. Morris & N. Mather (Eds.), *Evidence-based practices for students with learning and behavioral challenges* (pp. 163–192). New York: Routledge.

Mathes, P. G., & Babyak, A. E. (2001). The effects of peer-assisted literacy strategies for first-grade readers with and without additional mini-skills lessons. *Learning Disabilities Research & Practice, 16,* 28–44.

Mathes, P. G., & Fuchs, L. S. (1993). Peer-mediated reading instruction in special education resource rooms. *Learning Disabilities Research & Practice, 8,* 233–243.

Mazzocco, M. M. M. (2007). Defining and differentiating mathematical learning disabilities and difficulties. In D. B. Berch & M. M. M. Mazzocco (Eds.), *Why is math so hard for some children? The nature and origins of mathematical learning difficulties and disabilities* (pp. 29–47). Baltimore: Paul H. Brookes Publishing Co.

McGrew, K. S. (1993). The relationship between the WJ-R *Gf-Gc* cognitive clusters and reading achievement across the lifespan. *Journal of Psychoeducational Assessment* (Monograph Series: WJ-R Monograph), 39–53.

McGrew, K. S. (2005). The Cattell-Horn-Carroll theory of cognitive abilities: Past, present, and future. In D. P. Flanagan & P. L. Harrison (Eds.), *Contemporary intellectual assessment: Theories, tests, and issues* (2nd ed., pp. 136–182). New York: Guilford.

McGrew, K. S., Flanagan, D. P., Keith, T. Z., & Vanderwood, M. (1997). Beyond *g:* The impact of *Gf-Gc* specific cognitive abilities research on the future use and interpretation of intelligence tests in the schools. *School Psychology Review, 26,* 177–189.

McGrew, K. S., & Woodcock, R. (2001). *Technical manual: Woodcock-Johnson III.* Rolling Meadows, IL: Riverside.

McInnes, A., Humphries, T., Hogg-Johnson, S., & Tannock, R. (2003). Listening comprehension and working memory are impaired in children with ADHD irrespective of language development. *Journal of Abnormal Child Psychology, 31,* 427–433.

McKeown, M. G., & Beck, I. L. (2004). Direct and rich vocabulary instruction. In J. F. Baumann & E. J. Kame'enui (Eds.), *Vocabulary instruction: Research to practice* (pp. 13–27). New York: Guilford.

McLeskey, J., & Waldron, N. L. (1990). The identification and characteristics of students with learning disabilities in Indiana. *Learning Disabilities Research, 5,* 72–78.

McNeil, J., & Donant, L. (1982). Summarization strategy for improving reading comprehension. In J. A. Niles & L. A. Harris (Eds.). *New inquiries in reading research and instruction* (pp. 215–219). Rochester, NY: National Reading Conference.

Meichenbaum, D. H. (1977). *Cognitive-behavior modification: An integrative approach.* New York: Plenum.

Mercer, C. D., & Campbell, K. U. (1998). *Great Leaps Reading Program Grades K–2.* Gainesville, FL: Diarmuid.

Mercer, C. D., Campbell, K. U., Miller, M. D., Mercer, K. D., & Lane, H. B. (2000). Effects of a reading fluency intervention for middle schoolers with specific learning disabilities. *Learning Disabilities Research & Practice, 15,* 179–189.

Mercer, C. D., & Mercer, A. R. (1998; 2005). *Teaching students with learning problems* (7th ed.). Upper Saddle River, NJ: Pearson/Merrill Prentice-Hall.

Merzenich, M. M., & Sameshina, K. (1993). Cortical plasticity and memory. *Current Opinion in Neurobiology, 3,* 187–196.

Meyer, M. S., & Felton, R. H. (1999). Repeated reading to enhance fluency: Old approaches and new directions. *Annals of Dyslexia, 49,* 283–306.

Miller, A. D., Barbetta, P. M., Drevno, G. E., Martz, S. A., & Heron, T. E. (1996). Math peer tutoring for students with specific learning disabilities. *Learning Disabilities Forum, 21*(3), 21–28.

Miller, S. P., Butler, F. B., & Lee, K. (1998). Validated practices for teaching mathematics to students with learning disabilities: A review of literature. *Focus on Exceptional Children 31*(1), 1–24.

Miller, S. P., & Hudson, P. J. (2007). Using evidence-based practices to build mathematics competence related to conceptual, procedural, and declarative knowledge. *Learning Disabilities Research & Practice, 22,* 47–57.

Miller, S. P., & Mercer, C. D. (1993). Using data to learn about concrete-semi-concrete-abstract instruction for students with math disabilities. *Learning Disabilities Research & Practice, 8,* 89–96.

Miller, S. P., & Mercer, C. L. (1997). Educational aspects of mathematics disabilities. *Journal of Learning Disabilities, 30,* 47–56.

Miller, S. P., Mercer, C. L., & Dillon, A. (1992). Acquiring and retaining math skills. *Intervention, 28,* 105–110.

Miller, S. R., & Miller, P. F. (1995). Cross-age peer tutoring. A strategy for promoting self-determination in students with severe emotional disabilities/behavior disorders. *Preventing School Failure, 39*(4), 32–38.

Moats, L. C. (1983). A comparison of the spelling errors of older dyslexic and second-grade normal children. *Annals of Dyslexia, 33,* 121–139.

Moats, L. C. (2000). *Speech to print: Language essentials for teachers.* Baltimore: Paul H. Brookes Publishing Co.

Molfese, V.J., Beswick, J., Molnar, A., & Jacobi-Vessels, J. (2006). Alphabetic skills in preschool: A preliminary study of letter naming and letter writing. *Developmental Neuropsychology, 29* (1), 5–19.

Monroe, M. (1932). *Children who cannot read.* Chicago: University of Chicago Press.

Montague, M. (1992). The effects of cognitive and metacognitive strategy instruction on the mathematical problem solving of middle school students with learning disabilities. *Journal of Learning Disabilities, 25,* 230–248.

Montague, M. (1996). What does the "New View" of school mathematics mean for students with mild disabilities? In M. C. Pugach & C. L. Warger (Eds.), *Curriculum trends, special education, and reform: Refocusing the conversation* (pp. 84–93). New York: Teachers College Press.

Montague, M. (1998). Cognitive strategy instruction in mathematics for students with learning disabilities. In D. Rivera (Ed.), *Mathematics education for students with learning disabilities* (pp. 177–199). Austin, TX: Pro-Ed.

Montague, M. (2003). *Solve It! A mathematical problem solving instructional program.* Reston, VA: Exceptional Innovations.

Montague, M. (2006). Self-regulation strategies for better math performance in middle school. In M. Montague & A. Jitendra (Eds.), *Teaching mathematics to middle schools students with learning difficulties* (pp. 89–107). New York: Guilford.

Montague, M. (2008). Self-regulation strategies to improve mathematical problem solving for students with learning disabilities. *Learning Disability Quarterly, 31,* 37–44.

Montague, M., & Bos, C. S. (1986). The effect of cognitive strategy instruction on verbal math problem-solving performance of learning-disabled adolescents. *Journal of Learning Disabilities, 19,* 26–33.

Morin, V. A., & Miller, S. P. (1998). Teaching multiplication to middle school students with mental retardation. *Education and Treatment of Children, 21,* 22–36.

Mulcahy, R., Marfo, K., Peat, D., & Andrews, J. (1986). *SPELT: A strategies program for effective learning and thinking.* Calgary: University of Alberta.

Nagy, W. E., & Anderson, R. C. (1984). How many words are there in printed school English? *Reading Research Quarterly, 19,* 304–330.

Nagy, W. E., & Scott, J. A. (2000). Vocabulary processes. In M. L. Kamil, P. Mosenthal, P. D. Pearson, & R. Barr (Eds.), *Handbook of reading research* (Vol. 3, pp. 269–284). Mahwah, NJ: Erlbaum.

Nation, K. (2007). Children's reading comprehension difficulties. In M. J. Snowling & C. Hulme (Eds.), *The science of reading: A handbook* (pp. 248–265). Victoria, Australia: Blackwell Publishing.

National Assessment of Educational Progress. (2003). *NAEP mathematics report card for the nation and the states.* Princeton, NJ: Educational Testing Service.

National Assessment of Educational Progress. (2007). *NAEP 2006 mathematics report card for the nation and the states.* Princeton, NJ: Educational Testing Service.

National Center for Education Statistics. (2006). *NAEP questions.* http://nces.ed.gov/nationsreportcard/itmrls.

National Clearinghouse for Comprehensive School Reform. (2001). Taking stock: Lessons on comprehensive school reform from policy, practice, and research. *Benchmarks, 2,* 1–11.

National Commission on Writing in America's Schools and Colleges. (2003; 2004). *Neglected R: The need for a writing revolution.* Princeton, NJ: College Entrance Examination Board.

National Council of Teachers of English. (2004). *Beliefs about the teaching of writing.* Writing Study Group of the NCTE Executive Committee. Urbana, IL: Author.

National Council of Teachers of Mathematics. (2000). *Principles and standards for school mathematics.* Reston, VA: Author.

National Reading Panel. (2000). *Teaching children to read: An evidence-based assessment of the scientific research literature on reading and its implications for reading instruction.* Washington, DC: National Institute of Child Health and Human Development.

National Research Council. (2001). *Adding it up: Helping children learn mathematics.* J. Kilpatrick, J. Swafford, & B. Findell (Eds.), Mathematics Learning Study Committee, Center for Education, Division of Behavioral and Social Sciences and Education. Washington, DC: National Academy Press.

No Child Left Behind Act. Reauthorization of the Elementary and Secondary Education Act. PL 107-110, § 2102(4) (2001).

Ogle, D. M. (1986). K-W-L: A teaching model that develops active reading of expository text. *The Reading Teacher, 39,* 564–570.

Onken, J. S. (2002). *The effects of the Read Naturally Program on middle school students' oral reading fluency and reading comprehension skills in a residential treatment setting.* Unpublished capstone, Winona State University.

Owen, R. L., & Fuchs, L. S. (2002). Mathematical problem-solving strategy instruction for third-grade students with learning disabilities. *Remedial and Special Education, 23,* 268–278.

Palincsar, A. S., & Brown, A. L. (1984). Reciprocal teaching of comprehension-fostering and comprehension-monitoring activities. *Cognition and Instruction, 2,* 117–175.

Pardo, L. S. (2004). What every teacher should know about comprehension. *The Reading Teacher, 58,* 272–280.

Parente, R., & Herrmann, D. (1996). *Retraining cognition: Techniques and applications.* Gaithersburg, MD: Aspen Publishing.

Passolunghi, M. C., Cornoldi, C., & De Liberto, S. (1999). Working memory and intrusions of irrelevant information in a group of specific poor problem solvers. *Memory & Cognition, 27,* 779–790.

Passolunghi, M. C., & Siegel, L. S. (2001). Short-term memory, working memory, and inhibitory control in children with difficulties in arithmetic problem solving. *Journal of Experimental Child Psychology, 80,* 44–57.

Pellegrino, J. W., & Goldman, S. R. (1987). Information processing and elementary mathematics. *Journal of Learning Disabilities, 20,* 23–32, 57.

Perfetti, C. A. (1985). *Reading ability.* New York: Oxford University Press.

Perfetti, C. A. (1986). Continuities in reading acquisition, reading skill and reading disability. *Remedial and Special Education, 7*(1), 11–21.

Perfetti, C. A., Beck, I., Bell, L. C., & Hughes, C. (1987). Phonemic knowledge and learning to read are reciprocal. *Merrill-Palmer Quarterly, 33,* 283–319.

Perfetti, C. A., & Hogaboam, T. (1975). Relationship between single word decoding and reading comprehension skill. *Journal of Educational Psychology, 67,* 461–469.

Perfetti, C.A., Landi, N., & Oakhill, J. (2007). The acquisition of reading comprehension skill. In M. J. Snowling & C. Hulme (Eds.), *The science of reading: A handbook* (pp. 227–247). Victoria, Australia: Blackwell Publishing.

Phillips, D., & Crowell, N. A. (Eds.). (1994). *Cultural diversity and early education: Report of a workshop.* Washington, DC: National Academy Press.

Pikulski, J. J., & Chard, D. J. (2005). Fluency: Bridge between decoding and reading comprehension. *Reading Teacher, 58,* 510–519.

Pintrich, P. R., & De Groot, E. V. (1990). Motivational and self-regulated learning components of classroom academic performance. *Journal of Educational Psychology, 82,* 33–40.

Pittelman, S. D., Heimlich, J. E., Berglund, R. L., & French, M. P. (1991). *Semantic feature analysis: Classroom applications.* Newark, DE: International Reading Association.

Polloway, E. A., & Patton, J. R. (1993). *Strategies for teaching learners with special needs* (5th ed.). Columbus, OH: Merrill.

Pressley, M. (2000). What should comprehension instruction be the instruction of? In M. L. Kamil, P. B. Mosenthal, P. D. Pearson, & R. Barr (Eds.), *Handbook of reading research* (Vol. 3, pp. 545–561). Mahwah, NJ: Erlbaum.

Pressley, M., Almasi, J., Schuder, T., Bergman, J., Hite, S., El-Dinary, P. B., et al. (1994). Transactional instruction of comprehension strategies: The Montgomery County, Maryland, SAIL program. *Reading and Writing Quarterly: Overcoming Learning Difficulties, 10,* 5–19.

Quinn, P. C. (2004). Development of subordinate-level categorization in 3- to 7-month-old infants. *Child Development, 75,* 886–899.

Ramani, G. R., & Siegler, R. S. (2005, April). *It's more than just a game: Effects of children's board game play on the development of numerical estimation.* Poster presented at the biennial meeting of the Society for Research in Child Development, Atlanta, GA.

Raphael, T. (1986). Teaching question answer relationships, revisited. *The Reading Teacher, 39,* 516–522.

Raphael, T., Highland, K., & Au, K. (2006). *QAR now.* New York: Scholastic.

Raphael, T. E., Wonnacott, C. A., & Pearson, P. D. (July, 1983). *Metacognitive training in question answer relationships: Implementations in a 4th grade developmental reading program.* Report No. 284. Champaign: University of Illinois, Center for the Study of Reading.

Rasinski, T. V. (2004). Creating fluent readers. *Educational Leadership, 61*(6), 46–51.

Rasinski, T. V. (2006). Reading fluency instruction: Moving beyond accuracy, automaticity, and prosody. *Reading Teacher, 59,* 704–706.

Rasinski, T. V., Padak, N. D., McKeon, C. A., Wilfong, L. G., Friedauer, J. A., & Heim, P. (2005). Is reading fluency a key for successful high school reading? *Journal of Adolescent and Adult Literacy, 49*(1), 22–27.

Rathovan, N. (1999). *Effective school interventions.* New York: Guilford.

Read, C. (1971). Pre-school children's knowledge of English phonology. *Harvard Educational Review, 41*(1), 1–34.

Reid, D. K. (1988). *Teaching the learning disabled: A cognitive developmental approach.* New York: McGraw-Hill.

Rittle-Johnson, B., Siegler, R., & Alibali, M. (2001). Developing conceptual understanding and procedural skills in mathematics: An iterative process. *Journal of Educational Psychology, 93,* 346–362.

Rivera, D. P. (1996, Spring). Using cooperative learning to teach mathematics to students with learning disabilities, *LD Forum,* 1–9.

Rivera, D. P., & Smith, D. D. (1988). Using a demonstration strategy to teach mid-school students with learning disabilities how to compute long division. *Journal of Learning Disabilities, 21,* 77–81.

Rivera, D. P., & Smith, D. D. (1997). *Teaching students with learning and behavior problems* (3rd ed.). Boston: Allyn & Bacon.

Roberts, R., & Mather, N. (2007). *Phonic reading lessons: Practice.* Novato, CA: Academic Therapy.

Rohrbeck, C. A., Ginsburg-Block, M. D., Fantuzzo, J. W., & Miller, T. R. (2003). Peer-assisted learning interventions with elementary school students: A meta-analytic review, *Journal of Educational Psychology, 95,* 240–257.

Romani, C., Olson, A., & Di Betta, A. M. (2007). Spelling disorders. In M. J. Snowling & C. Hulme (Eds.), *The science of reading: A handbook* (pp. 431–447). Victoria, Australia: Blackwell Publishing.

Rose, T. L. (1984). The effects of two prepractice procedures on oral reading. *Journal of Learning Disabilities, 17,* 544–548.

Rose, T. L., & Sherry, L. (1984). Relative effects of two previewing procedures on LD adolescents' oral reading performance. *Learning Disability Quarterly, 7,* 39–44.

Rosenshine, B., & Meister, C. (1994). Reciprocal teaching: A review of the research. *Review of Educational Research, 64,* 479–530.

Rosenshine, B., Meister, C., & Chapman, S. (1996). Teaching students to generate questions: A review of the intervention studies. *Review of Educational Research, 66,* 181–221.

Rourke, B. P., & Conway, J. A. (1997). Disabilities of arithmetic and mathematical reasoning: Perspectives from neurology and neuropsychology. *Journal of Learning Disabilities, 30,* 34–46.

Samuels, S. J. (1979). The method of repeated readings. *The Reading Teacher, 32,* 403–408.

Scarborough, H. S. (1998). Predicting the future achievement of second graders with reading disabilities: Contributions of phonemic awareness, verbal memory, rapid naming, and IQ. *Annals of Dyslexia, 48,* 115–136.

Schumaker, J. B., Denton, P. H., & Deshler, D. D. (1984). *The Paraphrasing Strategy.* Lawrence, KS: The University of Kansas.

Schumaker, J. B., Deshler, D. D., Alley, G. R., Warner, M. M., & Denton, P. (1982). Multipass: A learning strategy for improving reading comprehension. *Learning Disabilities Quarterly, 5,* 295–304.

Schumaker, J. B., Deshler, D. D., Nolan, S., Clark, F. L., Alley, G. R., & Warner, M. M. (1981). *Error monitoring: A learning strategy for improving academic performance of LD adolescents* (Research Report No. 32). Lawrence, KS: University of Kansas Institute for Research in Learning Disabilities.

Scruggs, T. E., & Mastropieri, M. A. (2002). On babies and bathwater: Addressing the problems of identification of learning disabilities. *Learning Disability Quarterly, 25,* 155–168.

Semrud-Clikeman, M. (2005). Neuropsychological aspects for evaluating learning disabilities. *Journal of Learning Disabilities, 38,* 563–568.

Shamliyan, T. A., Duval, S., Du, J., & Kane, R. L. (2008). Just what the doctor ordered. A review of the evidence of the impact of computerized physician order entry system on medication errors. *Health Services Research, 43*(1), 32–53.

Shankweiler, D., Lundquist, E., Dreyer, L. G., & Dickinson, C. C. (1996). Reading and spelling difficulties in high school students: Causes and consequences. *Reading & Writing: An Interdisciplinary Journal, 8,* 267–294.

Sheffield, B. (1996). Handwriting: A neglected cornerstone of literacy. *Annals of Dyslexia, 46,* 21–35.

Shiah, R. L., Mastropieri, M. A., Scruggs, T. E., & Mushinski-Fulk, B. J. (1995). The effects of computer-assisted instruction on the mathematical problem solving of students with learning disabilities. *Exceptionality, 5*(3), 131–161.

Siegler, R. (1988). Individual differences in strategy choices: Good students, not-so-good students, and perfectionists. *Child Development, 59,* 833–851.

Siegler, R. S., & Shrager, J. (1984). Strategy choices in addition and subtraction: How do children know what to do? In C. Sophian (Ed.), *Origins of cognitive skills: The eighteenth annual Carnegie symposium of cognition* (pp. 229–293). Hillsdale, NJ: Erlbaum.

Silven, M., & Vauras, M. (1992). Improving reading through thinking aloud. *Learning and Instruction, 2*(2), 69–88.

Silver, E. A., & Marshall, S. P. (1990). Mathematical and scientific problem solving. In B. F. Jones & L. Idol (Eds.), *Dimensions of thinking and cognitive instruction* (pp. 265–290). Hillsdale, NJ: Erlbaum.

Simmons, D. C., & Kame'enui, E. J. (Eds.). (1998). *What reading research tells us about children with diverse learning needs: Bases and basics.* Mahwah, NJ: Erlbaum.

Sindelar, P. T., Monda, L. E., & O'Shea, L. J. (1990). Effects of repeated readings on instructional- and mastery-level readers. *Journal of Educational Research, 8,* 220–226.

Singer, B. D., & Bashir, A. S. (1999). What are executive functions and self-regulation and what do they have to do with language-learning disorders? *Language, Speech, and Hearing Services in Schools, 30,* 265–273.

Skinner, C. H., Turco, T. L., Beatty, K. L., & Rasavage, C. (1989). Cover, copy, and compare: A method for increasing multiplication performance. *School Psychology Review, 18,* 412–420.

Slavin, R. E. (1983). *Cooperative learning.* New York: Longman.

Sloutsky, V. M., & Yarlas, A. S. (2000). Problem representation in experts and novices: Part 2. Underlying processing mechanisms. In L. R. Gleitman & A. K. Joshi (Eds.), *Proceedings of the 22nd Annual Conference of the Cognitive Science Society* (pp. 475–480). Mahwah, NJ: Erlbaum.

Smith, C. R. (1997, February). *A hierarchy for assessing and remediating phonemic segmentation difficulties.* Paper presented at the Learning Disabilities Association International Conference, Chicago.

Smith, J. P. (1995). Competent reasoning with rational numbers. *Cognition and Instruction, 13,* 3–50.

Snow, C. E. (2002). *Reading for understanding: Toward an R &D program in reading comprehension.* Santa Monica, CA: Science and Technology Policy Institute. RAND Education.

Snow, C. E., Burns, M. S., & Griffin, P. (1998). *Preventing reading difficulties in young children.* Washington, DC: National Academy Press.

Sousa, D. A. (2005). *How the brain learns to read.* Thousand Oaks, CA: Corwin Press.

Spellings, M. (2006, February). *We must raise the bar in math instruction.* Testimony presented before the Senate, Health, Education, Labor, & Pensions Committee, Washington, DC.

Squire, L. R., & Schacter, D. L. (2003). *Neuropsychology of memory* (3rd ed.). New York: Guilford.

Stahl, S. A. (1999). *Vocabulary development.* Cambridge, MA: Brookline Books.

Stahl, S. A. (2004). What do we know about fluency? Findings of the National Reading Panel. In P. M. McCardle & V. Chhabra (Eds.), *The voice of evidence in reading research* (pp. 187–211). Baltimore: Paul H. Brookes Publishing Co.

Stahl, S. A., & Kapinus, B. (2001). *Word power: What every educator needs to know about teaching vocabulary.* Washington, DC: NEA Professional Library.

Stahl, S. A., & Stahl, K. A. D. (2004). Word wizards all! Teaching word meanings in preschool and primary education. In J. F. Baumann & E. J. Kame'enui (Eds.), *Vocabulary instruction: Research to practice* (pp. 59–78). New York: Guilford.

Stanovich, K. E. (1986). Matthew effects in reading: Some consequences of individual differences in the acquisition of literacy. *Reading Research Quarterly, 21,* 360–407.

Stauffer, R. B. (1969). *Directing reading maturity as a cognitive process.* New York: Harper & Row.

Steinberg, L., Dornbusch, S. M., & Brown, B. B. (1992). Ethnic differences in adolescent achievement: An ecological perspective. *American Psychologist, 47,* 723–729.

Stigler, J. W., & Perry, M. (1990). Mathematics learning in Japanese, Chinese, and American classrooms. In J. W. Stigler, R. A. Shweder, & G. Herdt (Eds.), *Cultural psychology: Essays on comparative human development* (pp. 328–353). New York: Cambridge University Press.

Strickland, D. S. (1991). Emerging literacy: How young children learn to read. In B. Persky & L. H. Golubchick (Eds.), *Early childhood education* (2nd ed., pp. 337–344). Lanham, MD: University Press of America.

Strickland, D. S., & Feeley, J. T. (1991). Development in the early school years.

In J. Flood, J. M. Jensen, D. Lapp, & J. R. Squire (Eds.), *Handbook of research on teaching the English language arts* (pp. 529–535). New York: Macmillan.

Stuebing, K. K., Barth, A. E., Cirino, P. T., Francis, D. J., & Fletcher, J. M. (2008). A response to recent reanalyses of the National Reading Panel report: Effects of systematic phonics instruction are practically significant. *Journal of Educational Psychology, 100,* 123–134.

Stylianou, D. A. (2002). On the interaction of visualization and analysis: The negotiation of a visual representation in expert problem-solving. *Journal of Mathematical Behavior, 21,* 303–317.

Sutherland, K. S., & Wehby, J. H. (2001). Exploring the relation between increased opportunities to respond to academic requests and the academic and behavioral outcomes of students with EBD: A review. *Remedial and Special Education, 22,* 113–121.

Suydam, M. N., & Higgins, J. L. (1977). *Activity-based learning in elementary school mathematics: Recommendations from research.* Columbus, OH: ERIC Center for Science, Mathematics, and Environmental Education.

Swanson, H. L. (1999). Reading research for students with LD: A meta-analysis of intervention outcomes. *Journal of Learning Disabilities, 32,* 504–532.

Swanson, H. L. (2001). Searching for the best model for instructing students with learning disabilities. *Focus on Exceptional Children, 34,* 1–15.

Swanson, H. L., & Beebe-Frankenberger, M. (2004). The relationship between working memory and mathematical problem solving in children at risk and not at risk for serious math difficulties. *Journal of Educational Psychology, 96,* 471–491.

Swanson, H. L., & Sachse-Lee, C. (2001). Mathematical problem solving and working memory in children with learning disabilities: Both executive and phonological processes are important. *Journal of Experimental Child Psychology, 79,* 294–321.

Swanson, H. L., Trainin, G., Necoechea, D. M., & Hammill, D. D. (2003). Rapid naming, phonological awareness, and reading. A meta analysis of the correlational evidence. *Review of Educational Research, 73,* 407–444.

Taboada, A., & Guthrie, J. T. (2006). Contributions of student questioning and prior knowledge to construction of knowledge from reading information text. *Journal of Literacy Research, 38*(1), 1–35.

Tallal, P., Miller, S. L., Bedi, G., Byma, G., Wang, X., Nagarajan, S. S. et al. (1996). Language comprehension in language-learning impaired children improved with acoustically modified speech. *Science, 5,* 81–84.

Tannenbaum, K. R., Torgesen, J. K., & Wagner, R. K. (2006). Relationships between word knowledge and reading comprehension in third-grade children. *Scientific Studies of Reading, 10,* 381–398.

Therrien, W. J. (2004). Fluency and comprehension gains as a result of repeated reading. *Remedial and Special Education, 25,* 252–261.

Therrien, W. J., & Kubina, R. M. (2006). Developing reading fluency with repeated reading. *Intervention in School and Clinic, 41,* 156–160.

Third International Mathematics and Science Study (TIMSS) 1999 Video Study (1999). U.S. Department of Education, Institute for Education Sciences, National Center of Education Statistics available at NCES web site: http://nces.ed.gov/timss.

Tomlinson, C. A. (2000). Differentiation of instruction in the elementary grades. *ERIC Digest EDO-PS-00-7.*

Tomlinson, C. A. (2006). *An educator's guide to differentiating instruction.* Boston: Houghton Mifflin.

Torgesen, J. K. (1997). The prevention and remediation of reading disabilities: Evaluating what we know from research. *Journal of Academic Language Therapy, 1,* 11–47.

Torgesen, J. K. (2007). Recent discoveries on remedial interventions for children with dyslexia. In M. J. Snowling & C. Hulme (Eds.), *The science of reading: A handbook* (pp. 521–537). Victoria, Australia: Blackwell Publishing.

Torgesen, J. K., Alexander, A. W., Wagner, R. K., Rashotte, C. A., Voeller, K., Conway, T., et al. (2001). Intensive remedial instruction for children with severe reading disabilities: Immediate and long-term outcomes from two instructional approaches. *Journal of Learning Disabilities, 34,* 33–58.

Torgesen, J. K., & Burgess, S. R. (1998). Consistency of reading-related phonological processes throughout early childhood: Evidence from longitudinal-correlational and instructional studies. In J. L. Metsala & L. C. Ehri (Eds.), *Word recognition in beginning literacy* (pp. 161–188). Mahwah, NJ: Erlbaum.

Torgesen, J. K., & Mathes, P. G. (2000). *Basic guide to understanding, assessing, and teaching phonological awareness.* Austin, TX: Pro-Ed.

Torgesen, J. K., Rashotte, C. A., & Alexander, A. (2001). Principles of fluency instruction in reading: Relationships with established empirical outcomes. In M. Wolf (Ed.), *Dyslexia, fluency, and the brain* (pp. 333–355). Parkton, MD: York Press.

Trabasso, T., & Bouchard, E. (2002). Teaching readers how to comprehend text strategically. In C. C. Block & M. Pressley (Eds.), *Comprehension instruction: Research-based best practices* (pp. 176–200). New York: Guilford.

Troia, G. A. (2002). Teaching writing strategies to children with disabilities: Setting generalization as the goal. *Exceptionality, 10,* 249–269.

Troia, G. A., & Graham, S. (2003). Effective writing instruction across the grades: What every educational consultant should know. *Journal of Educational and Psychological Consultation, 14,* 75–89.

Urso, A. (2008). Processing speed as a predictor of poor reading. Unpublished dissertation, University of Arizona, Tucson.

USA Today. (2005, July 4). *Report: State employees' lack of writing skills cost nearly $250M.* Associated Press.

Van de Walle, J. A. (2007). *Elementary and middle school mathematics* (6th ed.). New York: Longman.

van Garderen, D., & Montague, M. (2003). Visual-spatial representations and mathematical problem solving. *Learning Disabilities & Research, 18,* 246–254.

Wagner, R. K., & Barker, T. A. (1994). The development of orthographic processing ability. In V. W. Berninger (Ed.). *The varieties of orthographic knowledge 1: Theoretical and developmental issues* (pp. 243–276). Dordrecht, The Netherlands: Kluwer Academic.

Wahl, M. (2006). *Read Naturally.* Tallahassee, FL: Florida Center for Reading Research.

Walberg, H. J., & Tsai, S. L. (1983). Matthew effects in education. *American Educational Research Journal, 20,* 359–373.

Ward, M., & Sweller, J. (1990). Structuring effective worked examples. *Cognition and Instruction, 7*(1), 1–39.

Weedman, D. L., & Weedman, M. C. (2001). When questions are the answer. *Principal Leadership, 2*(2), 42–46.

Wentzel, K. R. (1999). Social-motivational processes and interpersonal relationships: Implications for understanding motivation at school. *Journal of Educational Psychology, 91,* 76–97.

White, T. G., Power, M. A., & White, S. (1989). Morphological analysis: Implications for teaching and understanding vocabulary growth. *Reading Research Quarterly, 24,* 281–290.

Whitehurst, G. J. (2002). *Evidence-based education* [Slide presentation]. Retrieved February 10, 2008 from www.ed.gov/offices/OESE/SASA/eb/evidence-based.pdf.

Wiig, E. H., & Semel, E. M. (1984). *Language assessment and intervention for the learning disabled* (2nd ed.). Columbus, OH: Charles E. Merrill.

Williams, D. D. (1986). *The incremental method of teaching algebra I.* Kansas City: University of Missouri.

Williams, J. K., Richman, L. C., & Yarbrough, D. B. (1992). Comparison of visual-spatial performance strategy training in children with Turner syndrome and learning disabilities. *Journal of Learning Disabilities, 25,* 658–664.

Wolf, M. (2007). *Proust and the squid: The story and science of the reading brain.* New York: HarperCollins Publishers.

Wolf, M., & Katzir-Cohen, T. (2001). Reading fluency and its intervention. *Scientific Studies of Reading, 5,* 211–238.

Wolf, M., Miller, L., & Donnelly, K. (2000). Retrieval, automaticity, vocabulary, elaboration, orthography (RAVE-O): A comprehensive fluency-based reading intervention program. *Journal of Learning Disabilities, 33,* 322–324.

Wolf, M., O'Brien, B., Donnelly Adams, K., Joffe, T., Jeffrey, J., & Lovett, M., et al. (2003). Working for time: Reflections on naming speed, reading fluency, and intervention. In B. Foorman (Ed.), *Preventing and remediating reading difficulties: Bringing science to scale* (pp. 355–379). Timonium, MD: York Press.

Wolfe, P. (2001). *Brain matters.* Alexandria, VA: Association for Supervision and Curriculum Development.

Wood, D. K., & Frank, A. R. (2000). Using memory-enhancing strategies to learn multiplication facts. *Teaching Exceptional Children, 32*(5), 78–82.

Woodward, J. (2004). Mathematics education in the United States: Past to present. *Journal of Learning Disabilities, 37,* 16–31.

Woodward, J., & Baxter, J. (1997). The effects of an innovative approach to mathematics on academically low-achieving students in inclusive settings. *Exceptional Children, 63,* 373–388.

Wylie, R., & Durrell, D. (1970). Teaching vowels through phonograms. *Elementary English, 47,* 787–791.

Xin, Y. P., & Jitendra, A. (2006). Teaching problem solving skills to middle school students with learning difficulties: Schema-based strategy instruction. In M. Montague & A. Jitendra (Eds.), *Middle school students with mathematics difficulties* (pp. 51–71). New York: Guilford.

Xin, Y. P., Jitendra, A. K., & Deatline-Buchman, A. (2005). Effects of mathematical word problem-solving instruction on middle school students with learning problems. *Journal of Special Education, 39,* 181–192.

Yopp, R. E. (1988). Questioning and active comprehension. *Questioning Exchange, 2,* 231–238.

Zentall, S. S. (1983). Learning environments: A review of physical and temporal factors. *Exceptional Education Quarterly, 4*(2), 10–15.

Zorzi, M., Priftis, K., & Umiltá, C. (2002). Brain damage: Neglect disrupts the mental number line. *Nature, 417,* 138–139.

Annotated Bibliography

Aaron, P. G., Joshi, R. M., & Quatroche, D. (2008). *Becoming a professional reading teacher.* Baltimore: Paul H. Brookes Publishing Co.

This comprehensive book provides a thorough discussion of what teachers need to know to teach reading most effectively. Research-supported instructional strategies are described for addressing problems in phonemic awareness, word recognition, vocabulary knowledge, and reading comprehension. As noted on the back cover, the book addresses the what, the how, and the why, of effective literacy instruction.

Allsopp, D. H., Kyger, M. M., & Loving, L. H. (2007). *Teaching mathematics meaningfully: Solutions for reaching struggling learners.* Baltimore: Paul H. Brookes Publishing Co.

A practical, research-based resource for educators, this book provides strategies adaptable for teaching math to students in Grades K through 12. Teachers will gain knowledge about how to work with students struggling with mathematics due to learning disabilities, ADHD, or other cognitive impairments. A key purpose of the book is to help teachers understand math in meaningful ways so that their teaching can be more effective.

Beck, I. L., McKeown, M. G., & Kucan, L. (2002). *Bringing words to life: Robust vocabulary instruction.* New York: Guilford.

This book provides a research-based framework and practical strategies for vocabulary development with children from early grades through high school. Instruction focuses on developing rich information about the words to be learned and enhances students' comprehension and language development. Guidance is provided in how to select words for instruction, how to develop student-friendly explanations and meaning activities, and how to get students actively involved in using, thinking about, and noticing words inside and outside the classroom.

Berch, D. B., & Mazzocco, M. M. M. (Eds.). (2007). *Why is math so hard for some children? The nature and origins of mathematical learning difficulties and disabilities.* Baltimore: Paul H. Brookes Publishing Co.

This edited book provides chapters by more than 35 internationally known experts in the areas of mathematics and learning disabilities research. It is comprehensive and multidisciplinary, providing research, teaching strategies, and insights into mathematical learning difficulties and disabilities. It will help researchers and educators develop an understanding of why students struggle with math and how best to help them learn.

Carnine, D. W., Silbert, J., Kame'enui, E. J., & Tarver, S. (2004). *Direct instruction reading* (4th ed.). Upper Saddle River, NJ: Pearson-Prentice Hall.

This practical guide to teaching reading using a direct instruction approach is based on the guidelines from the National Reading Panel. Direct instruction is a proven method, especially for vulnerable learners. The authors provide carefully sequenced procedures for teaching decoding, comprehension, content reading, and study skills. For example, the book discusses when a skill should be taught, what items to teach, how to correct errors, and the relationship among various reading skills. This text is designed to help teachers learn how to deliver explicit, systematic reading instruction.

Harris, K. R., Graham, S., Mason, L. H., & Friedlander, B. (2008). *Powerful writing strategies for all students.* Baltimore: Paul H. Brookes Publishing Co.

This book, which is based upon the authors' self-regulated strategy development approach, provides numerous lessons from 20 to 50 minutes each that are designed to improve student writing performance. It includes lesson plans and step-by-step guidelines for instruction, as well as additional support materials, such as cue cards, graphic organizers, and charts. It is appropriate for Grades K through 8.

MacArthur, C. A., Graham, S., & Fitzgerald, J. (Eds.). (2008). *Handbook of writing research.* New York: Guilford.

This is a comprehensive volume that synthesizes current knowledge on writing development in children and adolescents and the processes underlying successful learning and teaching. Leading researchers contributed to this book and present theoretical models, summarize available data on the effectiveness of major instructional approaches, and identify key directions for future research. The book includes a special section on cultural diversity, gender, special education, and bilingual learners.

Morris, R., & Mather, N. (Eds.). (2008). *Evidence-based interventions for students with learning and behavioral challenges.* New York: Routledge.

This edited book provides chapters on research-based intervention procedures for students with learning or behavior problems. Each chapter addresses a specific behavioral problem (e.g., depression, anxiety), learning problem (e.g., reading, mathematics), or a salient issue in the field (e.g., models of service delivery). All chapters are written by leading experts in the field who summarize the current knowledge regarding the best practices for intervention.

Acknowledgments

We would like to thank the *Essentials* series editors, Drs. Alan and Nadeen Kaufman, for their enthusiastic support of this book. Although the *Essentials* series typically focuses on assessment, the Kaufmans immediately saw the need for including a book on evidence-based instruction. They clearly recognize that, after testing, every evaluator wants to be able to develop appropriate educational recommendations. We appreciate their forward thinking and ongoing support for school psychology and education.

In addition, we would like to acknowledge the support, guidance, and helpful comments of our editor, Isabel Pratt. She provided encouragement, feedback, and somewhat flexible deadlines for which we are thankful. Deborah Schindlar, our production editor, managed the mountain of details connected with getting a book manuscript ready for publication, kept us on schedule, and answered each of our questions promptly. The efforts of all the staff working on our book at John Wiley are gratefully acknowledged. We would also like to express gratitude to each other for making this book a reality.

About the Authors

Barbara J. Wendling is an educator, author, and consultant specializing in assessment and instruction. She has taught in both general and special education settings and has an M.A. in learning disabilities. Her experience includes working in educational publishing in the areas of product management and development for both tests and instructional materials. She conducts presentations and workshops nationwide on topics related to assessment and evidence-based instruction. In addition, she serves as the Education Director for the Woodcock-Muñoz Foundation and has coauthored a number of publications related to the Woodcock-Johnson III, most recently the *Woodcock Interpretation and Instructional Interventions Program (WIIIP)*.

Dr. Nancy Mather is professor of learning disabilities in the department of Special Education, Rehabilitation, and School Psychology at the University of Arizona in Tucson. In addition to her teaching responsibilities, she conducts numerous presentations and workshops each year for conferences both nationally and internationally. She is a widely published author of tests, a reading program, books, book reviews, and articles. She is a coauthor of the *Woodcock-Johnson III* and has coauthored two books on the use and interpretation of this test. Her most recent books include: *Learning Disabilities and Challenging Behaviors, 2nd edition* (Mather & Goldstein, 2008) published by Paul H. Brookes Publishing Co. and a coedited book *Evidence-based Interventions for Students with Learning and Behavioral Challenges* (Morris & Mather, 2008) published by Routledge.

Index